Mediating Sustainability in the Consumer Society

This book sheds light on the role and impact of sustainability mediation, an effective tool for political authorities and business enterprises to persuade consumers of the integrity of their actions, products, and services.

In this era of ecological and societal crises fuelled by increasing consumption, sustainability has become a key buzzword and target to attain. Governments around the world argue that they will meet their sustainability goals through environmental actions, by enabling consumers to make better choices and expecting brands to respond accordingly. At the same time, consumers are overwhelmed by the messaging conveyed in sustainability marketing campaigns, often featuring misleading greenwashing, with political authorities, organisations, and business enterprises all having conflicting interests. In this complex scenario, mediation has become a crucial issue. This book offers a critical and multidisciplinary view of sustainability mediation from experts in the fields of philosophy, consumption research, media studies, fashion, design, and citizenship, offering a unique, holistic view. Each chapter highlights different and problematic aspects of the cultural narratives being communicated, for example, the necessity of growth and the notion of a green economy. They present current theories, methods, indicators, and strategies used to assess and measure the relation between mediation, behaviour, and sustainable development.

This book is of interest to scholars, researchers, and postgraduate students in all subject fields concerned with sustainability, including design, visual communication, fashion, consumption, media and journalism, and sustainable development.

Astrid Skjerven is Professor Emerita of Design Theory at the Department of Product Design, Oslo Metropolitan University (OsloMet), Norway.

Lisbeth Løvbak Berg is a researcher in the Sustainable Textile and Food Consumption Research Group at Consumption Research Norway (SIFO), Oslo Metropolitan University (OsloMet), Norway.

Liv Merete Nielsen is Professor Emerita of Design Education at the Faculty of Technology, Art and Design, Oslo Metropolitan University (OsloMet), Norway.

Dagny Stuedahl is Professor of Media Design in the Department of Journalism and Media Studies, Oslo Metropolitan University (OsloMet), Norway, and Henrik-Steffens Professor at Nordeuropa-Institut, Humboldt-Universität zu Berlin, Germany (2022–2025).

Routledge Studies in Sustainability

Reimagining Labour for a Sustainable Future
Alison E. Vogelaar and Poulomi Dasgupta

Waste and Discards in the Asia Pacific Region
Social and Cultural Perspectives
Edited by Viktor Pál and Iris Borowy

Digital Innovations for a Circular Plastic Economy in Africa
Edited by Muyiwa Oyinlola and Oluwaseun Kolade

Critical Sustainability Sciences
Intercultural and Emancipatory Perspectives
Edited by Stephan Rist, Patrick Bottazzi and Johanna Jacobi

Transdisciplinary Research, Sustainability, and Social Transformation
Governance and Knowledge Co-Production
Tom Dedeurwaerdere

Digital Technologies for Sustainable Futures
Promises and Pitfalls
Edited by Chiara Certomà, Fabio Iapaolo and Federico Martellozzo

Rethinking the Concept of Waste and Mass Consumption
Preserving Resources through Reuse, Repair and Recycling
Richard Waite

Mediating Sustainability in the Consumer Society
Edited by Astrid Skjerven, Lisbeth Løvbak Berg, Liv Merete Nielsen, and Dagny Stuedahl

For more information on this series, please visit: www.routledge.com/Routledge-Studies-in-Sustainability/book-series/RSSTY

Mediating Sustainability in the Consumer Society

Edited by
Astrid Skjerven, Lisbeth Løvbak Berg, Liv Merete Nielsen, and Dagny Stuedahl

Routledge
Taylor & Francis Group
LONDON AND NEW YORK

earthscan
from Routledge

First published 2025
by Routledge
4 Park Square, Milton Park, Abingdon, Oxon OX14 4RN

and by Routledge
605 Third Avenue, New York, NY 10158

Routledge is an imprint of the Taylor & Francis Group, an informa business

British Library Cataloguing-in-Publication Data
A catalogue record for this book is available from the British Library

Library of Congress Cataloging-in-Publication Data
Names: Skjerven, Astrid. | Berg, Lisbeth Løvbak. | Nielsen, Liv Merete. | Stuedahl, Dagny, editor.
Title: Mediating sustainability in the consumer society / edited by Astrid Skjerven, Lisbeth Løvbak Berg, Liv Merete Nielsen, and Dagny Stuedahl.
Description: Abingdon, Oxon ; New York, NY : Routledge, 2025. | Series: Routledge studies in sustainability | Includes bibliographical references and index.
Identifiers: LCCN 2024037963 (print) | LCCN 2024037964 (ebook) | ISBN 9781032492193 (hardback) | ISBN 9781032492216 (paperback) | ISBN 9781003392705 (ebook)
Subjects: LCSH: Sustainable development. | Environmentalism in mass media. | Consumer behavior—Environmental aspects. | Consumption (Economics)—Environmental aspects.
Classification: LCC HC79.E5 M4268 2025 (print) | LCC HC79.E5 (ebook) | DDC 338.9/27—dc23/eng/20241024
LC record available at https://lccn.loc.gov/2024037963
LC ebook record available at https://lccn.loc.gov/2024037964

ISBN: 978-1-032-49219-3 (hbk)
ISBN: 978-1-032-49221-6 (pbk)
ISBN: 978-1-003-39270-5 (ebk)

DOI: 10.4324/9781003392705

Typeset in Times New Roman
by codeMantra

Contents

Contributors

Louise Dennis is the Curator of the Museum of Design in Plastics (MoDiP), based at the Arts University Bournemouth, UK. MoDiP is the only UK-accredited museum with a focus on plastics and has been awarded Designated Outstanding Collection status by Arts Council England. Louise's research explores the value of the museum and its specialist focus, with a particular interest in the various relationships surrounding materiality and museum objects. Through her work with the museum, she aims to show the value of plastics materials when used appropriately and hopes that, by learning from the past, manufacturers, designers, and consumers can make better informed choices.

Tiziana Ferrero-Regis is Associate Professor of Fashion in the School of Design, Queensland University of Technology, Brisbane. Tiziana combines a professional background in the fashion industry and creative industries in Milan (including at Condé Nast – *Vogue Italy*), with a transdisciplinary background in fashion studies and sustainability. She has published widely on fashion and culture, and the Australian fashion and textile industry. Her research focusses on the social implications of sustainability in a local context through spatial and anthropological approaches. Her latest publication is *Staging Fashion: The Fashion Show and Its Spaces* (Bloomsbury, 2020); "Castoff from the West, Pearls in Kantamanto? A Critique of Second-hand Clothes trade", in the *Journal of Industrial Ecology*; and "#Instawool: Wool narratives of sustainability on Instagram", in *Fashion Practice.* Tiziana is the co-leader of the TextileR Group and a co-leader of the Circularity programme at the QUT Resilience Centre.

Ingrid Haugsrud is a PhD Candidate at Consumption Research Norway (SIFO), Oslo Metropolitan University (OsloMet). Her research interests lie within sustainable consumption – especially related to clothing in everyday life, theories of care, wardrobe studies, and consumption and childhood.

Ingun Grimstad Klepp is Professor of Clothing and Sustainability and an ethnologist who has worked at Consumption Research Norway (SIFO) at Oslo Metropolitan University (OsloMet) since 1999. She works with clothing and textiles and is central in developing the research field through advancing methods, projects, dissemination, knowledge and discourse about clothes, and their role in society and our lives, including clothing habits, laundry, lifespan, product development, value chains, and politics. For more information: https://clothingresearch.oslomet.nov).

Dörte Linke studied Scandinavian Studies, German Literature, and Theology at the Humboldt University in Berlin and at the University of Uppsala. She works as a research assistant in the Department of Nordic Studies, Humboldt-Universität zu Berlin in the field of Scandinavian literature. One focus of her research is on concepts of nature in literature, examining in particular in which ways literary texts negotiate knowledge as well as human self-reflection. Her dissertation "Reflexionen und Verwebungen. Wechselwirkungen von ›Natur‹ und ›Mensch‹ in der deutschen und dänischen Gegenwartsliteratur" was published in 2021. Another focus of her research is the relationship between theology and literature.

Rachel Matthews is Senior Lecturer in Fashion Marketing at Manchester Metropolitan University and was previously Head of the School for Design at the Australian College of the Arts in Melbourne. She is an educator and researcher whose work explores taste-making, change-making, and narratives of influence in fashion, through the networked conditions of the contemporary media landscape. As an educator, Rachel promotes responsible design pedagogies, and a critically optimistic vision of how creative practice can influence mindsets and challenge the status quo in pursuit of a better future.

Lisbeth Løvbak Berg is a Researcher in the Sustainable Textile and Food Consumption Research Group at Consumption Research Norway (SIFO), Oslo Metropolitan University (OsloMet.) She is also a member of the Media Practice Research Group and part of the GreenMet Initiative at OsloMet. She is further a member of the Union of Concerned Researchers in Fashion and the Sustainable Fashion Consumption Network. Trained as a fashion designer and maker, with a master's degree in fashion and sustainability from the MA Fashion Futures course at London College of Fashion, she has years of industry experience as an entrepreneur, university lecturer, and consultant before joining academia. Her research interests are design futuring, imaginaries and narratives of sustainability, consumption reduction, and product lifetimes. Her latest publications include "The Impact of Modes of Acquisition on Clothing Lifetimes"with Ingun Grimstad Klepp and Kirsi Laitala, in K. Niinimäki (2024) (Ed.), *Recycling and Lifetime Management in the Textile and Fashion Sector* and "Holding on or letting go: Conflicting narratives of product longevity" with Marie Hebrok in *Resources, Conservation and Recycling (2024).*

Liv Merete Nielsen is Professor Emerita of Design Education at the Faculty of Technology, Art and Design, Oslo Metropolitan University (OsloMet). Her main interest is design education for a greener tomorrow including design education of the general public in their role as consumers. She has promoted design literacy for the general public through books, articles, and her role as chair for the design part of National Curriculum for schools in Norway. She is chairing the *Design Literacy International Network* (DLIN) and is a member of the convening group EdSIG in *Design Research Society* (DRS). Since 2008, she has been section editor of the journal *FormAkademisk*.

Cecilie Sachs Olsen is Professor of Art and Society at Oslo Metropolitan University. Her work is practice-based and revolves around developing creative methods for urban research and exploring how artistic practice can be used as a framework to analyse and re-imagine urban development, space, and politics. Cecilie was the chief curator of Oslo Architecture Triennale 2019, which used fiction, art, and performance to explore degrowth as alternative social and spatial structures that question the supremacy of economic growth as the basis of contemporary societies. She is also the co-founder of the urban performance collective zURBS.

Astrid Skjerven is Professor Emerita of Design theory at the Department of Product Design, Oslo Metropolitan University (OsloMet), Norway. In 2017–2023, she was head of the planning and implementation of the PhD programme *Innovation for Sustainability*. Her fields of interest are Nordic design in a global perspective, everyday aesthetics, and cultural sustainability. She is a member of the International Sustainable Development Research Society (ISDRS), and OsloMet's representative in Sustainable Development Solutions Network (SDSN). She is a board member of the scientific journals *Sustainable Development* and *FormAkademisk*. She has published articles in *Scandinavian Journal of Design History*, *Kunst og Kultur*, *Formakademisk*, *Sustainable Development*, and other scientific journals. She has been the editor of the books *Transatlantic Discourses in Nordic Design* (Bloomsbury, 2014), *Design for a Sustainable Culture: Perspectives, Practices and Education* (Routledge, 2017), and *Gender and the Sustainable Development Goals* (Routledge, 2022).

Paige Street is a PhD candidate and research assistant the the RMIT University School of Fashion & Textiles in Melbourne, Australia. Her PhD project investigates the downstream processes and labour involved in the trade of used clothing exported from Australia, aiming to understand how these practices can support a just and circular fashion system. Her research work thus far has focused on governing and transforming the fashion system through product stewardship, degrowth, social activism and design intervention. She has research experience on projects at the local, state, national and international scale, including work for the Australian Fashion Council, Salvos Stores, and the United Nations Environment Programme. She holds a Master of Philosophy from the Queensland University of Technology.

Dagny Stuedahl is Professor of Media Design in the Department of Journalism and Media Studies, OsloMet, and Henrik-Steffens professor at Nordeuropa-Institut, Humboldt-Universität zu Berlin (2022–2025). With a background in Nordic ethnography, she has focused on youth, identity, and digital media. She has especially focused on cultural heritage and museum institutions' engagements with youth, co-design methodologies, and design anthropology approaches. Her latest publications are "Design Anthropological Approaches in Collaborative Museum Curation", in the *Journal of Design Studies*, and (with Mariana Mata Passos and Raquel Ribeiro dos Santos) *Power and Rebellion in Participatory Practices* (Materiais Diversos, 2023). Stuedahl is co-leader of the research group Media Practice, and part of the GreenMet Initiative at OsloMet.

Camille Z. Thisell is a Researcher and Lecturer at the University of Inland Norway, concentrating on Ecomedia literacy. Her research examines the evolving demands and expectations for sustainable development competencies within the audiovisual industry, particularly in the realms of education, leadership, and operational footprint.

Arne Johan Vetlesen is Professor of Philosophy at the University of Oslo. His main interests are ethics, social theory, and environmental philosophy. He has published 30 books, among them *Evil and Human Agency* (Cambridge U.P., 2005), *A Philosophy of Pain* (Reaktion Books, 2009), *The Denial of Nature* (Routledge, 2015), *Cosmologies of the Anthropocene* (Routledge, 2019), and *Animal Lives and Why They Matter* (Routledge, 2023).

Preface

It all started with a classic case of greenwashing. A professor at Oslo Metropolitan University was engaged as a model for a magazine article on sustainable fashion design. During the photoshoot, it became evident to her that the clothes were far from sustainable. She sent an op-ed about this to the newspaper that publishes the magazine, which was brave enough to publish it. It caused a watershed of grateful comments by designers who were frustrated about the increasing degree of greenwashing. Colleagues at the university instantly agreed to arrange a seminar on the topic with external and internal contributors. It attracted researchers, students, and representatives from organisations and businesses that all actively took part in the discussion. Since then, the self-established group, which has given itself the name *GreenMet*, has organised biannual seminars on various aspects of sustainability, with international and national contributors. Thus, an independent forum for dialogue on sustainability was created which made it possible to establish a multidisciplinary discourse without bindings. This means that mediation from groups that do not have any organisational or political power can be successful. This book is a spin-off of these experiences, which we hereby share with an international audience.

Introduction

Astrid Skjerven, Lisbeth Løvbak Berg, Liv Merete Nielsen, and Dagny Stuedahl

Introduction

Sustainability is one of the main buzzwords of our time. With the looming climate and nature crises, no society, organisation, group, or individual can avoid taking a stand on the phenomenon, which makes it necessary to adapt production, consumption, behaviour, attitudes, and culture to living within planetary boundaries. The UN Sustainability Goals (UN, 2015), laws, and regulations are responding to these crises and are trying to facilitate a green transition. Both businesses and consumers need to adapt to these new measures. At the same time, these measures, including the UN Sustainable Development Goals, are critiqued for perpetuating the current growth-based economic system (e.g., Liverman, 2018; Sultana, 2018), which is the main driver of the degradation of nature we are witnessing. Further critiques of the development agenda include its basis on Western ideals and the use of "nation based, quantitative, contradictory, development indicators" (Liverman, 2018). It is also a fact that the concept of sustainable development, as well as its indicators, is understood in different ways. At the same time, political authorities, organisations, and business enterprises may have conflicting interests. In this scenario, sustainability constitutes a *wicked problem* that cannot be solved with quick fixes and universal solutions.

In this situation, mediation is a crucial issue. While the individual consumer and citizen depend on concrete and reliable information in order to relate to sustainability, the dynamics of mediation constitute a sphere where many interests assert themselves in order to attract the attention of the recipient. Mediation is an effective tool for stakeholders to persuade the recipients of the eminence of their actions, products, and services. The communication channels include advertisements, articles and essays, news, discussions, and other expressions of meanings and take place on various platforms. The main media channels are owned by a few media corporations who have their interests in the matter and have the power to control and manipulate messages. Computerisation and lately artificial intelligence make it easy to generate and transform facts and arguments. Thus, mediation of truth has become a relative matter, and information has become a matter of construction, technological infrastructure, design, and performance, all to the benefit of the messenger. For the media audience, the number of messages conveyed

DOI: 10.4324/9781003392705-1

is overwhelming and often confusing. This has led to a state of frustration and indifference. Some have taken to activism by using alternative and sometimes unlawful ways of expression.

General awareness of the need for change is rising in institutions, companies, and the public. Still, public discussion and political action tend to stay on the surface level of incremental change. It is often simplistic, limited to superficial slogans, and *greenwashing* is a growing problem. Greenwashing, or misleading the public to believe that a company or other entity is doing more to protect the environment than it is, has become a common phenomenon and an important tool in order to keep up with the expectations of the customers and the authorities. Still, the core media messages throughout society remain based on progress as growth and increased consumption. This even includes several of the main international measures, like the UN Sustainable Development Goals.

While there are a large number of scientific articles available, the number of books in the field of mediation in the perspective of sustainability is remarkably low and these tend to be either handbooks or focused on a particular discipline.

The Mediation of Sustainability: Development Goals, Social Movements, and Public Dissent, edited by Ben Harbisher (2023), examines the way Sustainable Development Goals initiatives have been disseminated. It questions to what extent sustainability narratives are being supported and how they are represented; how saving the environment can be made pertinent to someone who has no access to clean food or running water; and why local initiatives are overshadowed by multinationals whose attempts to rectify the damage their goods have done gains more credible reportage.

Josh Hawley's recently published book *The Tyranny of the Big Tech* (Hawley, 2021) addresses the immense power of the big computer companies Google, Facebook, Amazon, and Apple, mostly from an American perspective. He claims that these mega-corporations are the gravest threat to American liberty in decades and that there is a need for recovering the link between liberty and democratic participation.

In his book *Greenwashing: Foundations and Emerging Research on Corporate Sustainability and Deceptive Communication* (2022), Agostino Vollero examines the understanding of greenwashing, provides a systematic review of available literature, and reflects on theoretical approaches and research trends. Additionally, specific case studies that offer lessons in avoiding the greenwashing trap are explored and construct a view of the future in this context. The book is a broad and updated presentation of the topic of greenwashing but only briefly addresses the societal context.

Toby Miller and Walter Murdoch's book *Greenwashing culture* (2017) reveals the high environmental costs of culture production and weighs its institutional complicity with the black art of greenwashing. The book presents a highly needed analysis of this often-overlooked theme.

The Routledge Handbook of Environmental Journalism (Sachsman & Valenti, 2020) provides a thorough overview of environmental journalism around the world. It displays how, despite the dramatic changes in the news industry, environmental journalists remain key to bringing stories to light across the globe. With contributions from around the world broken down into five key regions, this book provides support for today's environmental reporters. With its special focus point, it does not deal with societal matters of mediation.

Nicole Starosielski and Janet Walker's book *Sustainable Media: Critical Approaches to Media and Environment* (2016) explores the many ways that media and environment are intertwined, from the exploitation of natural and human resources during media production to the installation and disposal of media in the landscape; from people's engagement with environmental issues in film, television, and digital media to the mediating properties of ecologies themselves. It is a broad overview of the societal role of mass media but tends to be outdated in today's context of mediation.

In *Ecomedia Literacy: Integrating Ecology into Media Education* (Lopez, 2020), the author provides key resources that will enable media educators to apply ecomedia concepts to their curricula. By reconceptualising media education, this book connects ecology, environmental communication, ecomedia studies, environmental humanities, and eco-literacy to bridge media literacy and education for sustainability. The book is an essential read for educators and scholars in the areas of media literacy.

Communicating Sustainability by Mary Robertson (2017) is a book of evidence-based strategies for making sustainability vivid, accessible, and comprehensible. To do this, it brings together research from a range of specialities including cognitive psychology, visual perception, communication studies, environmental design, interpretive exhibit design, interpretive signage, wayfinding, storytelling, courtroom litigation, information graphics, and graphic design to illustrate not only what approaches are effective but also why they work as they do.

Donna J. Haraway's book *Staying with the Trouble: Making Kin in the Chthulucene* (2016) is a classic in ecofeminism. She offers provocative ways to reconfigure our relations to the Earth and all its inhabitants. She eschews referring to our current epoch as the Anthropocene, preferring to conceptualise it as what she calls the Chthulucene, as it more aptly and fully describes our epoch as one in which the human and nonhuman are inextricably linked in tentacular practices. Learning to stay with the trouble of living and dying together on a damaged earth will prove more conducive to the kind of thinking that would provide the means to building more liveable futures. Theoretically and methodologically driven by the signifier SF – string figures, science fact, science fiction, speculative feminism, and speculative fabulation.

Design as a means for enhancing sustainable development is discussed in Astrid Skjerven and Janne Beate Reitan's book *Design for a Sustainable Culture: Perspectives, Practices and Education* (2017). It explores the relationship between sustainability, culture, and the shaping of human surroundings by examining the significance and potential of design as a tool for sustainable development.

A staple in the field of fashion and sustainability, the *Routledge Handbook of Sustainability and Fashion* (2015), edited by Kate Fletcher and Mathilda Tham, presents contributions from a diverse range of disciplines on the various interconnected actors in the fashion space and their positive and negative impacts, including topics such as fashion media, business models, and the role of science and technology.

Global Perspectives on Sustainable Fashion (2019), edited by Alison Gwilt, Alice Payne, and Evelise Anciet Rüthschilling, explores fashion sustainability through the lens the local action from six regions of the world: Latin America, North America, Europe, Asia, Southeast Asia and Oceania, and Africa and the Middle East.

Alice Payne's book *Designing Fashion's Future: Present Practice and Tactics for Sustainable Change* (2021) focused on sustainability mediated through design and discusses various design approaches to counter overconsumption and proposes a more radical change of redefining fashion design as a network of actors rather than a top-down approach, opening up the definitions of sustainability, fashion, and design, to encompass the complexities of the various fashion systems.

Design Materials and Making for Social Change: From Materials We Explore to Materials We Wear (2023), edited by Rebecca Earley and Rosie Hornbuckle, examines design research for change through the lens of materials and their interconnectedness with the social. The volume spans topics such as homelessness, the impact of colonialism, climate change, and the changing complexities of collaborating across disciplines and with various stakeholders.

Accelerating Sustainability in Fashion, Clothing and Textiles (2024), edited by Martin Charter, Bernice Pan, and Sandy Black, has a distinctive business-led approach to sustainability mediation. In this book, five business case studies are presented along with chapters analysing the current state of affairs in fashion and the potential for fostering a different consumer culture through activism, diversity, and localism.

Fashion Media and Sustainability: Encouraging Ethical Consumption via Journalism and Influencers (2021) by Anastasia Denisova, destined for policymakers, suggests regulating the fashion media landscape, including its vocabulary and affiliated links across journalism and other media platforms such as social media.

Pioneering New Perspectives in the Fashion Industry: Disruption, Diversity and Sustainable Innovation (2023), edited by Elaine L. Ritch, Catherine Canning and Julie McColl, is a textbook for marketing students. It introduces fashion sustainability issues, consumer sustainability perspectives along with more traditional fashion marketing topics such as online retail.

This book aims to shed light on the role and impact of mediation of sustainability; to create awareness in society; and to investigate the different stakeholder roles involved in this mediation, including the media industry and the public sector, social groups, and individuals. It seeks to highlight the diversity of areas where mediating sustainability is of key importance to achieve the deep change necessary to succeed in the green transition and to discuss alternative forms of mediation and communication. The book offers a multidisciplinary view from experts in the fields of philosophy, consumption research, media studies, and design studies, among others. As such, it offers a more holistic view than previous publications.

The book is divided into four thematic parts, which are closely related: Ethics, Consumption, Mediation, and Literacy. Ethics are a foundational factor in sustainability and the mediation of it. A green transition requires production and access to unbiased information, organisational and personal responsibility as well as honesty and empathy. Overconsumption, as a result of overproduction, is the main cause of most environmental problems. Despite knowledge of its damaging effects, the "use and discard" mentality is still ruling. Communication, understood as the way we communicate, discuss, and respond to messages on sustainability, is the basis for the implementation of degrowth and other undertakings. In the flora of messages of "green" products and services, it is often difficult to differentiate between facts and greenwashing. Literacy in the form of basic knowledge, consciousness, and citizenship are vital for the understanding of the situation and how we can relate to it. Both general education and mediation contribute to such literacy.

Part 1: Ethics

Chapter 1 "Sustainability and Its Discontents: Recovering the Sources of Value", by Arne Johan Vetlesen, is based on his GreenMet lecture "The Problem of Growth". This chapter constitutes the point of departure for all the following chapters. It addresses how economic growth has been regarded as indispensable for political and social progress in Western societies. The basic question of what it would mean to abandon the growth paradigm is met by great resistance in spite of the knowledge of its ecological and human costs. The author argues that the resistance is multi-dimensional, nourished by a sense of entitlement among individuals perceiving themselves as consumers rather than as citizens that form a political collective. Although there is widespread support for "a greener future", achieving it is impossible without facing the systemic conflict between a growth-driven economy and ecology, between our present levels of consumption and the dwindling resources on Earth. The chapter analyses how this conflict plays out in each one of us as well as systemically in the constellation of consumers, corporations, and authorities.

Sustainable urban development requires not only factual knowledge but also emphatic attention to environmental needs. In Chapter 2 "Sustainability Discourses and the Question of Democracy", Cecilie Sachs Olsen argues that the main question is how we can adapt our way of looking at urban form to identify, question, and transform the power relations, neglects, and injustices that are at the root of our socio-ecological predicament. In her chapter, she develops the idea of "an urban attention ecology", defined through our ability to attend to urban form in ways that better address social and ecological injustices and crises. The author uses her curation of the Oslo Architecture Triennale 2019 as a starting point to discuss the challenges and potentials for critical spatial practice in developing an urban attention ecology.

Camille Z. Thisell in Chapter 3 "Exploring Norway's Audiovisual Industry: A Study on Communicated Engagement in Sustainable Practices" addresses small- and medium-sized audiovisual enterprises in Norway. The fundamental purpose of the chapter is to raise awareness of and spark debate on the meaning of "green production". The collection and publication of data related to environmental issues in media production is vital indicators for sustainable transitions. It presents a study of the status of mediated sustainability activities in 21 Norwegian audiovisual small and medium-sized companies owned by international corporations. The main discovery is that they have disclosed minimal information about sustainable practices, which challenges the stated policy objectives of their parent corporations. This raises doubts about the advancement of sustainable development among these companies. The author argues that a unified green European standard for sustainable audiovisual production is needed to ensure consistent and transparent reporting and foster genuine progress in sustainability efforts.

Part 2: Consumption

Chapter 4 "Who Can Stop the Greenwashing", by Ingun Grimstad Klepp and Ingrid Haugsrud, addresses the impotence and frustrations caused by greenwashing. Governments are hoping to meet their sustainability goals by calling for consumers to make better choices and expect brands to respond accordingly. Consumers are currently overwhelmed by the amount of information conveyed in sustainability marketing campaigns, complaining that it is far too much to deal with. Trust in sustainability marketing and labelling schemes is low. The question asked is how to prevent greenwashing. It uses The Norwegian Consumer Agency warning that the Higg Materials Sustainability Index (Higg MSI) tool in the form of a consumer-facing label could not be used in marketing in Norway to discuss this. Both the industry and consumer authorities can stop greenwashing, but only the authorities have the will to do so. Consumers neither have the will nor the possibility to differentiate between greenwashing and other green claims and want the authorities to stop greenwashing. This constitutes a wicked circle that as yet has not been broken.

Rachel Matthews and Tiziana Ferrero-Regis in Chapter 5 "Future of Sustainable Fashion Communications: From Marketing Messages to the Mediation of Mutable Meanings" argue that both fashion and the marketing of it are driven by increasing consumption, and the two activities are reinforcing each other. They ask whether it is possible to rebalance and reconcile two systems – fashion and marketing – both based on growth, with the industry's central concerns with sustainability. It examines the strategies of three existing fashion brands (Ganni, Bode, and A.BCH) who are each taking different approaches to communicate the meaning of sustainable fashion for their brands. This chapter concludes with a discussion on how the findings can be used for teaching and implementing sustainable fashion marketing for future fashion systems.

Part 3: Communication

Business enterprises are often associated with a lack of responsibility for sustainable development and with marketing their products to customers conceived as passive recipients. Astrid Skjerven in Chapter 6 "Creating Sustainability by Myth-making: IKEA's Advertising Campaigns 'The Trash Collection' and 'The Life Collection'" challenges this conception in her case study of two of IKEA Norway's advertising campaigns from 2021 to 2022. She discusses whether the campaign was purely an example of "greenwashing" or it might have contributed to a higher awareness of environment-friendly consumption in the market and among the staff at IKEA Norway. In particular, the narrative and mythological means used to influence consumers have been investigated. Her interpretation is that the campaigns can be regarded as myths in the sense of a wished truth where myth-maker IKEA and the myth recipients, i.e., the consumers, can interact in order to contribute to a green transition.

Instagram is a relatively new communication platform which gives the account holder a certain freedom to publish messages and communicate with its readers. In Chapter 7 "Cultivating Responsibility through Instagram: Fashion, Revolution, and Narrative", Paige Street argues that knowing how to respond to and take responsibility for structural injustices is one of the most urgent problems of our time, and that social media platforms can be used as spaces to make responsibility-taking accessible and intelligible to a large audience. Using the global activist organisation Fashion Revolution as a case study, she analyses how consumers are invited to respond through its campaigns. This can be seen to invoke affective and neoliberal gestures of responsibility-taking, calling upon consumers to feel for their clothes and the people who made them. On the other hand, the affective turn might overlook direct attention to the institutional context which creates structural injustice in the fashion industry.

Activism is a growing phenomenon among young people who care about the environment and have experienced that traditional communications do not work. This can take many forms. Dörte Linke in Chapter 8 "Imagination and Agency: On the Role of Fiction in Ecological Discourses", analyses the role and impact of the so-called Letzte Generation, which calls for civil resistance. She asks how messages and demands like those of "Letzte Generation" can be mediated on the Internet to influence and change how humans act in the real world. The chapter addresses the role of fiction in and for ecological discourses and the action taken by society to implement them. It discusses how the dualistic separation between humans and "nature" can be broken down and rethought, and whether storytelling can facilitate a more sustainable way of living. By analysing the writings of central researchers in the field, the chapter displays how fiction can invite and contribute to reflection on humanity's relationship with the environment, based on the example of "Letzte Generation".

Part 4: Literacy

In Chapter 9 "Redefining Digital Literacy for Sustainable Mediation", Dagny Stuedahl displays that digital technology has been regarded as a non-polluting business and therefore used to solve the climate crisis. This has proven not to be the case, as media can also be used to increase consumption. The author states that the technology and its algorithms are increasingly driven by tech giant companies who have consumption as the main goal. Consumerism contains both increasing production of hardware with an equal increasing problem of healthy production. In the last decade, there has been a growing discussion on sustainable ways of designing technologies. Several perspectives for sustainable technology design, such as repairable technologies have been introduced. This chapter discusses how media studies may contribute to the discussion, by focusing on questions of sustainable digital infrastructure and by arguing for including critical understandings of technology in the concept of media literacy.

Museums play an important role in the dissemination of knowledge to the general public. Currently, many of them are engaged in sustainability issues. In Chapter 10 "Communicating Sustainable Uses of Plastics in a Museum Setting: The Case of the Museum of Design in Plastics", Louise Dennis takes her point of departure in how museums traditionally are places that communicate often complicated ideas and concepts to a wide-ranging audience. Dennis addresses how museums more recently have become places to mediate and to generate conversations, with the acknowledgement that the visiting public are not "without knowledge" but bring important experience to the meaning-making process. The chapter discusses the role of mediation in a museum setting to explore the sustainable use of plastics, a contested material family. Its case study explores how a deep focus on a single material family can help visitors understand its value.

All forms of sustainability mediation contribute to our sustainability literacies, but also seemingly unrelated messages, mediated through arenas such as education contribute to our worldviews and hence how we also see sustainability. In the final chapter of this anthology, "Indigenous Approaches to Mediation of the Climate and Nature Emergency: A Conversation with Vanessa Andreotti", Lisbeth Løvbak Berg explores Indigenous perspectives on sustainability through the lens of education. The perspectives presented build on a critique of modern-colonial worldviews, mediated through both formal and informal education, that uphold unsustainable ways of living. While the chapter presents a stark critique of modernity, through the work of Andreotti and her Gesturing Towards Decolonial Futures Arts / Research Collective, it also conveys a message of hope and a call to action to mediate other ways of being in the world that opens the door to other perspectives and alternatives for the future.

This book is a contribution to the current discourse on the topic of sustainability mediation, destined for researchers of the field in academia and the industrial and public sectors. It will serve as an introduction to the topic and a basis for further studies and research for scholars, PhD students and post-graduate students in media and journalism, design, education, marketing, communication, media, and sustainability studies. It will hopefully pave the way for developing alternatives that support a more sustainable society.

References

Charter, M., Pan, B. & Black, S. (Eds.) (2024). *Accelerating Sustainability in Fashion, Clothing and Textiles*. Routledge.

Denisova, A. (2021). *Fashion Media and Sustainability: Encouraging Ethical Consumption via Journalism and Influencers.* CAMRI Policy Briefs and Reports. London: University of Westminster Press.

Earley, R. & Hornbuckle, R. (2023). *Design Materials and Making for Social Change: From Materials We Explore to Materials We Wear*. Taylor & Francis.

Fletcher, K. & Tham, M. (Eds.) (2015). *Routledge Handbook of Sustainability and Fashion.* London: Routledge.

Gwilt, A., Payne, A. & Ruthschilling, E. A. (2019). *Global Perspectives on Sustainable Fashion*. Bloomsbury Visual Arts.

Haraway, D. J. (2016). *Staying with the Trouble - Making Kin in the Chthulucene*. Duke University Press.

Hawley, J. (2021). *The Tyranny of Big Tech*. Regnery Publishing.

Lopez, A. (2020). *Ecomedia Literacy: Integrating Ecology into Media Education*. London: Routledge.

Liverman, D. M. (2018). Geographic perspectives on development goals: Constructive engagements and critical perspectives on the MDGs and the SDGs. *Dialogues in Human Geography*, *8*(2), 168–185. https://doi.org/10.1177/2043820618780787.

Miller, T. & Murdoch, W. (2017). *Greenwashing Culture*. London: Routledge.

Payne, A. (2021). *Designing Fashion's Future: Present Practice and Tactics for Sustainable Change.* Bloomsbury.

Ritch, E. L., Canning, C. & McColl, J. (Eds.) (2023). *Pioneering New Perspectives in the Fashion Industry: Disruption, Diversity and Sustainable Innovation.* Leeds: Emerald.

Robertson, M. (2017). *Communicating Sustainability*. London: Routledge.

Sachsman, D. & Valenti, J. A. (Eds.) (2020). *Routledge Handbook of Environmental Journalism*. London: Routledge.

Skjerven, A. & Reitan, J. B. (Eds.) (2017). *Design for a Sustainable Culture: Perspectives, Practices and Education*. London: Routledge.

Starosielski, N. & Walker, J. (Eds.) (2016). *Sustainable Media: Critical Approaches to Media and Environment*. London: Routledge.

Sultana, F. (2018). An(Other) geographical critique of development and SDGs. *Dialogues in Human Geography*, *8*(2), 186–190. https://doi.org/10.1177/2043820618780788.

UN. (2015). *17 Sustainable Development Goals*. https://sdgs.un.org/sites/default/files/publications/211617%20Goals%2017%20Partnerships.pdf.

Vollero, A. (2022). *Foundations and Emerging Research on Corporate Sustainability and Deceptive Communication.* London: Emerald.

Part 1
Ethics

1 Sustainability and its discontents

Recovering the sources of value

Arne Johan Vetlesen

Sustainable development: The career of a concept

The term «sustainable development» was introduced to the general public in the 1987 report of the "World Commission on Environment and Development", commonly referred to as the "Brundtland Report", since it was chaired by the then Norwegian Prime Minister Gro Harlem Brundtland. Like the Club of Rome's landmark study of 1972, *Limits to Growth*, authored by Donella H. Meadows et al., the Brundtland Report focused on the possibility that modern industrial society is using up its source materials at an alarming rate, which cannot be maintained for much longer without major change. How to meet this challenge?

The Brundtland Report gives a twofold response. On the one hand, it recognises that economic growth is necessary in order to bring greater prosperity to the developing world, i.e., to the countries that historically have not enjoyed the growth in prosperity, measured in GDP, that the leading industrial nations in the world have done, especially since WWII. In this way, continued economic growth of a kind that will benefit the countries hitherto lagging behind as well as those already most affluent is tied to a sense of entitlement and so to a notion of justice: growth would be unjust if it does not correct the historical imbalance between the poor and the rich, taken globally.

On the other hand, the development facilitated by continued economic growth "overall" has to become sustainable. In stating that this constitutes a "must", the Report clearly tries to tackle the problem concerning the "using up" of (limited) source materials (non-renewable natural resources) that the Club of Roma raised with such alarm in 1972, finding considerable public resonance (Meadows et al. 1972). The ecological imbalance caused by taking more from nature than nature is allowed to regenerate and replenish – that is, systemic overshoot – must be contained before it is too late and the consequences become irreversible and beyond human control. What is required is that development be "sustainable": it must be such as to "meet the needs of the present without compromising the ability of future generations to meet their own needs" (Brundtland et al. 1987: 326). Again, a notion of justice is being appealed to, if largely implicitly – namely, the idea that it would be unjust to future (not-yet-born) generations if present ones were to "use up" resources to an extent that leaves less for future humans than has been enjoyed by those now living.

DOI: 10.4324/9781003392705-3

The injustice would be that of generational egoism, if you like (a moral term not employed by Brundtland). Of course, the preference for the present over the future, giving more weight to a desire that can be fulfilled now than one that can only be fulfilled later, is well-known in economics and psychology alike as the problem of discounting, and is viewed as a profound propensity in human nature. What is novel is the context: the ways in which future human beings will likely suffer as a result (however unintended) of the tendency of living humans to put their interests first.

As far as UN-initiated reports go, the Brundtland Report was soon to inspire a number of important declarations about policy changes, nationally as well as globally. Thus, the high-profile 1992 UN Rio Earth summit endorsed a declaration setting out 27 principles of "sustainable development" and recommended that every country produce a national strategy to achieve these results. In the same spirit, a few years later, the Treaty of Amsterdam embraced sustainable development as integral to the aims of the EU, and a comprehensive Sustainable Development Strategy was established in 2001.

Academically no less than institutionally, the notion of "sustainable development" has enjoyed almost unprecedented success, being cited by scientists, politicians, and business leaders all around the world. Nevertheless, the notion and the thinking behind it has had a number of detractors ever since it was launched. They argue that its popularity is in large part due to its vagueness, coupled with a have-your-cake-and-eat-it quality. It is difficult to come out against the goals endorsed in the two prime terms, "sustainability" and "development". What is more, it has the ring of good news to all concerned – future as well as present-day humans, the poor as well as the affluent, environmentalists as well as investors – that one can reach both goals at the same time, indeed (to put it more strongly) the one goal presupposes the other, and vice versa.

Whether that is really so, or simply too good to be true, is a question I will return to below. For now, consider one example showing how the elusive nature of the concept has been sought tackled by avoiding to define it and instead to substitute a set of goals in its place. So, in their book *Implementing Sustainable Development*, William Lafferty and James Meadowcroft argue: "Sustainable development indicates an interdependent concern with: promoting human welfare; satisfying basic needs; protecting the environment; considering the fate of future generations; achieving equity between rich and poor; and participating on a broad basis in decision-making" (2000: 19). It is easy to agree with critics who point out that in amounting to such an all-encompassing list of policy goals acceptable to everyone and offending nobody, the concept is made into a slogan emptied of analytical precision and political bite.

A somewhat more substantial deployment can be witnessed in the "Environmental Sustainability Index" worked out by the Davos-based World Economic Forum, now applied to more than 100 countries. Here, environmental sustainability is defined in terms of five elements (see Esty et al. 2001):

1 The condition of ecological systems such as air, soil and water.
2 The stresses to which those systems are subject, including their levels of pollution.

3 The impact of such stresses upon human society, as measured in terms of factors such as the availability of food and exposed to disease.
4 The social and institutional capacity of a society to cope with environmental hazards.
5 The capacity to create stewardship of global public goods, especially the atmosphere.

Obviously, these are very general statements, abstracting from the highly varied contexts and countries within which the five elements need to be observed.

A striking feature of the policy goals adopted on a worldwide basis since the Brundtland Report is the axiom that development and sustainability are compatible: to succeed, development needs to be sustainable; the requirements for sustainability are such as to facilitate development, not slow it down, let alone forbid it.

To render "development" more concrete, we need to see that it has two different meanings. Development can simply mean economic growth, as measured by GDP, in which case, it applies in principle to all countries. But it can also be taken in a more restricted sense, referring to the economic processes that help take people out of poverty. As Anthony Giddens (the prominent British sociologist known for his affiliation with Tony Blair's "Third Way" policies in the 1990s) points out in his 2011 book *The Politics of Climate Change*, this is the sense in which we contrast the "developing" countries with the "developed" ones, adding that in the first sense of the term, considered simply as GDP-measured economic growth, "development" never stops (2011: 62): the more economic growth, the better as far as development is concerned.

The argument of the Brundtland Report is premised on the all-important distinction between so-called developed and developing countries. Giddens remarks that "growth is much less important to the former than the latter", holding that "developed" countries "may continue to expand their economies, but the need for growth is much less pressing" (2011). By contrast, Giddens states, "for the poor countries there is a *development imperative*":

> It is not only that they have the right to become richer, but that such a process has direct implications for sustainability. Poverty is closely associated with population expansion, one of the root causes of the pressure that is now threatening resources.
>
> (2011)

The poorer countries must be allowed to reach a "certain level of wealth", the more exact definition of which "has to be negotiated politically". What is clear, though, Giddens continues, is that "wherever possible, such as through technology transfer, reductions in emissions – at least relative to past practices in the developed countries – should be sought" (2011: 63). Indeed, the dangers involved in climate change as caused to a large extent by the burning of fossil fuels "will determine in large part how far 'development' today can mimic the trajectories followed by the existing industrial countries". Despite the fact that the outcome of those trajectories is today "under immense pressure", Giddens maintains that "a certain "licence to pollute" has to be acknowledged" (2011).

The false promise of decoupling

I have quoted Giddens extensively because his views are representative of the political and academic consensus: the problems posed by climate change can, and should, be solved within the framework provided by "sustainable development", politically and economically so as well as analytically. It is not only that "development" and "sustainability" are perfectly compatible, indeed mutually dependent but also that the sort of policies that the goal of "sustainable development" recommends will allow us to tackle climate change. This being so, whatever changes the problem of climate change forces upon us, they will not be such as to undermine what the poorer countries are morally entitled to: the "right to become richer" and "a license to pollute".

I see Giddens' highly representative position – though perhaps more so in political circles than in academic ones – as a case of wishful thinking. The compatibility between sustainable development and the need to tackle climate change does not stand up to closer scrutiny; it does not survive a reality check.

To be sure, Giddens himself declares that he will avoid using the notion of "sustainable development" in the remainder of *The Politics of Climate Change*. However, his reasons for doing so have nothing to do with the reality check I have in mind. Rather, Giddens' dissatisfaction is to do with the notion being "more of a slogan than an analytical concept"; indeed, it is "something of an oxymoron" (2011: 71). Nevertheless, "sustainability" is regarded by Giddens as a useful notion, "although itself a little slippery to define, since it concerns an indefinite future. We don't know what technological innovations will occur down the line, and hence assessments of the limits of the earth's resources usually operate under a question-mark" (2011: 61).

I shall come back to the role played by technology in a moment. Before I do so, we should note that Giddens pays some attention to what he calls "over-development", a problem presumably corresponding to that of the "under-development" (my term, not Giddens') seen in poor countries. "Over-development" as understood by Giddens, then, must be acknowledged as a "possibility in the affluent societies". His reasoning is that "the continued expansion of the economy may well bring benefits, but at the same time the problems of affluence tend to pile up". The implication, Giddens goes on to observe, is "not that economic growth has to stop, but that it should not be pursued irrespective of its wider consequences" (2011: 63).

Given this summary of Giddens' view, one thing seems clear: economic growth should continue. It should do so as a matter of moral right in "developing" countries, and it should do so in the "developed" ones with a concern for "the wider consequences", although what exactly these are remains unspecified in Giddens' discussion.

What I find "slippery" and lacking in analytical as well as political bite is not so much the notion of "sustainable development" as such, but Giddens' own position, especially concerning the pivotal issue of the relationship between economic growth and climate change. It all boils down to a very simple question: Is economic growth part of the solution to climate change, or is it part of the problem causing it, even reinforcing it?

To see what is at issue here, recall Giddens' statement that "assessments of the limits of the earth's resources usually operate under a question-mark", the reason being that "we don't know what technological innovations will occur down the line". Characteristically, Giddens does not talk about the limits of the earth's resources as something absolute, that is, as constituting a condition whose primacy over all others needs to be recognised. Instead of focusing head-on on the ecological limits as such, Giddens relativises them in a twofold manner: by connecting them with our assessments of them, and by making the validity of those assessments conditional on future technologies, the when, where, and what of whose impacts we in principle cannot know or predict with much certainty. The effect is that a cloud of relativity and uncertainty is made to hang over any mention of the limits of the earth's resources.

Yet there is no denying that "growing the economy" means putting natural resources under more stress, exploiting them to meet the demands of the world's poor and rich alike, enabling the former to adopt the lifestyle and the patterns of consumption enjoyed by the latter, this being their right, one whose lack of realisation would amount to injustice and hence be morally unacceptable (to recall Giddens' statement). Now, goes the argument that I take Giddens to implicitly rely on, if the exploitation of the earth's resources may intensify so as to meet the demands of the poor and the rich alike without harming sustainability, this is so because new technologies will be much less environmentally harmful than the ones deployed in the era of fossil-fuels driven industrialism. In other words, technological innovation is the key to the promise of continued, never-ending economic growth on a finite planet; it will allow us to produce, consume, and distribute ever-more goods, for ever-more people, without inducing the unacceptable cost of ruining the planet humans depend upon.

Although Giddens refrains from going into this issue in any detail, his view appears to rely heavily on the idea that technologically driven de-materialisation – whereby production and consumption become less resource-intensive per unit of output – is required for the world economy to enjoy constant growth in the foreseeable future. If only technology will help us change *how* we go about using natural resources for human purposes, talk about there being "intrinsic" and absolute limits to that use will prove groundless, proof of misguided techno-pessimism the very moment its opposite is what may save us.

To be sure, the notion of "decoupling" in play here is intriguing: as economic output by way of new, non-fossil-based technologies becomes progressively less dependent on material throughput, the economy can continue to grow without crossing ecological limits or running out of resources. The idea that technological progress will resolve environmental problems is attractive for all sorts of reasons, not least psychological ones: it provides welcome reassurance in rejecting system-related critique and so-called alarmism out of hand, since if technological innovations are the solution, there is no need to engage in any serious changes in our individual lifestyles and collective practices. Indeed, the constellation "more economic activity – less environmental damage" suggests a win-win situation. It therefore fits nicely with the idea we looked at above: rather than being contradictory and in conflict, development and sustainability are mutually dependent – you cannot have the one without presupposing the other. Crucially, both elements – taken as goals, even matters of entitlement for those concerned – are made possible by continued economic growth (to recall Giddens' argument).

Economist Tim Jackson comments on the promise of "decoupling" in his book *Prosperity without Growth* (published one year prior to Giddens' book yet conspicuously ignored there). Jackson points out that there is as yet no credible, socially just, ecologically sustainable scenario of continually growing incomes for a world of seven, eight, or nine billion people. It is entirely fanciful to suppose that "deep" emission and resource cuts can be achieved without confronting the structure of market economies – the very confrontation that the Brundtland Report, followed through the years by scholars such as Giddens, sought to avoid. Nowhere, argues Jackson, is there any evidence that *efficiency can outrun scale* in the way it must do if is to be compatible with sustainability. Far from acting to reduce the throughput of goods, technological progress serves to increase productivity input by reducing factor costs. The phenomenon of "rebound" attests to this: money saved through energy efficiency gets spent on other goods and services (see Jackson 2010: 86, 88, 95).

What prevents "enough is enough" from happening is not a lack of knowledge or moral character in the individual consumer. It is the structural reliance of the market system itself on continued growth: on investments continuing to bring profit, on profits continuing to grow. The twin objectives of growth and profit – whereby profit is both growth-dependent and growth-driving – are the system-immanent key characteristics of a capitalist economy, and they happen to be exactly the traits resulting in capitalism's incompatibility with the planetary key characteristics of limits and finiteness. Recent decades have taught us that, as capitalism goes global, all human needs are directed towards the market and all cultures are forced to strive for the very instrument – the market – that relentlessly robs humans of their ability to survive by their own efforts and skills and to live lives that do not in total lead to an overload of the global carrying capacity – the limit that is threatened by the limitlessness of the market and the insatiability of commercialised needs spread by 24/7 advertising. The cycles of creative destruction attest to this, giving the lie to the rhetoric of a win-win alliance between capitalist economy and sustainability, between what is good for the market and what is good for the planet. The harsh reality is that product lifetimes plummet as durability is systematically designed out of consumer goods and obsolescence is designed in. It's not only that everybody has to have a smartphone but also that you have to buy a new one ever-more often – what is ideologically sold as consumer choice is instead a matter of sheer technological compulsion, there being no option to keeping up with the newest technology and the newest model. In a word, quality is sacrificed to volume throughput. As Jackson observes, the throw-away society is not so much a consequence of consumer greed as a structural prerequisite for survival – survival of the capitalist system, that is. To an ever greater – not smaller – extent, "the institutions of consumer society are designed to favour a particularly materialistic individualism and to encourage the relentless pursuit of consumer novelty because it is exactly what's needed to keep the economy growing" (Jackson 2010: 163).

The impossibility of infinite exponential growth on a finite planet may appear obvious to most people. But it has failed to gain traction in neoclassical economic theory, contradicting as it does its very foundation. Herman Daly, perhaps the world's most prominent ecological economist, has noted that economics will remain "autistic" as long as it ignores the fact that "the economy is a subsystem of the ecosystem", and that the containing ecosystem is finite, non-growing and materially closed (Daly 2007: 2). The fact is that the pattern of scarcity has changed: Manmade capital (labour, technologies) has become relatively plentiful, and remaining natural capital is becoming more and more scarce, subject to over-efficient exploitation to the point of depletion. Manmade and natural capital are complements, not substitutes (as the dominant theoretical paradigm informing and helping justify current practice would have it). As Daly insists, "when factors are complements then the one in short supply is limiting", i.e., natural capital with its flow of natural resources and flux of natural services. To illustrate: "the fish catch used to be limited by a number of fishing boats and fishermen, now it is limited by remaining stocks of fish and their reproductive capacity; cut timber is no longer limited by saw mills, but by standing forests" (2007: 28, 252). The upshot is as unambiguous as it is anathema to the advocates of business-as-usual coupled with techno-optimism: Any attempt, by way of decoupling or otherwise, to marry economic growth and environmental sustainability will fail because premised on an unrealistically high degree of eco-technological efficiency increase. Regrettably, Daly's well-taken criticisms of neoclassical economic theory's autistic separation from any material content and thus from limits – unchallenged in the Brundtland Report – stop short of a fundamental rejection of capitalism, relying instead on the feeble hope for "a broad moral awakening among capitalists".

As yet, there is no sign of such a thing. To give an example, as the world is receiving the one wake-up call after the other concerning the ecological disaster caused by the ever-increasing global plastic binge, corporations like Exxon-Mobile Chemical and Shell Chemical have just decided to invest more than 180 billion dollars to build new facilities that will help fuel a 40% rise in plastic production in the next decade, exacerbating a plastic pollution crisis that scientists warn already risks "near permanent pollution of the earth", affecting the entire marine food chain. In June 2017, an investigation carried out by *The Guardian* revealed that a million plastic bottles are bought around the world every minute, with the large majority ending up in landfill or the sea; globally, only 10% of plastics are being recycled (see Taylor 2018: 12). Plastic is a telling example of what happens when scientists, based on their most recent findings, sound the alarm bell, with business leaders and politicians responding with statements expressing their "deep concern" with the "serious problems" that have been documented: the problem gets worse. With a few exceptions, this holds for the various problems – designated as so many "challenges" – identified in the Brundtland Report 30 years ago: since then, they have become worse.

Subscribing to technology optimism

Giddens and Brundtland share the kind of routine technology optimism that is characteristic of political and business elites around the world. It is an axiom of faith that humanity will manage the planet – and itself – towards the required transition to sustainability. The mentality in question is captured with great precision in a book written 40 years ago by David Ehrenfeld, *The Arrogance of Humanism*. I take it that the key assumptions Ehrenfeld listed then ring familiar today as well: that all problems are soluble; that they are so by people; that many problems are soluble by technology, and if not be technology alone, then by politics or economics; that whenever a catastrophe is threatening to happen, knowledge of that fact will motivate people to work together for a solution before it is too late; that while some resources are finite, all finite or limited resources have substitutes such as will be found and developed in time to avert a catastrophic outcome; and that, no matter what sort of danger or risk humanity will be confronted with, human civilisation will survive (see Ehrenfeld 1978: 16–17).

Ehrenfeld is especially concerned with the dialectical process whereby a solution to one problem generates a set of problems that eventually preclude solutions. His conclusion, based on a number of case studies in a wide range of fields, is that a technological solution is never complete and hence is a quasi-solution. Each quasi-solution generates a residue of new techno-social problems arising from incompleteness, augmentation, and secondary effects. The new problems will proliferate at a faster rate than solutions can be found to meet them. The resulting increased complexity will in its turn increase costs, decrease resources, require even greater control, and lead to the inertia of social institutions (1978: 107). More than 30 years before the notion of "ecosystem services" gained traction outside the circle of economists, holding that "you cannot manage what you do not measure" and that therefore the way to ensure that endangered ecosystems, habitats, and species be saved is to put a price tag on them, Ehrenfeld observed that "finding a value for some part of nature is no guarantee that it will be *rational* for us to preserve it – the reverse may hold" (1978: 202). Anticipating every argument currently employed in the case for ecosystem services, Ehrenfeld writes:

> It does not occur to us that nothing forces us to confront the process of destruction by using its own uncouth and self-destructive premises and terminology. It does not occur to us that by assigning only instrumental value to diversity we merely legitimize the process that is wiping it out, the process that says, "The first thing that matters in any important decision is the magnitude of the dollar costs and tangible benefits". [...] I am referring not just to the effort to put an actual price on biological diversity but also to the attempt to rephrase the price in terms of a nebulous survival value.
>
> (Ehrenfeld 1993: 118)

Allow me to mention here just one of many concrete examples that corroborate Ehrenfeld's argument. In 1973, the applied mathematician Colin Clark wrote a paper about the economics of killing blue whales. The question examined was whether it was economically advisable to halt the Japanese whaling of this species to give blue whale time to recover to the point where they could become a sustained economic resource. The conclusion Clark arrived at was that in fact it was economically preferable to kill every blue whale left in the oceans as fast as possible and reinvest the profits in growth industries rather than to wait for the species to recover to the point where it could sustain an annual catch. To take a more recent example, consider the fate of the rhino in Africa, being one of the "iconic" animals (alongside the polar bear, the tiger, and the orangutang) whose dramatic decline in numbers has received worldwide attention in the last decade. Having reached an all-time-high price in the international market – and be it a black one – poaching of the rhino has tripled in several areas. The market mechanism of supply and demand operates to the effect that as poaching increases, the numbers of rhinos plummet; and the fewer rhinos there are, the more money will be paid for each exemplar being killed, the endpoint being that the very last rhino will command the highest price ever paid for one. In other words, allowing the market to set the price yields the opposite result of that defended by the advocates of putting a price tag on endangered wild animals: the speeding up of the process of extinction. Whether one wants to call this unintended consequence proof of the sometime perversity of the free-market mechanism, or simply the way it works, run-of-the-mill like, yet for the most part inconspicuously so, is a moot question. The fact of the matter is that it's simply how the market works.

Ecosystem services

As Christophe Bonneuil and Jean-Baptiste Fressoz remind us in their book *The Shock of the Anthropocene*, the concept of sustainable development derives from the notion of "maximal sustainable yield" conceived by (ecological) fishery science in the 1950s, which in its turn was inspired by the notion of "sustainable (*nachhaltig*) management" developed by German forestry science in the eighteenth century. As Bonneuil and Fressoz point out, all three notions are based on presuppositions that today are proven wrong in that they no longer obtain: "The Anthropocene cancels the peaceful and reassuring project of sustainable development" (2016: 22).

I think that the point can be put even more strongly: the success of the notion of sustainable development, measured in terms of its world-wide impact on policies adopted (and those not adopted) during the last three decades, is partly responsible for having led us into the Anthropocene, understood as a danger zone of unprecedented magnitude as far as multi-dimensional ecological catastrophe is concerned. In keeping with Daly's critique, the notion of "sustainable development" has helped maintain belief in the possibility of perpetuating economic growth by means of a bit more "conservation" of the environment, conveniently neglecting the warnings over the impossibility of indefinite growth on a finite planet that stemmed from not only the famous *Limits to Growth* report published by the club of Rome in 1972, but also the work dating back to the 1960s by the economist Nicholas Georgescu-Roegen on entropy and degrowth, captured in what he called "the fallacy of endless substitution", i.e., the fallacy found in the neoclassical school (on which the Brundtland Report tacitly relies) as well as in Marxist economics, failing to recognise the way in which an economy driven by the twin imperatives of growth and profit is bound to undermine resources for which this planet has no substitutes – the fallacy of (mis)treating as mere means, as perfectly replaceable, what is in fact indispensable (see Georgescu-Roegen 1971).

In other words, only by refusing to seriously consider the implications of these insights was it possible to go on pretending that the three crucial dimensions could be mutually negotiated within a growth-driven capitalist economy: namely the economic, the social and the environmental. The failure is a twofold: the economy is not placed within the social, which in itself is framed by a thousand feedback loops within the biosphere and the Earth system. Indeed, the related notions of a "green economy" and of "ecosystem services", in vogue since the 1990s, demonstrate the unwillingness to take on board the bad news: that we have to do with limits, not opportunities; with systemic problems such as require overturning the entire economic framework, not business challenges of a kind wedded to sustaining what has become unsustainable. To the extent that "ecosystem services" – those yielded for humans by, say, bees active in pollination – now are singled out as object of markets, the biosphere, the hydrosphere, and the atmosphere are made to appear as mere subsystems of the financial and commodity sphere, thus turning the actual ecological order of primacy on its head: regarding as fixed and unchangeable the current capitalist economic system and the imperatives inseparable from it, and as perfectly elastic and manipulable for human purposes (as expressed in insatiable needs and desires) the material substratum on which all economic activities rely, called "nature". In effect, the social system that desperately needs to change is placed beyond critique, whereas what can only be further changed at the cost of degradation, depletion, and extinction is subject to ever-intensifying exploitation, rendering the current trajectory self-destructive.

That said, it is easy to see why "green growth" and "ecosystem services" became buzzwords in the wake of the Brundtland Report. Both concepts hold the promise of using the market to solve whatever problems the market has failed to solve thus far – recalling Sir Nicholas Stern's oft-cited statement that climate change is a matter of the biggest "market failure" in history. To be sure, the market economy was for a long time criticised for externalising its true costs as far as the values provided by nature are concerned, so that a problem like deforestation failed to be accounted for within the given cost/benefit calculus – i.e., the more rapidly and comprehensively deforestation takes place, the better economically speaking, with supply meeting demand, GDP increasing, etc., tacitly presupposing that there will always be "more for the taking". Thus, the thinking behind ecosystem services may be said to change the situation radically in declaring everything affected in/by the economy an "internal" aspect of it and so needing to be accounted for in a manner doing justice to its true importance for the system as a whole. And indeed, this is the logic that allowed the pioneering economist in the field, Robert Costanza, to assess the annual value of the services rendered by the biosphere at about $33 billion, or twice the world's GDP. The point about ecosystem services being that they are valuable, the only way to demonstrate the value in question is to measure it qua monetary value, allowing for the perfect commensurability that market transactions crave, in effect subjecting nature *in toto*, in all its qualitative and life-(re)generating dimensions and processes, to quantification. As Bonneuil and Fressoz remark, all values of nature, even those far upstream from production and including the most spiritual (renamed "cultural services"), thus enter an accounting logic, as illustrated by the adopted policy of International Union for Conservation of Nature to present nature as "the largest company on Earth" (see Bonneuil and Fressoz 2016: 55).

Resistance to giving up on growth

Given this background, what we need to ask is: What would it mean to abandon the growth paradigm that we have seen the notion of sustainability to rely upon, and why is there so much resistance to doing so? To what extent is such resistance culturally entrenched, and in that sense running deeper than simply reflecting the self-interest of commercial players?

The growth paradigm as we know it involves two distinct yet intertwined forms of exploitation, that of inner and outer nature, i.e., human and natural capital, respectively. Whereas the harm inflicted by inner-directed exploitation entails *burnout* as suffered by the humans affected, that inflicted by outer-directed exploitation entails *overshoot*, resulting in loss of biodiversity and extinction of species.

There is little doubt, then, that a society wedded to ever-increasing growth carries costs for the human individuals involved as well as for the wider natural world – costs that nowadays are felt by more and more people on all continents. This prompts the question: Is it worth it?

For all its pertinence, such a question may assume a degree of free choice that is simply not enjoyed by those hardest hit by burnout as caused by the psychosomatic stress of keeping up with current demands on performance in the workplace. Although working less hours, as part of a desire to counter requests for increased productivity, may seem a good idea to many people, one conducive rather than detrimental to enhanced quality of life, working less is simply not an option. Most of us feel compelled to go on as cogs in the machine of growth for the simple reason of sustaining ourselves and our families. It doesn't make a real difference that we have lost all illusions about growth being tantamount to progress and the good life, or that we lament the degradation of nature, including the places we live and love, that is the "external" cost of perpetuating the growth machine we are part of.

The picture is more complicated, however. While there is widespread recognition of the two-dimensional costs of growth alluded to, inasmuch as the costs are directly experienced, there is also a high degree of resistance to change course. There are many reasons for such resistance, some of them "rational" in the sense of being tied to self-interest, economic, or otherwise. For my purposes, a source of resistance that deserves particular attention is what I designate "a sense of entitlement".

Generally and across class divisions, we are being socialised into the role of consumer in a market-driven society. From an early age, we learn to take it for granted that nature is there for humans to exploit and that, provided we can afford it, all sorts of commodities on the (legal) market are free for us to enjoy, whether it be driving a diesel SUV, flying to Thailand for Easter holidays or eating red meat four days a week. I learn to see myself as deserving all sorts of experiences and goods that are available to me, partly for the simple fact that we humans are exceptional creatures – intellectually, morally, and legally – vis-a-vis all other creatures, and partly because as an individual, I have worked hard to get what I want. The sense of entitlement justifies consumerism morally speaking, and sees to it that its current form – that of being implicated in systemic overshoot – is being embraced by the individual and transmitted from one generation to the next (see Vetlesen 2021).

This is not to say that no criticism of entitlement thus understood and acted upon exists. It does, and that very fact underscores the self-understanding of our society as free, tolerating that individuals may be committed to different and even conflicting values. Nonetheless, most people are immune to critiques of consumerism as a way of life: giving pride of place to freedom of choice and hence individual autonomy, the trump values presented as guaranteed by the free market, the mindset of entitlement makes sure that the burden of argument rests with those voicing the criticism, daring to question my actions on moral or political grounds, thereby interfering with the way I exercise my freedom. Indeed, the taboo against so-called moralisation is culturally entrenched. Insisting on one's right to enjoy individual freedom of choice is simply the default position, immensely powerful at that. Moreover, defenders of the sanctity of consumer choice tend to neglect the role of advertising in creating the "needs" allegedly met by the market; needs whose subtle fabrication renders them imposed rather than authentic.

In her book *Psychological Roots of the Climate Crisis,* British psychoanalyst Sally Weintrobe observes that each of us is conflicted, with a caring and an uncaring part. She describes the triumph of neoliberalism as a case not only of deregulating the market (rolling back the welfare state by way of privatisation and outsourcing), but also, more fundamentally, of "deregulating the morals of a nation". This involves a two-pronged approach: "boost the uncaring part that wants to override limits" (say, by encouraging the sense of right to have it all, turning selfishness and greed into a timeless "truth" about human nature) and "undermine the caring part that says no to that" (Weintrobe 2021: 114).

Whereas Weintrobe puts more emphasis on neoliberalism than I have done here, her depiction of its rise to dominance since the reign of Margaret Thatcher, swiftly spreading to other European countries, sits well with what I have argued about the successful career of "sustainability" in the same period: the Brundtland notion of sustainability was never meant to challenge neoliberalism – indeed, it has proved to be all-too-readily adopted and co-opted by it, seamlessly and without friction.

But hasn't the damage done by the growth-obsessed economy that we are implicated in become increasingly visible, for all to see, during the last decades? The overshoot and burnout I referred to, manifesting the over-exploitation of both natural and human capital, are both taking their toll, increasingly so. Why doesn't this double damage – to the natural world, and to us humans as part of it – cause more conflict and more protest? What about resistance?

Weintrobe's assessment is worth quoting in full. Neoliberalism, she points out,

> talked up the virtues of shameless conspicuous consumption; it sanctioned omnipotent "as if" thinking by promoting extensive disavowal of the damage the neoliberal economy was doing. As neoliberalism's damaging effects rose, it worked harder than ever to hide and obscure the damage. Mass media ignored the damage, advertising "greened" it and the science community that told us about it started to be discredited and vilified. Neoliberal culture infantilized and regressed people, encouraging them to be less mature and less responsible than they are capable of being; it seduced them into believing they could continue with business as usual. It used every trick in the psychological toolkit to persuade us we need not change when only change will prevent systems' collapse. It drew society into a collective psychosis that people are now starting to wake up from.
>
> (Weintrobe 2021: 114)

According to Weintrobe, then, neoliberal culture is attacking our will to care about each other – and, I would add, our will to care about the non-human others that go to make up the natural world. At the individual level, we are inclined to resist the idea that culture can influence us without our awareness; we do not want to admit that we are far less free than we like to think when it comes to what we understand by freedom, and that the way we enact the culturally upheld sense of entitlement to "have it all" is in fact deeply problematic, psychologically as well as ecologically, for intrapsychic as well as environmental reasons. This being so, what is required if we are to find a way out is what is so difficult and steeped in denial – namely, to rid ourselves of the belief that, while others may be affected by culture or what used to be called "ideology", we are far too smart. As Weintrobe insists, we need to tolerate uncertainty, muddle and doubt; we need to see our collusion and how deeply we are invested in it. In short, we need to be mature, to admit and confront our responsibility and guilt, and to recognise the need for *reparation* in Melanie Klein's sense: to realise the loss we have inflicted, the good we have spoiled by way of taking too much without giving back (see Klein 1988).

When is enough enough?

The sense of entitlement I have talked about is wedded to the promise that "more" is always "better", and that there will always be more and more for everyone. One could say that up to a point, as long as there is still an insufficiency, the "more" delivered by growth – in production and consumption – will translate into a "better", meaning improvement in the life of those affected. But what if there is already excess? Where, exactly, do we go from "enough", in the sense of "enough is enough", to a situation of excess such that adding more – perpetual growth – fails to be a true improvement? Where the "more" promised is a blatantly false promise, doing more harm than good?

In his recent book *Post Growth: Life after Capitalism*, Tim Jackson argues that the inability to know where the point constituting "enough" is reached, and the inability to know how to stop when we get there, are the two "critical flaws at the heart of capitalism" (2021: 13, 151). Jackson holds that "green growth", understood as the sort of growth compatible with – or dictated by – sustainability is dressed up as "better growth" in all sorts of ways: "better technology, more innovation, greater efficiency" (2021: 39). As we saw above, in an earlier book Jackson showed that the decoupling that this promise relies upon, is simply not happening. This being so, the faith in green growth, far from being a way out of crisis, helps make matters worse, amounting as it does to the message that "only growth can deliver us from the mess that growth itself has landed us in" (2021).

Besides the unwillingness of many of us to admit the seriousness of the mess we are part of, there is a lack of imagination when it comes to envision a good life that is not based on ever-increasing consumption in the material sense, but instead seen for what it is: detrimental to such a life. Kate Soper speaks about the need for exerting pressure to "simplify and settle for a less materially encumbered and work-driven existence: decisions not to buy but to do without" (2020: 173). On Soper's view,

> The zeal for money and material possessions that is such a prevalent feature of market societies, is not an inherent feature of human nature, but compensatory at least to some extent for the absence or loss of other less tangible goods (for love, friendship, respect, security, justice, trust.
>
> (2020: 149)

Central to Soper's case for "an alternative hedonism" is the reappraisal of *craft*, that is to say, of work not made for sale but simply for the pleasure of making or gift giving, insofar as such works embody an intrinsic "hand-value" not found in commodities made for profit (see Soper 2020: 102).

Hence, the particular skills required for making a work of craft are not simply the "means" to achieve some desired end-result. Transcending mere instrumentality, such skills are meaningful in themselves, providing a sense of mastery and purpose in those acquiring and performing them, and attracting the admiration of others. With craft, to become good at what one is doing is not an individual project, but something genuinely social, involving others in the role of masters to be respected for their rich experience in dealing with all the "how to..." questions that the novice faces, and that can only be transmitted from one generation to the next in the form of practice and so by way of example: "look how I do it, and try for yourself". Besides helping maintain vital relationships between different generations, craft brings about works esteemed for their durability; taking pride in being made to last, to sustain being used by more than one generation, say, the table made by my father, or by my grandfather, allows all members of the family to cherish something in common, of shared value. By being one of its kind, made at a particular point in time and by a loved one, those to whom such a table is passed on will feel a special responsibility for it, a commitment to helping keep it as intact as possible, both to heed the person who made it and to help ensure that future owners/users will learn to value it as well. When things are made to endure, to have a future linked up with a known past, they help accomplish something important in three dimensions: they connect the present with the past, they are kind to the environment and they are carriers of inter-generational bonds.

Reinvigorating craft, then, has a lot going for it both ecologically and socially. But it is also a project that is up against a number of obstacles. Turnover is everywhere on the rise, amplified by planned obsolescence and advertising's mantra that the new model is always preferable to the old one, even though it's not old at all. We are encouraged to throw away things long before they get the chance to be worn out; we acquire the newest model fully aware that we will keep it for ever shorter periods of time. In the course of a few decades, we have gone from a situation where one set of furniture would be used by several generations, to one where each generation will change their furniture several times, to use an example offered by Jean Baudrillard in his early book *The System of Objects,* published in 1968. As consumers, we become complicit in the companies' relentless endeavour to increase profits by speeding up the cycle of production and consumption.

"Growing the economy" in a material, quantifiable sense harbours a double loss, that of quality and that of experience. As the types and numbers of human-made things to meet some alleged human "need" or desire are everywhere on the rise, the time spent attending to, using and developing what might qualify as a relationship with each one of them decreases. Never before in history was the relationship between human owner/user and object owned/used so short-lasting, shallow, and wasteful. If "materialism" is a concept meant to show up the value of things – not necessarily in their own right, but for us, their users – a less materialistic culture than ours may never have existed. To dispose of things ever more quickly is clearly to hold each one of them in disrespect and to consider them devoid of intrinsic value. Indeed, the shallowness of the instrumental value with which consumer items are associated is such as to belie the very meaning of value, of something being treated – respected – as value-able, able to carry value. The result is a historical situation that makes for a stark contrast with Hannah Arendt's conception of the "common world" in her book *The Human Condition*. Arendt conceived the "artificial", meaning the human-made world of artefacts, ranging from buildings to furniture and works of art, as capable of bringing about a tangible permanence in a world otherwise shot through with the transience of life, bound to the cycle of life and death. The most admired works of human hands and human imagination – think of Michelangelo or Leonardo – are those that succeed in transcending the here and now – transitoriness – of its creator as well as its physical origins.

Of course, the capacity for transcendence Arendt ascribes to great works of art in particular involves a number of qualities, durability, and longevity being but two of them, and beauty a third one – always remember how closely the functional and the aesthetic are interconnected. Perhaps only now we start to recognise their true value and importance, at the moment of their demise, as it were. To make the point by shifting from works of art to use-objects (both helping make up Arendt's "common world"), that the new generation of furniture outlasts its predecessor or the new model of smartphone lasts longer than those before it is precisely *not* the point. The fabricated, advertising-driven demand for the new over the old, for novelty as such, as a quasi goal in itself, a fetish, in the last decades has been effectively divorced from the goal of improving quality as measured by durability; divorced, that is, from both the mindset of the craftsman – the made product/artefact as eminently usable for its given purpose as well as worthy of admiration for the skills it embodies – and the object's immanent standards of excellence. The world made of stuff these days is one prone to undermine the aspiration to permanence at every turn, depriving us – both as makers, owners and users – of the chance to build attachment and loyalty to artefacts as so many particular things, each with their peculiar trajectory; as things to rely upon not only in functional terms but in affective ones as well, born of a shared past, that of me-and-my-grand-dad's table; things to be dedicated to insofar as they lay a claim on us to uphold their value in the rich sense going beyond their sheer instrumentality. Therefore, to hold – as is often said – that we live in an excessively "materialistic" society is to get it wrong: we are not as materialistic as we should be if the term refers to building relationships of depth and longevity with things we use such as furniture. But again, for such human–object relationships to aspire to depth and be genuine sources of memory, meaning, and identity, they need to be made to last and to be carriers of beauty as well as functionality – if not, they fail to live up to their potential to inspire the bond alluded to. Deliberately making things that are meant to be shallow and short-lived is a matter of disrespect to the objects themselves as well as to the human producers/users involved.

Reparation and the myth of production

Above I invoked Melanie Klein's notion of reparation understood as the need to right past wrongs. Reparation is premised on the admission of responsibility and guilt for having played a part in causing that something good has been spoiled: spoiled to the point of degradation or extinction as a consequence of my greed, egoism, etc. In the present context, what is typically played out as between individuals in the psychoanalytic setting Klein has in mind – say, between mother and child – must be raised to a cultural and so collective level. This means that a "we", not an individual "I", is behind the harm wrought – a "we" in the form of what I have called a culture of entitlement, justifying the harm as "worth it". It also means that in the case I focus on here, the "other" ("object" in psychoanalytic terminology) being harmed is the natural world instead of a human other.

In *Rekindling Life*, French philosopher Baptiste Morizot observes that a key feature of our present-day society is that it "cancels out the timeless motif of a *debt* toward the nonhuman milieu, a motif omnipresent in the animist cultures that do not believe in the fable according to which they produce the manioc they cultivate" (2022: 87f.). This cancellation is the work of what Morizot terms "the myth of production" so powerful in our culture, alleging that we humans are the sole source of value, unique in producing the goods needed to meet our needs and so, ultimately, to secure our survival; only thanks to our own capacities and efforts can we flourish and persist on planet Earth. To cancel the notion of a debt towards the nonhuman natural world, then, is to effect a "deregulation of limits in the exploitation of the milieu" (2022). Morizot elaborates:

> It is precisely because animist hunter-gatherers acknowledge their debt to the forest for their very survival that they recognize the forest as a giving environment, and thus that their social form can spontaneously impose *limits* on everyone in the use of the commons – that is, on the products of the dynamics of the living world. Recognition of the debt induces very powerful social mechanisms that establish forms of durability.
>
> (Morizot 2022: 88)

That ours is culture wedded to the myth of production in Morizot's sense should be clear from my above analysis. Looking upon ourselves as producers of our own substance, rather than as having received it from the natural world, encourages the belief that "we owe nothing to anyone". Hence, as Tim Jackson observed, we are at a loss to answer the question about limits, to know when the point constituting "enough" is reached. This makes for a stark contrast with cultures committed to the need to *restore* something to the milieu that keeps us alive; the need, that is, to "maintain sufficient vitality in that milieu for it to regenerate and keep on giving" (Morizot 2022: 88). This need is being denied in our culture. As a result, gratitude towards the gifts of the natural world is rendered inconceivable, at best a relic of superstitious and occult beliefs, at worst downright irrational. True, showing such gratitude openly to nonhuman creatures such as trees may be tolerated among children. But it raises suspicion of being less than fully "rational" if displayed by adults. Variation among individuals aside, the big picture is that as a culture we have shifted, meaning progressed, from a "mythical" worldview to a modern scientific one (to use Max's Weber's distinction) where humans and human-initiated activities are considered the sole locus of value.

To be sure, there is a difference between my above discussion of reparation and Morizot's conception of debt. Whereas Morizot talks about the natural world in its life-regenerating aspects, I have talked about the value of entities – artefacts – brought about by us, exemplarily by way of craft. Analytically, this difference goes back to the well-known Aristotelian distinction between two kinds of entities: the grown and the made. The difference of emphasis aside, however, Morizot and I are making the same point: we are in debt to both the natural world and to the "common world" erected thanks to humans as craftsmen, artisans, and artists. The tree, as well as the table made from it, is a genuine loci of value – value-able, able to embody value – and thus something we should treat with respect and gratitude. It is incumbent on me that I do what I can to sustain such value as encountered in something – in other living creatures, or in man-made objects – brought about independently of me yet depending on me for its (their) continued intactness. A truly sustainable culture is one made up of individuals sharing this double commitmen

Bibliography

Arendt, Hannah, 1958. *The Human Condition.* Chicago, IL: The University of Chicago Press.

Baudrillard, Jean, 1996 [1968]. *The System of Objects*. London: Verso.

Bonneuil, Christophe and Jean-Baptiste Fressoz, 2016. *The Shock of the Anthropocene.* London: Verso.

Brundtland, Gro Harlem et al., 1987. *Our Common Future.* Oxford: Oxford University Press.

Daly, Herman, 2007. *Ecological Economics and Sustainable Development.* Cheltenham: Edward Elgar.

Ehrenfeld, David, 1978. *The Arrogance of Humanism.* Oxford: Oxford University Press.

Ehrenfeld, David, 1993. *Beginning Again.* Oxford: Oxford University Press.

Esty, Daniel et al., 2001. *Environmental Sustainability Index.* Davos: Davos World Economic Forum.

Georgescu-Roegen, Nicholas, 1971. *The Entropy Law and the Economic Process.* Cambridge, MA: Harvard University Press.

Giddens, Anthony, 2011. *The Politics of Climate Change.* Cambridge: Polity Press.

Grusovnik, Thomaz et al. eds., 2021. *Environmental and Animal Abuse Denial.* London: Rowman & Littlefield.

Jackson, Tim, 2010. *Prosperity without Growth.* London: Earthscan.

Jackson, Tim, 2021. *Post Growth. Life after Capitalism.* Cambridge: Polity Press.

Klein, Melanie, 1988. *Love, Guilt, and Reparation and Other Works 1921-1945.* London: Virago.

Lafferty, William and James Meadowcroft eds., 2000. *Implementing Sustainable Development.* Oxford: Oxford University Press.

Meadows, Donella et al., 1972. *Limits to Growth.* New York: New American Library.

Morizot, Baptiste, 2022. *Rekindling Life: A Common Front.* Cambridge: Polity Press.

Orange, Donna M., 2017. *Climate Crisis, Psychoanalysis, and Radical Ethics.* New York: Routledge.

Soper, Kate, 2020. *Post-Growth Living. For an Alternative Hedonism.* London: Verso.

Taylor, Matthew, 2018. "Warnings of "disastrous" plastic binge." *The Guardian Weekly* 5 January: 12.

Vetlesen, Arne Johan, 2021. "Denial as a sense of entitlement: Assessing the role of culture." In Grusovnik et al., 2021: 35–53.

Weintrobe, Sally, 2021. *Psychological Roots of the Climate Crisis.* New York: Bloomsbury Academic.

2 Sustainability discourses and the question of democracy

Cecilie Sachs Olsen

In this chapter, I discuss the mediation of messages of sustainability from the perspective of democracy. I am concerned with how the theories and practices of democracy will fare in a climate-changing world, and I believe that the ways in which messages of sustainability are mediated have a key role to play. Sustainability is mediated through various discourses, defined here as systems of meaning ascribed to objects and events. Meaning can be communicated through language, but discourses also condition interpretation and sense-making in relation to actions, interactions and material artefacts (Wetherell et al. 2001). Since they organise social relations, discourses also dictate conduct (and our interpretation of that conduct) in everyday life. Some analyses show that the "successes" of sustainability discourses when it comes to dictate conduct across different fields and contexts reside in the term "sustainability" being an empty signifier that allows for multiple interpretations and contingency of meaning (Brown 2016; Laclau 1990, 2005).

This becomes very clear in the Norwegian context, which this chapter focuses on. Sustainability discourses in Norway are particularly strong, representing consensual and hegemonic power relations and systems of rule that are historically and culturally constituted. The reason for this is twofold. First, Norway is a consensus-based democracy characterised by its high levels of political and social trust (Wollebæk et al. 2012). Second, the idealisation of nature has been a central element of Norwegian nation-building since the nineteenth century. Hence, instead of remaining solely the purview of an oppositional civil society realm or social movement, the field of environmentalism was adopted at an early stage of the state itself, becoming a key aspect of Norwegian statecraft (Lahn and Rowe 2015). With the coining of the term "sustainable development" in the Brundtland Report, launched by the Norwegian Prime minister Gro Harlem Brundtland in 1987, Norway cemented its international role as a climate leader. Yet, Norway is caught in what by some is called "The Norwegian Paradox" (Faarstad and Aasen 2022) whereby Norway pertains to be a climate leader on the one hand, and a major oil and gas exporter on the other. As I demonstrate in this chapter, within this setting "sustainability" risk becoming an empty signifier and thus reveals its Janus-faced nature.

On the one side of the Janus-faced nature of sustainability, the term might offer radical potential because it enables evermore diverse critiques of economic systems and brings sustainability debates into the realm of politics. On the other side,

DOI: 10.4324/9781003392705-4

it might advance consensus around dominant political-economic interests and thus evacuate any proper political dimension from environmental debates. Hence, while the openness and ambiguity of the term "sustainability" might be the reason for its success as a discourse, it raises important questions concerning the democratic implications of how messages of sustainability are mediated: Does the urgency of climate change relegate sustainability issues to a terrain beyond dispute and thus foreclose democratic debate? Does the mobilisation of change as inevitable and universally beneficial infuse a post-democratic situation by masking what needs to change and thus work to sustain business-as-usual? Might sustainability discourses reinvigorate democracy by empowering emancipatory thought and action?

The chapter discusses different responses to these questions from two main perspectives. First, I draw on Machin's (2022) analysis of different political imaginaries of climate change to grasp and contrast the different ways in which the relation between different sustainability discourses and democracy can be understood. Second, I foreground, with reference to various scholars, the importance of enabling the expression of disagreement and difference as a prerequisite for a democratic approach to sustainability issues (see i.e. Kenis and Lievens 2015; Machin 2013, 2020; Mouffe 2022; Rancière 1999; Swyngedouw 2010, 2018). On this basis, I distinguish between three sustainability discourses in which the relationship between messages of sustainability and democracy takes distinct forms. These are the *technical*, *liberal*, and *political* sustainability discourse. The *technical* sustainability discourse is illustrated through the campaign "The Clock Is Ticking Toward 2030" (2020) by the Norwegian wind power company Norwegian Wind (Norsk Vind). Here, the present climate conundrum is staged through the mobilisation of apocalyptic climate change imaginaries in which "we" are all victims of forces beyond our control. The aim is to prompt a rational consensus around the technical solution of wind power. The urgency of taking action leaves no room for democratic deliberation.

In the *liberal* sustainability discourse, the "we" of the people is not constituted as "universal victims" but rather as a heterogeneity of voices that are all agents of change. This discourse is illustrated through the campaign "Say Hi to Change" (2018) by the Norwegian state-owned multinational energy company Equinor (former Statoil and StatoilHydro). Celebrating diversity and equality through a presentation of consensual harmony, the campaign promises an improvement of democratic representation and participation as a key to tackle issues of climate change.

Finally, the less dominant *political* sustainability discourse does not put forward a single and straightforward solution to sustainability challenges, but rather insists on a plurality of conflicting demands that contest the status quo. This discourse is illustrated through the theatre performance "Society under Construction" (Oslo 2019) by the German theatre group Rimini Protokoll. The performance presents individual and situated stories of sustainability that contest neoliberal approaches to the environment and insist on the formation of alternatives.

My discussion of the Norwegian Wind and Equinor campaigns is based mainly on document analysis of commercial videos released by the companies as part of their campaigns. The analysis also includes newspaper articles and reports concerning the campaigns as well as official statements from company spokespersons. My discussion of Rimini Protokoll's theatre performance is based on my own experience as an audience of the performance as well as documentary material from the performance, including a full transcription of the manuscript. I acknowledge that the medium and the experience of the videos for the campaigns and the performance differ greatly. The videos are about two minutes long while the performance is almost two hours long and watching a video and participating in a theatre performance are two quite different experiences. However, the focus of my discussion is the discursive space produced through the examples, and this space is constituted by both medium and message. Hence, I consider the difference in medium and experience not as a problem for my analysis but as an integral part of it.

I proceed as follows: first, I outline the potentials and challenges that discourses around sustainability might pose for democracy. I then discuss the three examples of the technical, liberal, and political sustainability discourse and their democratic implications. Finally, I conclude that although none of these discourses can address the complexity of sustainability issues in their entirety, they all contain valid and valuable insights into the role of sustainability discourses in shaping the trajectories of democratic politics and life. Yet, I also contend that the political sustainability discourse is the only one that celebrates the openness of democracy and the political plurality around sustainability.

Situating sustainability discourses and democracy

In the era of the Anthropocene, when the interconnections and impact of human actions and various serious environmental challenges are brought to attention, ecological consciousness appears to be on the rise. Everyone, from artists and activists to corporate businesses and multinational companies, is now declaring their dedication to work towards a more sustainable future (Ergene et al. 2020; Machin 2020; Tyszczuk and Smith 2018). As Gunder (2006: 214) observes, sustainability has come to "act as an empty name or label of an ideal that many can believe and identify with. Yet, in doing so, sustainability accommodates a wide range of contestable discourses, each vying to articulate its definite meaning". As mentioned in the introduction, these discourses have different democratic implications. Some discourses might support approaches rooted in radical democratic potential, while others might work to evacuate any proper democratic dimension from sustainability debates. In this part, I further unpack these different implications by which sustainability discourse matter for democracy. In many ways, we live in times in which institutional representative democracy is more widespread than ever (Wilson and Swyngedouw 2014). All manner of issues and problems concerning sustainability are mediated, made visible and politicised, from the unsustainable re-engineering of the climate to the heroic resistances of indigenous peoples, from fracking to the garbage left on the sidewalk, from the plight of the whale to sustainable lifestyle preferences. At the same time, critics have long observed that discourse around the need for more "sustainable" futures in the face of pending environmental catastrophe signals a range of populist manoeuvres that infuse a so-called post-democratic condition (see e.g. Badiou 2008; Castree 2009; Mouffe 1992; Swyngedouw 2010).

The diagnosis of post-democracy has dominated many debates about the condition and perspectives of Western representative democracies (see e.g. Badiou 2008; Castree 2009; Crouch 2004; Mouffe 1992; Rancière 1995; Swyngedouw 2010; Žižek 2000). The gist of the diagnosis is the argument that democracy in Western countries has been compromised by a managerial governance logic structured under neoliberalism. This governance logic is, according to prominent critics such as Mouffe and Rancière, post-political and post-democratic because it narrows political debate through consensus-generating processes. For Mouffe (2000), the problem with consensus politics is that it ignores the persistence of antagonistic positions. She warns that it is not possible to achieve general political consensus without obfuscating and repressing remaining deep differences in world-views and political values between ideologies, which – if unrecognised – will inevitably resurface in destructive forms. To mitigate these destructive tendencies, democracy needs instead to move towards pluralism and agonism – an open struggle between different ideological adversaries – which she argues is the basis for a vibrant democracy. Rancière sees democracy less through the prism of adversaries, and more as a struggle for subjectivation and inclusion by newly emerging identities who, as yet, do not have an equal voice. However, he agrees with Mouffe that democracy depends on the political struggle for the maintenance of pluralism, difference, disagreement, and conflict, which the managerial and neoliberal idea of a universal consensus seems to annul.

Coming back to how sustainability discourse infuses this post-democratic tradition, critics such as Swyngedouw (2010) observe that discourses concerning climate change have been relegated to a consensual terrain beyond dispute as the need for more sustainable futures is framed as a global humanitarian cause. This consensual terrain is furthermore enforced by a perceived inevitability of capitalism and the market economy as the basic organisational structure of the social and economic order, for which there is no alternative.

The consensual approach to sustainability can be seen in relation to the fact that the emergence of sustainability discourses in the 1970s and 1980s coincides with the expansion of neoliberalism in the West and beyond (Ergene et al. 2020). The merging of these two processes, the emergence of sustainability discourses and the expansion of neoliberalim, is evident in the so-called techno-managerial perspective on sustainable development. This perspective foregrounds how sustainability could be achieved by corporate strategies and "sustainable" or "green" growth, linking and consolidating contradictions of social equity and of economic versus ecological benefits in sustainability (Banerjee 2011).

What makes this techno-managerial mediation of sustainability post-democratic is that it works to sustain and advance dominant political-economic interests and does not permit conflictual debates around possible alternatives (see i.e. Machin 2020, 2022; Wilson and Swyngedouw 2014). As Yusoff and Gabrys (2011, p. 519) observe, sustainability discourse is to a large extent dominated by "neoliberal approaches to the environment, which actively attempt to disable the imagination of alternatives, outside of economic systems of environmental governance and the valuation of natures that capital can 'see'". Westman and Broto (2022) contend that the problem with these neoliberal approaches is that they are guided by a form of thinking that explains everything in advance, thus excluding any form of knowledge or experience that does not fit its prescription. Hence, while sustainability discourses are cloaked in emancipatory terminology, they are often linked with consensual democracy approaches that prevent the flourishing of radical ideas that might enable a systemic challenge to the status quo. As a result, sustainability discourses risk reproducing assumptions and values of mainstream discourses, rather than changing them.

Another post-democratic aspect of sustainability discourses is what Machin (2022) defines as a "skeptical democratic imaginary". Here, a growing number of voices question whether democracy is at all suitable for tackling environmental concerns and risks, demanding that policy should instead be guided by experts. Expertise, particularly in the form of scientific knowledge, is praised for transcending the petty quarrels and quibbles of politics and point to the "rational" and "effective" way forward towards sustainability. As Machin (2022) argues, this sceptical approach to democracy is problematic because it ignores that while science and expertise can alert us to environmental issues, there will always be disagreements about the implications of their discoveries. Leaving no room for such disagreements not only can be detrimental to the legitimacy of political decisions but also ignores individual experiences and diverse forms of knowledge production.

There are also critics who question whether science and expertise alone can provide effective responses to environmental problems. They argue that the problem is not too much democracy, but too little (Machin 2022, p. 5). Hence, they advocate for expanding democratic representation by incorporating other forms of expertise and the participation of lay citizens (see i.e. Deese 2019; Goodman and Morton 2014; Plumwood 1995). Following the ideas of theorists of deliberative democracy (i.e. Habermas and Rawls), the argument goes that by engaging both citizens and experts in discussion, environmental policy will be rendered more inclusive, legitimate, and rational. This rationalist conception of democracy, then, is premised on the idea of a free and unconstrained public deliberation for all, which, in turn, depends on a given equality of voices (Machin 2020). However, as Rancière (1999) points out, equality is not a given, but a contingent that must be taken as a supposition and constantly verified by opening up scenes of demonstration and enunciation. Insisting upon consensual dialogue, then, risk becoming a repressive norm in itself because it fails to address, challenge, and deconstruct the social categories that maintain relations of power and domination.

Westman and Broto (2022, p. 1335) furthermore observe that personal narratives are almost entirely absent from sustainability discourse, as is emotions (suffering, frustration, joy, or loss) that may inspire resistance or change. Sustainability discourse, they argue, is predominantly interested in supposedly rational and transferable frameworks and roadmaps for "moving forward", and thus fails to build on situated experience. This is problematic because, as Tully (2001) observes, attempting to facilitate inclusive environmental debates is not a matter of conforming to an allegedly universal rationality about the way forward. Rather is about attempting to grasp the many different and situated practices, beliefs and knowledges constitutive of different ways of being and living in and with the environment. This means, as Machin (2022) points out, that forums for environmental debate can never be fully rational nor entirely inclusive. Instead, they are rowdy spaces that manifest not only clashes of interests but also clashes of ways of being and living. By focusing on universal rather than situated experiences of, for example, climate change, sustainability discourse, then, risks ignoring a plurality of perspectives and values, and fails to provide an alternative for action that can truly challenge the dominance of neoliberal perspectives. In turn, the democratic insistence on maintaining pluralism, as envisioned by Mouffe and Rancière, is severely compromised. However, to be fair, there is a growing recognition within sustainability discourse of the need to focus on plural perspectives, such as those of disadvantaged populations. But, as Westman and Broto (2022) point out, these populations are seldom recognised as something other than passive, vulnerable groups. What is needed, they argue, is knowledge perspectives that, rather than examining the life conditions of vulnerable groups, develop knowledge from their perspectives. Machin (2022) accordingly advocates the promotion of a so-called radical democratic imaginary that celebrates pluralism, encourages participation, and facilitates and legitimises the expression of differences. While this radical imaginary has much in common with the concern to protect and foster an inclusive democracy by including both experts and lay people, the difference is that it does not align democratic procedures with a specific set of environmental outcomes. Instead, the radical democratic imaginary insists on the openness of democracy by driving democratic participation around which various alternatives circulate, and thereby also by refusing to suppress the contestation between differences on which democracy is ultimately based (Mouffe 1997). However, as Machin (2022) observes, while the radical democratic imaginary offers an important alternative for approaching the connection between sustainability and democracy, it does not circulate widely in the dominant sustainability discourse.

In this short review, I have discussed how various sustainability discourses shape approaches to democracy. What emerges from this discussion is that sustainability discourse might not only be expressive of post-democratic tendencies but also, as Swyngedouw (2010) asserts, that sustainability discourse is among the key arenas through which a post-democratic frame is forged, configured, and entrenched. In the following, I demonstrate and discuss in more detail this argument by distinguishing between three forms of sustainability discourse – the technical, liberal, and political – and evaluating their democratic implications. These three are of course not the only sustainability discourses, nor are they rigidly fixed. However, I have chosen to focus on them in this chapter because they illustrate well how the mediation of messages of sustainability might have different democratic implications. I also want to emphasise that these three are not supposed to be reductive categories nor normative ideals, but rather analytical tools that can be used to approach the different assumptions, expectations, fears, and desires that circulate in sustainability discourse and how these configure democratic (im)possibilities.

The technical sustainability discourse

In January 2020, a giant clock, 15 metres wide and 3.5 metres tall, was erected in a windmill park in Jæren, Norway. A few weeks later, an identical clock was erected in the middle of Oslo City Centre. The clock also appeared in TV commercials, on billboards, on social media and in airports in what is the largest national campaign for wind power in Norwegian history (Norsk Vind 2020a). The illuminated digital numbers on the clock were counting down to 2030, the declared "tipping point" at which the world's carbon emissions, according to the UN, must be halved in order to avoid climate disaster. In the TV commercial for the campaign (see Norsk Vind 2020b), the sound of the dramatic ticking of the clock is set against the backdrop of images of an apocalyptic and dystopian future that presents a clear threat to civilisation as we know it, unless urgent and immediate remedial action is undertaken. The narrator in the commercial speaks with the authority of an expert presenting the viewer with undisputable facts: "The climate crisis is a global challenge that we all have the responsibility to solve. We have to do more. And we have to do it faster". As he speaks, we see the threat that faces us if we do not comply: the disintegration of icebergs, the rise of the ocean, ravaging floods, forest fires, and burnt waste lands. While there does not seem to be an immediate redemption of this immanent disaster, there is one technical solution that will help us move forward: "Land based wind is clean energy that will make a difference now" the narrator asserts as the clock keeps ticking in the background.

The Norwegian Wind campaign, "The Clock Is Ticking Towards 2030", illustrates well what I call the technical sustainability discourse. The TV commercial mobilises expert knowledge alongside apocalyptic imaginaries of dystopian futures in order to assert a rational consensus around a technical solution to environmental problems: the production and erection of more wind turbines. Without this technical intervention, the campaign contends, climate disaster is inevitable.

As O'Brien (2018) observes, the pursuit of climate mitigation through technological innovations tends to ignore the conflicts, tensions, and contradictions that arise in transformation processes. There has, for example, been significant mobilisation among local organisations and activists against Norwegian Wind, and wind power more generally. Protesters point to how the erection of wind turbines will have detrimental impacts on "untouched" nature and might cause major environmental problems on a local scale (Nilsson 2018). However, as Swyngedouw (2010) observes, the use of expert knowledge and apocalyptic images is very powerful in disavowing or displacing any forms of disagreement around the proposed solution. Accordingly, the campaign positions clean wind energy as the only practical way forward, side lining what is portrayed as the petty quarrels and quibbles of politics. "I hope this will help us clarify the message that we cannot wait when it comes to producing more renewable energy" (author's translation), the CEO of Norwegian Wind states on the company's webpage for the campaign (Norsk Vind 2020a). He further explains that he is fully aware that there has been some resistance towards land-based wind power because of the consequences for natural landscapes. However, as he concludes, "the climate does not have time to wait for us to finish the debate" (Norsk Vind 2020a, author's translation).

The campaign can be seen to produce what Swyngedouw calls a "depoliticized imaginary" (2010, p. 219). That is, it forecloses the possibility of a proper political debate that might enable the negotiation around choosing one alternative over another. Instead, the campaign demands that different positions succumb to the superior wisdom of expertise because the urgency of the situation leaves no time for debate. The campaign further negates different positions and opinions by presenting climate change as a global humanitarian cause that elevates the interests of "the people" to the level of the universal. The "we" in the campaign is portrayed as universal victims suffering from processes beyond our control. This "universal we" cuts across the idiosyncrasies of different, heterogeneously constituted, opinions, experiences, and interests by distilling a common threat or challenge to both Nature and Humanity.

The universal threat of climate change that is depicted in the TV commercial is constructed as exterior to society – as an environmental problem and not as a social problem. While the commercial readily acknowledges the part-anthropogenic process of carbon emissions and thus the human impact on nature, the related ecological problems are externalised as the emphasis is put on the causal power of nature to derail civilisations. Carbon emissions here become the stand-in for the totality of climate change calamities, and therefore it suffices to halt the emissions to return to "normal" life as we know it. As the narrator in the commercial points out: "Placing wind turbines in nature has its costs, but it is nothing compared to the price we and future generations will have to pay if we can't change the effects of climate change in time".

By externalising the threat of climate change, the commercial reinforces a nature-society dichotomy. In his thesis about the production of nature, Neil Smith (2008, p. 245) refers to the construction of this dichotomy as a form of "nature-washing". He argues that "nature-washing" has partly taken over for the corporate "greenwashing" that absorbed green politics in the 1990s, recoding environmentalism for the purpose of capitalist profit. Through "nature-washing", nature becomes a new super determinant of our social fate: "It might well be society's fault for changing nature, but it is the consequent power of that nature that brings the apocalypse" (Smith 2008). "Nature-washing" then, turns the question of *causality* in the sustainability argument on its head: the focus is not on the unsustainability of human activity, but on the effects of nature on human activity. According to Millar and Mitchell (2017), this is an ideological move that does not accurately describe what is at stake in the Anthropocene. Instead, it legitimates a denial of culpability. The increasing carbon emissions just *are,* and there is nothing we can do about them, except perhaps erecting wind turbines to reduce the emissions so that life as we know it can continue.

Within the technical sustainability discourse, then, environmental problems are framed not as results of the "system" (of unevenly distributed power relations, of the overuse of resources and the unjust exploitation of people and nature) but are externalised and blamed on an outsider – the abstract idea of "carbon emissions". This abstraction might serve to confuse the problem at hand and hinder collective strategies to address it. Furthermore, the scientific expertise concerning "the facts of climate change" are used as a trump card to settle all arguments and insist that wind power is the right solution. This approach, however, is problematic because it turns the potential questioning of this proposed solution into a scientific rather than political disagreement. Scientific in the sense that the discussion is reduced to a conflict between those who believe in anthropogenic climate change and those who deny it, rather than a wider political contestation around the meaning and implications of climate change, and the struggle over who gets to decide.

To illustrate the move from a political towards a scientific disagreement: The play on fear in the campaign was fiercely criticised and the Consumer Authority (Forbrukertilsynet) received hundreds of complaints (Giæver 2020). Activists accused the campaign for compromising their fight for the climate by playing on a one-sided evocation of fear and parents criticised the campaign for an unnecessary fearmongering that might be harmful for children (Kalstad 2020). Replying to the critique, the spokesperson for Norwegian Wind asserted that the people *should* be scared as the campaign is based on "pure facts" stemming from the IPCC (Kalstad 2020). Nevertheless, the Consumer Authority ruled that the campaign was illegal because it "employs frightening means or is likely to cause fear or anxiety" amongst children (The Marketing Control Act 2016). The PR company behind the campaign called the ruling "a dramatic regulation of the freedom of speech" (Giæver 2020, author's translation), questioning why The Consumer Authority should meddle in how the facts of climate change are presented to children.

What emerges here is a strategy in which the PR company turns any disagreement concerning the meaning and implications of the campaign into a matter of accepting or denying "the facts" of climate change. This is an effective strategy to foreclose political debate because, to borrow a metaphor from Rancière (1999, p. xii), the conflict is staged as a disagreement between one who says white and one who says black. However, as Rancière points out, political disagreement is "the conflict between one who says white and another who says white but does not understand the same thing by it or does not understand that the other is saying the same thing in the name of whiteness" (1999, p. x). Political disagreement, then, involves "a dispute over the object of discussion and over the capacity of those who are making an object of it" (1999, p. xii).

To sum up, the technical sustainability discourse leaves little room for democracy understood as the promotion of plural and conflicting perspectives and the negotiation between alternatives. Focusing on resolving urgent and narrowly defined problems, democracy is seen as valuable only to the extent that it aligns with technical, efficient, and solution-oriented approaches. Disagreement concerning these approaches is displaced because the underlying rationale is that technical solutions constitute the best and right way forward and therefore serve goals that are self-evident and unambiguous. Faced with dominant forces beyond our control, there is not time for lengthy discussions around alternative forms of action.

The liberal sustainability discourse

In 2018, the Norwegian state-owned petroleum company Statoil changed its name to Equinor. Dropping "oil" from its name and replacing it with the combination of "equi" (the starting point for words like equal, equality and equilibrium) and "nor" (signalling the company's Norwegian origin), the company wanted to reflect its commitment to become a responsible "broad energy company" focusing on renewable energy (Equinor 2018a). The rebranding was accompanied by the advertising campaign "Say Hi to Change" that was broadcasted on social media and on national billboards and television. The TV-commercial of the campaign (see Equinor 2018b) tells stories of change, including babes in arms, a cartoon butterfly emerging from a chrysalis, a teenage punk in opposition to her conservative-looking mother, and a young man trying on a dress. Throughout the commercial, we see portraits of people from all walks of life and corners of the world, dealing with change in various ways. The narrator tells us that since we are born, our stories are stories of change. Change can be painful and hard he replies to a teenager complaining about the pimples suddenly covering his face, but it can also be liberating and beautiful he cheers as the young man poses in a dress. "We all change and so the world changes. Even a big company like Statoil changes" the narrator continues. And as the imagery reflects the changes of the world, including climate change and extreme weather events, the narrator ensures us that "along the way, we [Statoil] realized we had a responsibility to change. To search for a better balance. And we're evolving from an oil and gas company into a broad energy company. Cheering for diversity and equality".

In contrast to Norwegian Wind's promotion of expert knowledge as a driver in forging consensus around technical solutions to address climate change, Equinor foregrounds its belief in the power of personal freedom and rights, democratic representation and participation as a key to tackle environmental issues. As such, the Equinor campaign is a good example of what I call the liberal sustainability discourse. Where the technical sustainability discourse is formed against the impersonal and abstract enemy of carbon, the liberal sustainability discourse is formed around the mobilisation of personal stories of change. The notion of sustainability is here wielded for the positive empowerment and recognition of "the people", rather than the technocratic expert-rationalities of the technical sustainability discourse. The Equinor campaign furthermore breaks with doom-laden narratives of apocalyptic futures of which we are all potential victims, portraying instead a narrative of hopeful futures that recognises the power of personal transformation, multiplicity, and difference. The "we" referred to in the Equinor commercial are not "universal victims" of forces beyond our control, but rather empowered agents for change. Hence, beyond the delivery of change to protect ecosystems through a green energy push, the changes depicted in the commercial represent a new liberal agenda for social justice.

Social justice has long played a key role in sustainability discourses, particularly regarding the distribution of responsibilities, rights, and mutual obligations between nations (Patterson et al. 2018). The Equinor campaign accordingly highlights its commitment to climate justice by (re)presenting a broad segment of society through which difference and equity are approached in multiple ways: between privileged and disadvantaged groups within society, between genders, between ethnicities, between the global North and South, and across generations. At the same time, what emerges in the commercial is a focus on autonomy and liberty in which the concept of difference constitutes the idea of a multiplicity of uniquenesses. This multiplicity simply indicates the acknowledgement of the existence of diverse particularities in society at the expense of a critical questioning of these differences. Laclau and Mouffe (2001, p. 115) call this conception "a closed system of differences". Instead of seeing difference as a complex relational process sustained by domination and control, it is here understood as a series of distinct and fixed categories that can be held together by a harmonious and unifying ideal.

The harmonious and unifying ideal promoted in the commercial revolves around the self-fulfilling, resilient, and self-made neoliberal subject. For example, in one of the stories portrayed in the Equinor commercial, we meet a young girl practising tumbling and dance skills on a balance beam. In the beginning of the commercial, the girl stumbles and falls and the narrator talks about the necessity to "try, fail, learn and try again". By the end of the commercial, the girl manages to do the tricks without falling and we see her posing in front of a wall of medals. The narrator concludes by foregrounding the need to always search for a better version of ourselves. The neoliberal subject that emerges here then is a subject that is led by the market to reproduce, expand, and reinforce competitive relations between themselves. Such competitive relations are often premised on inequality rather than equality, including explicit acts of violence and exploitation as well as more subtle systems of repression and control (Lorber 2001; Yodanis 2004). However, the commercial glosses over such unequal relations by focusing on a harmonious togetherness and individual resilience.

By promoting win-win change narrative, the commercial constructs change as apolitical, inevitable and universally beneficial: the chrysalis becomes a butterfly, the young gymnast becomes a champion, the students become educated, and so on. However, as Blythe et al. (2018) point out, cultural and social differentiation means that people are unevenly able and willing to take up opportunities of transformation. Moreover, transformative actions often involve trade-offs that disproportionately affect already marginalised or vulnerable groups. Calling on individuals and communities to build their own resilience furthermore shifts the burden of response to global environmental change from the systemic drivers of global change (such as multinational companies like Equinor) towards individuals as the most appropriate drivers of transformational change (Ayers and Huq 2013; Dodman and Mitlin 2013; O'Brien 2015). As Fabinyi et al. (2014) observe, such assertions have significant implications for who we collectively perceive as appropriate actors to enable change, and which interventions we prioritise. Rather than acknowledging Equinor's major role in the extraction of fossil fuels, the company appears in the commercial as one individual among many. By positioning itself not as the cause of the problem of climate change, but as one of the effected individuals, the new Equinor gives the impression of representing not only an improved version of Statoil but also, to some extent, a more democratised version. As Fischer (2000, p. 42) points out: "in choices about how we want to live together … the experts [or, in this case, the company] are only fellow citizens". The notions of fellowship and democracy that is evoked here is one of an untroubled, undivided, cohesive, and resilient community in which companies and citizens alike "do their part" to change the world and make it a better place to live.

However, the shared imperative of change in the commercial masks plural notions of what exactly needs to change. As Westman and Broto (2022) point out, the promotion of change tends to articulate transformation objectives along established ideas of progress. That is, change is aligned with established notions of social improvement and progress, thereby cementing their underpinning values. Blythe et al. (2018) accordingly observe a tendency in which transformation is used as a loose description that directs effort towards building the resilience of the existing system rather than transforming it, and, as a consequence, providing yet another means to justify business-as-usual approaches. Indeed, files published by the environmental lawyer ClientEarth (2021) point to how the world's biggest fossil fuel companies, including Equinor, use advertising to "greenwash" their ongoing contribution to climate change. Johnny White, one of client Earth's lawyers, states to *The Guardian*: "We're currently witnessing a great deception, where the companies most responsible for catastrophically heating the planet are spending millions on advertising campaigns about how their business plans are focused on sustainability" (Carrington 2021). The analysis by ClientEarth accordingly shows that while Equinor has talked of growing renewable capacity tenfold by 2026, renewables are only planned to be 4% of its energy by that date.

To conclude this part, the liberal sustainability discourse moves away from the focus on presumably unambiguous technical solutions to environmental problems towards ambiguous notions of personal and individualised change. While promising a democratic approach to sustainability focusing on inclusivity, diversity, and equality, the liberal sustainability discourse effectively communicates universal demands for societal change alongside established ideas of progress, while at the same time obscuring a plurality of struggles in favour of cemented ideas and interests. Hence, in the same vein as the technical sustainability discourse, this discourse promotes what Swyngedouw (2010, p. 219) calls a "sort of mobilization without political issue" where the sentiment is that we must change radically, but within the contours of the existing ideas of progress so that nothing really has to change. According to Swyngedouw, such sentiments infuse not democracy, but rather a post-political and post-democratic situation. What is promoted is not conflicting struggles for various forms of change, but a harmonious and one-directional change in which everyone knows their place and happily performs their resilience within the boundaries of the existing system.

The political sustainability discourse

In 2019, the performance *Society under Construction* by the German theatre collective Rimini Protokoll visited the National Theatre in Oslo. The performance explored the construction site as a model of a (post-)democratic society, extracting individual stories and personal experiences from large-scale construction processes that cause ecological degradation and social injustice. For the performance, the main stage of the National Theatre was turned into a global construction site with scaffoldings, sandhills, piles of bricks, and construction containers. Yet, what was being built – the building itself – remained curiously absent, irrelevant even. Instead, the audience was introduced to what normally remains unnoticed: the many people and fates that are entangled up in processes of construction. Divided into groups and following a guide to various "stations" at the construction site, the audience met ordinary people (not actors) in the roles of storytellers telling their own stories: A Romanian construction worker talking about illegal employment and existential angst; the former head engineer for Berlin's BER Airport reconstructing how he became a scapegoat for the government, for supposedly designing a default smoke-extraction system; an investment consultant drawing up a cost-benefit analysis of investments in "concrete gold"; a lawyer revealing tactics for how to fight supplementary claims by subcontractors; an economist warning a government delegation from Ethiopia against copying the unsustainable urban development of Singapore; a lawyer from Transparency International detailing cases of corruption in the Norwegian construction industry that resulted in poisoned forests and contaminated drinking water; a Chinese migrant worker telling about exploitation and poor living conditions; and a biologist demonstrating how ant colonies build more successfully than humans by doing things together rather than solely looking out for individual interests.

Society under Construction was the opening performance of the Oslo Architecture Triennale 2019, which used theatre and performance to explore the radical idea of an "architecture of degrowth". Degrowth is an idea and social movement acting as a powerful call to reject the obsession with economic growth and seek out alternative forms of sustainability in which social and ecological flourishing matters most (see e.g. Gorz 1975; Kallis 2018; Latouche 2009). By revealing the structural problems of growth, including the destructive and extractive processes of "development" (Demaria et al. 2019; Kallis and March 2015; Paulson 2017), degrowth constitutes a rupture with the status quo, which might open the possibility for broader social and political configurations. Degrowth, in this sense, is not simply an affirmative idea that signifies the opposite of growth. Rather it can be described as "a horizon chartered through confrontation with hegemonic worldviews" (Kallis and March 2015, p. 362). This is an open-ended horizon that evolves through confrontation with the existing one, in order to open up new imaginaries and spaces (D'Alisa et al. 2014). In contrast to the two previously discussed campaigns, the performance was not centred around one-directional calls for action and change. Instead, it explored the contestation between different perspectives, views and experiences involved in – literally – the construction of an unsustainable status quo. The performance, then, illustrates well what I call the political sustainability discourse.

The political sustainability discourse aligns with the previously mentioned "radical democratic imaginary" (Machin 2022, p. 7). I define "the political" as a space in which interests and understandings are negotiated and where disagreement and dissent are expressed, which, in turn, can produce conflicts and tensions (Mouffe 2005). As such, the political challenges what is taken-for-granted and demarcated as visible and invisible (Rancière 2013 [2004]). Hence, the political sustainability discourse envisages the openness of politics to a plurality of conflicting demands that contests the prevailing political regime "all the way down" (Tønder and Thomassen 2005, p. 4). For example, in the performance, climate change is portrayed not as an external threat stemming from nature and processes beyond our control, but as a direct consequence of human activities and modes of production. Hence, climate change is moved from the realm of scientific debate to the realm of political debate. In the performance, then, nature is not the ultimate legislator, and the question is not whether you are with a universal us or against a universal us in the fight against climate change. Instead, the performance unpacks the links between environmental problems, social injustice, and the dominant discourses of progress and development, such as the structure of the world economy, amassed wealth, logics of investment, and policies of perpetual growth. The audience is faced with the different personal and ecological fates tangled up in these structures and discourses: unfinished airports, exploitative migrant work, the blaming on individuals for systemic failures, air conditioning systems that cause a rise in temperature, billion tons of sand needed to build artificial islands, and the reliance on fossil sources for the continuous urbanisation of the world.

Because these issues are internal to how we organise ourselves as a society, they are likely to be issues over which various perspectives clash. The storytellers in the performance make a point out of telling the audience not to believe the other storytellers as the audience rotate between them. For example, the investment consultant, after having played a game with the audience in which they "slip into the role of investors", ends the session with the following request: "Please follow the signs to Transparency International, where the lawyer Andreas Riegel will tell you all sorts of conspiracy theories about us investors. Don't believe him!" (Kaegi 2019). In a similar vein, the lawyer would ask the audience to not believe the corrupt decision-makers that would be the next stop for the audience.

As illustrated, *Society under Construction* did not aim to convince the audience of one story, vision, idea, or alternative as the right one. On the contrary, when encountering the many personal stories in the performance, the audience had to draw their own observations and conclusions without the reassuring presence of a principal narrative to refer to. The performance accordingly defied any notions of a generic "we" and thereby also the idea that there can be one "correct" solution that is satisfactory to everyone. The point is not simply that multiplicity exists, as in the Equinor commercial, but recognising that this multiplicity is a place of disagreements between various experiences, opinions, demands and struggles that stem from different histories and territories. By developing knowledge from various perspectives, from the migrant worker to the investment consultant, the performance unpacked how various structures of power are embedded in labour relations, racialised spaces, Western conventions, and multiple other forms of inequalities.

Rimini Protokoll is known for working with "ordinary people" rather than with professional actors in their performances. These people are often referred to as "experts of everyday life" (Behrendt 2003). In contrast to the authority granted to technical expertise in the Norwegian Wind commercial, *Society under Construction* embraces a plurality of ways of knowing and experiencing a world shaped by rampant inequality and global environmental crisis. Here, disagreement is not seen as incompatible with effective responses to environmental problems, but as the very condition for tackling these problems because it enables ever-more diverse critiques of the economic system. Where the Norwegian Wind and Equinor commercials present climate change as a unitary problem with a single solution, *Society under Construction* enables contestation over its meaning and implications and therefore resists the foreclosure of political disagreement around sustainability issues and challenges. So, if the technical sustainability discourse dismisses democracy by placing technical interventions in a terrain beyond political dispute, and the liberal sustainability discourse promises a democratic approach in which everyone are winners, the political sustainability discourse recognises that democracy is an ongoing project that is founded upon the expression of disagreements and differences. Although there is no guarantee of the outcome, and the refusal to close down disagreements may frustrate those who champion green ends, the focus on plurality and contestation around sustainability issues may, as Machin (2020, 2022) observes, enable both a healthy democracy and a more profound socioecological transformation.

At the end of the performance, the stortytellers gather in a collective act of imagination concerning alternative futures: "Imagine a future where housing is only built for the price segment that actually needs it" the investment consultant suggests. "Imagine houses that were built with regenerative resources" the urban scholar says. "Imagine politicians who see construction projects with longer perspective than their own electoral terms" the lawyer proposes (Kaegi 2019). What is expressed here is not simply a desire for change but also a direction for this change through broader reconfigurations of social and material possibilities.

Conclusion

In this chapter, I have distinguished between three discourses that mediate messages of sustainability in very different ways. My aim was not to capture the entirety of sustainability discourses, nor was it to assess the validity and importance of the messages presented in the three examples. Furthermore, I certainly do not want to frame all attempts to engage with disastrous or catastrophic mediations of climate change as negative, nor condemn approaches that bring equity and social justice to the forefront of sustainability debates. What I have done, however, is to discuss the implications of sustainability discourses for democracy.

In the technical sustainability discourse, questions of democracy are transcended through a focus on forging rational consensus around technical solutions. Unless we – the universal victims of this pending catastrophe – come to an agreement and take immediate action, natural disasters will bring an end to life as we know it. Rendering environmental problems as external to society, this discourse forecloses disagreement and debate and leaves little room for scrutinising our own actions and ways of living.

If democracy is irrelevant and doomed in the technical sustainability discourse, it is all the more alive and kicking in the liberal sustainability discourse. This discourse promises to deepen and extend democracy by focusing on empowerment, justice, and difference and highlighting the potential of "the people" to generate societal change. Yet, what emerges here is an understanding of democracy as a blueprint of the good society which is disconnected from situated experiences and struggles. The notion of "change" is conceived as a generic and universal change involving everyone, obscuring questions and disagreements around what exactly needs to change and how that change might affect different people in different ways. Hence, while focusing on the "perfect" democracy and liberal idyll in which everything and nothing must change, this discourse risks foreclosing democratic possibilities by re-instating rather than rethinking status quo.

Finally, the political sustainability discourse brings democracy to life through the formation and contestation around different perspectives, alternatives, and experiences. Personal stories feature here not as an ensemble of harmonious multiplicity in a common world, but as an aggregation of multiple subjects, creating multiple and conflicting worlds. Refusing to suppress the contestation of differences on which democracy is based, environmental problems are not presented as external technical problems in need of a straightforward solution, nor as a unifying common cause. Instead, environmental problems emerge as political issues around which alternative, dynamic, and conflicting socio-economic perspectives and projects circulate (Kenis 2018; Machin 2013). Rather than simply reaffirming the status quo and reiterating conventional assumptions about the possibilities for social transformation, the political sustainability discourse highlights that our environmental practices and ways of being could always be otherwise. As such, it keeps alive a democratic politics and the possibility of finding alternative ways to live, act, and interact.

The path towards sustainability is a matter of contestation. No definite map is provided, nor is there a final end point. It is also not possible to reach a sustainable ecological equilibrium that works for everyone. Yet, while there is no one right thing to do, something must be done. What then is to be done? In line with Purcell (2013), I want to conclude by highlighting the importance that the answers to this question revolve around "democracy". As demonstrated in this chapter, I understand democracy as an open-ended process that acknowledges the contingency of any sustainability project and enables the recurrence of political disagreement that allows us to conceive of alternatives to the status quo and demand their implementation. As Machin (2020, p. 168) highlights, disagreement should be seen as a generative source of democratic possibility. This means that there cannot be a one-size-fits-all approach to sustainability, but that every action could be done differently and that we must revisit, again and again, the question of our ways of living.

References

Ayers, J., & Huq, S. (2013) 'Adaptation, development, and the community', pp. 201–214. In J. Palutikof, S. L. Boulter, A. J. Ash, M. Stafford Smith, M. Parry, M. Waschka, & D. Guitart (eds.) *Climate Adaptation Futures*. Oxford: Wiley-Blackwell.

Badiou, A. (2008) 'Live Badiou – Interview with Alain Badiou, Paris, December 2007', pp. 136–139. In O. Feltham (ed.) *Alain Badiou – Live Theory*. London: Continuum.

Banerjee, S. B. (2011) 'Embedding sustainability across the organization: A critical perspective.' *Academy of Management Learning & Education* 10, 719–731.

Behrendt, E. (2003) *The Experts of Everyday-Life*. https://www.rimini-protokoll.de/website/en/text/the-experts-of-everyday-life.

Blythe, J., Silver, J., Evans, L., Armitage, D., Bennett, N. J., Moore, M.-L., Morrison, T. H., & Brown, K. (2018) 'The dark side of transformation: Latent risks in contemporary sustainability discourse.' *Antipode* 50(5), 1206–1223.

Brown, T. (2016) 'Sustainability as empty signifier: Its rise, fall, and radical potential.' *Antipode* 48(1): 115–133.

Carrington, D. (2021, April 19) '"A great deception": Oil giants taken to task over "greenwash" ads.' *The Guardian*. https://www.theguardian.com/business/2021/apr/19/a-great-deception-oil-giants-taken-to-task-over-greenwash-ads.

Castree, N. (2009) 'The environmental wedge: Neoliberalism, democracy and the prospect for a new British left', pp. 222–33. In P. Devine, A. Pearman, & D. Purdy (eds.) *Feelbad Britain – How to Make It Better*. London: Lawrence and Wishart.

ClientEarth (2021, March 25) *The Greenwashing Files*. https://www.clientearth.org/projects/the-greenwashing-files/.

Crouch, C. (2004) *Post-Democracy*. Cambridge: Polity Press.

D'Alisa, G., Demaria, F., & Kallis, G. (eds.) (2014) *Degrowth: A Vocabulary for a New Era*. London/New York: Routledge.

Deese, R. S. (2019) *Climate Change and the Future of Democracy*. Luxembourg: Springer.

Demaria, F., Kallis, G., & Bakker, K. (2019) 'Geographies of degrowth: Nowtopia, resurgences and the decolonialization of imaginaries and places.' *Environment and Planning E: Nature and Space* 2(3), 431–450. https://doi.org/10.1177/2514848619869689.

Dodman, D., & Mitlin, D. (2013) 'Challenges for community-based adaptation: Discovering the potential for transformation.' *Journal of International Development* 25(5), 640–659.

Ergene, S., Subhabrata, B., & Hoffman, A. J. (2020) '(Un)sustainability and organization studies: Towards a radical engagement.' *Organization Studies*, 1–17. https://doi.org/10.1177/0170840620937892.

Equinor (2018a, March 15) *Statoil to change name to Equinor*. https://www.equinor.com/news/archive/15mar2018-statoil.

Equinor (2018b, March 15) *Thank you, Statoil! It's been a pleasure*. [Video] Youtube. https://www.youtube.com/watch?v=hwLKEl9G_W0.

Fabinyi, M., Evans, L., & Foale, S. J. (2014) 'Social-ecological systems, social diversity, and power: Insights from anthropology and political ecology.' *Ecology and Society* 19(4), 28. https://doi.org/10.5751/ES-07029-190428.

Faarstad, F. M., & Aasen, M. (2022) 'Climate change doesn't win you a climate election: party competition in the 2021 Norwegian general election.' *Environmental Politics* 32(4), 732–742.

Fischer, F. (2000) *Citizens, Experts, and the Environment*. Durham & London: Duke University Press.

Giæver, H. (2020, February 5) 'Forbrukertilsynet mener omstridt klimareklame var ulovlig.' *Dagens Næringsliv*. https://www.dn.no/markedsforing/forbrukertilsynet/try-rad/

norsk-vind/forbrukertilsynet-mener-omstridt-klimareklame-var-ulovlig-try-sier-tilsynet-lar-seg-pavirke-av-aktivister/2-1-750816.

Goodman, J., & Morton, T. (2014) 'Climate crisis and the limits of Liberal democracy? Germany, Australia and India compared', pp. 229–252. In B. Isakhan, & S. Slaughter (eds.) *Democracy and Crisis: Democratising Governance in the Twenty-First Century.* Lonodn/New York: Palgrave Macmillan.

Gorz, A. (1975) *Ecologie et politique* [Ecology and Politics]. Paris: Le Seuil.

Gunder, M. (2006) 'Sustainability: Planning's saving grace or road to perdition?' *Journal of Planning Education and Research* 26(2), 208–221.

Kaegi, S. (2019) 'Society under construction.' *E-flux.* https://www.e-flux.com/architecture/overgrowth/282655/society-under-construction/.

Kallis, G. (2018) *Degrowth.* Newcastle upon Tyne: Agenda Publishing.

Kallis, G., & March, H. (2015) 'Imaginaries of hope: The utopianism of degrowth.' *Annals of the Association of American Geographers* 105(2), 360–368. https://doi.org/10.1080/00045608.2014.973803.

Kalstad, L. M. (2020, January 29) 'Mange klager på klimaklokke – mener den teller ned til dommedag.' *NRK Rogaland.* https://www.nrk.no/rogaland/mange-klager-pa-klimaklokke-_-mener-den-teller-ned-til-_dommedag_-1.14872670.

Kenis, A. (2018) 'Post-politics contested: Why multiple voices on climate change do not equal politicisation.' *Environment and Planning C: Politics and Space* 37(5), 831–848.

Kenis, A., & Lievens, M. (2015) *The Limits of the Green Economy: From Reinventing Capitalism to Repoliticising the Present.* London/New York: Routledge.

Laclau, E. (1990) *New Reflections on the Revolution of Our Time.* New York: Verso.

Laclau, E. (2005) *On Populist Reason.* New York: Verso.

Laclau, E., & Mouffe, C. (2001) *Hegemony and Socialist Strategy* (2nd edition). London/New York: Verso.

Lahn, B., & Rowe, E. W. (2015) 'How to be a 'front-runner': Norway and international climate politics', pp. 126–146. In B. Carvalho, & I. B. Neumann (eds.) *Small States and Status Seeking. Norway's Quest for International Standing.* London/New York: Routledge.

Latouche, S. (2009) *Farewell to Growth.* Cambridge: Polity.

Lorber, J. (2001) *Gender Inequality* (2nd edition). Los Angeles, CA: Roxbury.

Machin, A. (2013) *Negotiating Climate Change: Radical Democracy and the Illusion of Consensus.* London: Zed Books.

Machin, A. (2020) 'Democracy, disagreement, disruption: Agonism and the environmental state.' *Environmental Politics* 29(1), 155–172.

Machin, A. (2022) 'Climates of democracy: Skeptical, rational, and radical imaginaries.' *WIREs Climate Change* 13(4), e774. https://doi.org/10.1002/wcc.774.

Millar, S., & Mitchell, D. (2017) 'The tight dialectic: The anthropocene and the capitalist production of nature.' *Antipode* 49(s1), 75–93.

Mouffe, C. (1992) 'Preface: Democratic politics today.' In C. Mouffe (ed.) *Dimensions of Radical Democracy: Pluralism, Citizenship and Community* (pp. 1–14). London: Verso.

Mouffe, C. (1997) 'Decision, deliberation, and democratic ethos.' *Philosophy Today* 41(1), 24–30.

Mouffe, C. (2000) *The Democratic Paradox.* London: Verso.

Mouffe, C. (2005) *On the political.* New York/London: Routledge.

Mouffe, C. (2022) *Towards a Green Democratic Revolution.* New York/London: Verso.

Nilsson, Å. (2018, November 12) 'Massiv protest mot vindkraftturbiner.' *Bergen og Hordaland Turlag.* https://www.bergenoghordalandturlag.no/artikler/nyheter/15187-massiv-protest-mot-vindkraftturbiner/.

Norsk Vind (2020a, January 13) *Norsk Vind setter opp Norges største klimaklokke*. https://valinor.no/activities/norsk-vind-setter-opp-norges-storste-klimaklokke/.

Norsk Vind (2020b, January 13) *The clock is ticking toward 2030 – Web version/Norsk Vind (English version)*. [Video]. Youtube. https://www.youtube.com/watch?v=WZ7aQPOmDi0.

O'Brien, K. (2015) 'Political agency: The key to tackling climate change.' *Science* 350(6265), 1170–1171.

O'Brien, K. (2018) 'Is the 1.5°C target possible? Exploring the three spheres of transformation.' *Current Opinion in Environmental Sustainability* 31, 153–160.

Patterson, J. J., Thaler, T., Hoffmann, M., Hughes, S., Oels, A. Chu, E., Mert, A., Huitema, D. & Burch Sand Jordan, A. (2018) 'Political feasibility of 1.5°C societal transformations: The role of social justice.' *Current Opinion in Environmental Sustainability* 31, 1–9.

Paulson, S. (2017) 'Degrowth: Culture, power and change.' *Journal of Political Ecology* 24, 425–666. https://doi.org/10.2458/v24i1.20882.

Plumwood, V. (1995) 'Has democracy failed ecology? An ecofeminist perspective.' *Environmental Politics* 4(4), 134–168.

Purcell, M. (2013) *The Down-Deep Delight of Democracy.* Hoboken, NJ: Wiley-Blackwell.

Rancière, J. (1995) *On the Shores of Politics.* London: Verso.

Rancière, J. (1999) *Disagreement: Politics and Philosophy*. Minneapolis: University of Minnesota Press.

Rancière, J. (2013 [2004]) *The Politics of Aesthetics.* London: Bloomsbury Academic.

Smith, N. (2008) *Uneven Development: Nature, Capital, and the Production of Space* (3rd edition). Athens: University of Georgia Press.

Swyngedouw, E. (2010) 'Apocalypse forever?' *Theory, Culture and Society* 27, 213–232.

Swyngedouw, E. (2018) 'CO2 as neoliberal fetish: The love of crisis and the depoliticized immuno-biopolitics of climate change governance', pp. 295–307. In D. Cahill, M. Cooper, M. Konings, & D. Primrose (eds.) *The SAGE Handbook of Neoliberalism.* Thousand Oaks, CA: SAGE.

The Marketing Control Act (2016) https://www.forbrukertilsynet.no/english/the-marketing-control-act – Chapter 3.

Tønder, L., & Thomassen, L. (2005) 'Introduction: Rethinking radical democracy between abundance and lack', pp. 1–13. In L. Tønder, & L. Thomassen (eds.) *Radical Democracy: Politics between Abundance and Lack*. Manchester: Manchester University Press.

Tully, J. (2001) 'An ecological ethics for the present', 147–164. In B. Gleeson, & N. Low (eds.) *Governing for the Environment: Global Problems, Ethics and Democracy.* New York: Palgrave.

Tyszczuk, R., & Smith, J. (2018) 'Culture and climate change scenarios: The role and potentials of the arts and humanities in responding to "the 1.5 degrees target".' *Current Opinion in Environmental Sustainability* 31, 56–64.

Westman, L., & Broto, V. C. (2022) 'Urban transformations to keep all the same: The power of Ivy discourses.' *Antipode* 54(4), 1320–1343. https://doi.org/10.1111/anti.12820.

Wetherell, M., Taylor, S., & Yates, S. J. (eds.) (2001) *Discourse Theory and Practice: A Reader.* London: Sage.

Wollebæk, D., Ejolras, B., Steen-Johnsen, K., & Ødegård, G. (2012) 'After Utøya: How a high-trust society reacts to terror – Trust and civic engagement in the aftermath of July 22.' *Political Science & Politics* 45(1): 32–37.

Wilson, J., & Swyngedouw, E. (eds.) (2014) *The Post-Political and Its Discontents.* Edinburgh: Edinburg University Press.

Yodanis, C. L. (2004) 'Gender inequality, violence against women, and fear: A cross-national test of the feminist theory of violence against women.' *Journal of Interpersonal Violence* 19(6), 655–675.

Yusoff, K., & Gabrys, J. (2011) 'Climate change the imagination." *WIREs Climate Change* 2, 516–534.

Žižek, S. (2000) *The Ticklish Subject: The Absent Centre of Political Ontology.* London: Verso.

3 Exploring Norway's audiovisual industry

A study on communicated engagement in sustainable practices

Camille Z. Thisell

Introduction

Film and television productions in the audiovisual industry have been identified as significant contributors to carbon emissions. The carbon footprint generated by high-budget productions such as *Iron Man* or *Pirates of the Caribbean* can be as high as 3,370 metric tons per day of filming. Moreover, an average hour of TV, like the multi-camera show *Shall We Dance* produced by Nordisk Film TV in Norway, based on the British television series Strictly Come Dancing, can generate a carbon footprint of 5.7 tons CO2e (Sustainable Production Alliance & Producers Guild of America Foundation, 2021; Priestley, 2022), resulting in an estimated 6,000 metric tons CO_2 emissions footprint for a 24-episode series. To put this into context, Norway's CO_2 emissions per capita per year, based on consumption, were 8.3 metric tons in 2021 (www.ourworldindata.org).

This study points to an opportunity for improvement: Norwegian audiovisual small- and medium-sized enterprises (NAV-SMEs) should improve their reporting frequency and depth to align with higher international standards, such as the Corporate Sustainability Reporting Directive (CSRD)(Directive (EU) 2022/2464, 2022; NOU 2023:15, 2023). SMEs like Nordisk Film TV and across all industries are gaining increasing recognition worldwide for their pivotal role in addressing climate change and realising the UN Sustainable Development Goals (SDGs) (Kardosa, 2012; Koirala, 2018; Searcy, 2022). There is limited information on how different SMEs in Norway and globally contribute to the UN Agenda 2030 (Revell et al., 2010; Koirala, 2019) and what sustainable development principles they implement. According to recent studies, there are 142,493 audiovisual companies in Europe (Grassman & Gouttefarde, 2020) and 2,877 registered film and audiovisual businesses in Norway (Babun & Holmqvist, 2018). The cultural and creative industries in Europe generate around €457 billion annually, representing nearly 4% of the European GDP (European Commission, 2022b). Meanwhile, the audiovisual sector alone generate approximately €46,9 billion each year, surpassing the added value of sectors like aerospace (€45,7b) and iron and steel (€41,5b) (AV Data 4 Europe, n.d.). These numbers underscore the importance of understanding how audiovisual companies in Europe and Norway are working to reduce their CO_2 emissions, as

DOI: 10.4324/9781003392705-5

well as any initiatives or regulations aimed at reducing CO_2 emissions from the audiovisual industry in Europe and Norway.

In this chapter, the results of a 2020/2021 study are revealed, which explored the transparency and accountability of environmentally conscious practices and sustainability claims made on webpages and annual reports of NAV-SMEs using the SDGs as a proxy. The study found that the communicated commitment to sustainable development, the implementation of the SDGs, and the measurement and reporting of the generated CO_2 footprints by selected NAV-SMEs was inadequate, despite the sustainable development objectives of their parent companies. It is thus unclear to what extent the subsidiaries have implemented sustainable practices.

The chapter explores existing research on sustainable development in the audiovisual industry, identifying key trends, challenges, and opportunities for sustainable development in small and medium-sized companies. This contributes to the dialogue on embracing sustainability measures with a systems-thinking approach, essential for achieving long-term sustainability objectives. The research findings can also guide future policies and practices promoting sustainable development in the audiovisual industry.

The environmental impact of the audiovisual industry

We currently have a limited understanding of the significant factors that contribute to the social and environmental impact of the audiovisual industry, dispiriting a circular transformation. The research in media on sustainability issues in the audiovisual industry has mainly centred on examining the communication of environmental concerns in films and television and their influence on audience behaviour and policy. This includes exploring how popular media, films, and television shape our understanding of environmental issues.

Navigating Ecomedia research trends

Cubitt (2005) explores the intersection between media, technology, and ecology in his book *Ecomedia*. He also starts a scholarly discussion on the environmental impact of popular media materialities through his work. In *Digital Rubbish* (2011), Jennifer Gabrys examines the components utilised in producing media devices and their significant environmental impact. Similarly, Jane Bennett's (2010) research on vibrant materialities and Jussi Parikka's *The Geology of Media* (2015) emphasise the importance of the materials, while Pietari Kääpä (2018) discusses environmental management, emphasising the importance of both the content and operational practices of media companies in addressing environmental issues. *Sustainable Media*, edited by Starosielski and Walker (2016), advocates for rethinking media practices to promote environmental sustainability and responsible production and consumption. In the Nordics, commissioned feasibility and case studies have been performed (Brunklaus & Eriksson, 2015; Wu et al., 2017; Helsing & Wu, 2018; Fritsche, 2020), with subsequent recommendations on how to improve the environmental work in the film industry, prompting that transport, electricity, fuel, accommodation, travel, and waste have the most significant environmental footprint. Olsberg & Barnes (2014) analyse the impact of fiscal incentive schemes on European film and audiovisual production. Fritsche (2020) found that involving the production team in planning and promptly communicating a clear environmental strategy from top management enables eco-friendly decisions and efficient implementation of practices, which is further supported by the research of Rodriguez and Ricart (1997) and Epstein and Roy (1998). Research performed in Europe and the US is the study *Greening the European Audiovisual Industry* (Grassman & Gouttefarde, 2020), commissioned by the European Commission, including a general overview of the audiovisual value chain regarding environmental challenges together with an analysis of the most significant impacts in each area. This study provides a cost analysis of the transition to a green audiovisual industry. It also includes a definition of further research data that will be useful in validating the most critical steps needed to reduce significant impacts in each area of production, distribution, and consumption. Victory (2015) identifies environmental initiatives on set and highlights the role of an eco-manager, while Heidsiek (2014) focuses on the CO_2 footprint in the industry, together with capturing unique French and Belgian funding schemes at that time.

The footprint of the film- and television industry

The report *Close up Carbon Emissions of Film and Television Production* (2021) estimates carbon footprints of scripted and non-scripted production collected between 2016 and 2019. It mobilises stakeholders to take significant action and accelerate operational change by providing industry insights into high-impact areas. A total of 266 television series were included in the report, from scripted and unscripted shows to single and multi-camera TV series, shot in major filming cities around the world, together with 161 feature films, ranging from tentpole movies (expensive productions expected to generate significant revenue) to medium and small films. The report was released by the Sustainable Production Alliance (SPA) and Producers Guild of America Foundation (2021), with member companies Amazon Studios, Amblin Partners, Disney, Fox Corp., NBCUniversal, Netflix, Participant, Sony Pictures Entertainment, ViacomCBS, and WarnerMedia, showing global data (Figure 3.1) from the *Production Environmental Accounting Report* (*PEAR*).

As per the findings shown in Figure 3.1, small productions with a budget of USD$20 million and below have a carbon footprint of 391 metric tons. In contrast, medium productions, with budgets between USD$20–40 million, have a carbon footprint of 769 metric tons. Large productions, with budgets between USD$40–70 million, have a carbon footprint of 1,081 metric tons. In comparison, tentpole films like *Barbie*, *Iron Man*, and *Pirates of the Caribbean* have an average carbon footprint of almost 3,370 metric tons per day of filming, which can significantly impact the environment. Please note that the *PEAR* report's calculation includes direct emissions (scope 1) from fuel consumption and indirect emissions (scope 2) from electricity purchases, air travel, and accommodations. However, it does not account for the carbon footprint generated during pre-production or post-production

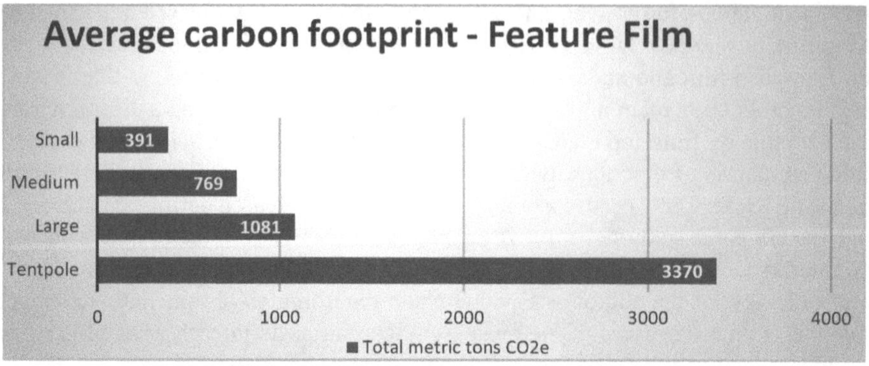

Figure 3.1 Average carbon footprint, categorised by their shooting budget – *Production Environmental Accounting Report* (*PEAR*).

periods, the manufacturing of technical equipment, or the use of devices and other technical products to consume film or audiovisual content. It is worth noting that these factors are repeatedly excluded from industry CO_2e calculators.

The collected data indicates that the most significant environmental impact comes from the fuel used in production vehicles and generators to power sets and location base camps. This represents about 58% of scripted dramas and single-camera series carbon footprint.

The most significant factor for multi-camera series is utilities, and for unscripted TV, air travel is the most significant contributor to emissions (Sustainable Production Alliance & Producers Guild of America Foundation, 2021; Spangler, 2021).

Studies performed by the BAFTA's industry-backed screen industry organisation for environmental sustainability, based in the UK, have shown that data from the Albert carbon calculator and certification toolkit indicate that producing an average hour of TV contributed 5.7 metric tons (or 5,700 kg) CO_2e (Priestley, 2022). In perception, the average household in Norway emits just under 1 kg CO_2e per hour, reflecting the total amount of greenhouse gases emitted from various consumption activities such as transportation, food production, and energy use (www.ourworldindata.org, 2021).

Albert further presents a more nuanced picture of CO_2e divided into the following programme genres: Comedy, Sport, Children, News and Current Affairs, Factual, Entertainment, and Drama, where sports programming has the lowest average emissions of any genre (2021) with the average hour of filming emitting 0.7t CO2e/h (Wearealbert, 2021).

The combined results from *Albert carbon calculator* and *PEAR* are shown in Figure 3.2.

Net-zero and carbon offsets

The European Green Deal has set an ambitious target of achieving net-zero, climate neutrality by 2050, while promoting inclusive procedures and a circular

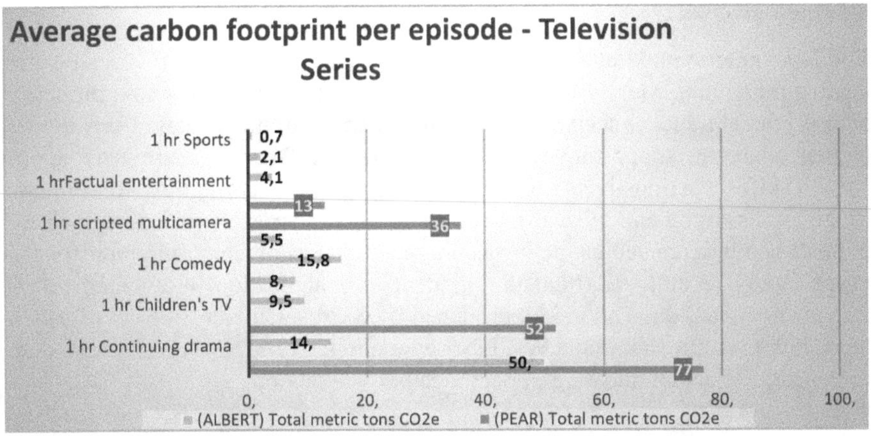

Figure 3.2 Average carbon footprint per hour of content – *Albert carbon calculator* & *PEAR*.

economy. (European Commission., n.d.). The concept of net-zero involves achieving a balance between anthropogenic greenhouse gas emissions and removal or offset. Carbon offsets provide a means of compensating for inevitable greenhouse gas emissions, enabling organisations to offset their carbon footprint and claim carbon neutrality. Carbon capture and storage (CCS) has emerged as a viable solution for mitigating CO_2 emissions, but it requires proper regulation and monitoring to address potential risks. Climate offsets incentivise investment and technological innovation that are instrumental in achieving the goal of net-zero.

Applicable green incentives to the audiovisual industry could be providing clean and renewable energy like mobile batteries, solar panel chargers, and fuel-efficient fleets to eliminate on-site emissions and provide a more efficient continuous power source for productions when on location. Albert, the screen industry organisation for environmental sustainability, offers "Creative offsets" as the "easiest way to take action", but they also warn not to "just offset" all emissions since that will lead to the Albert certification not being granted (www.wearealbert.org, n.d.).

The word "offset" has a semantic implication, leading us to interpret it as the emissions are entirely neutralised or cancelled out. It is important to exercise caution when supporting carbon offset projects and avoid using misleading or unverified claims of carbon neutrality to prevent greenwashing (Gallou, 2022). Communities relying on offset companies may suffer if genuine sustainability practices are neglected. Unsubstantiated carbon neutrality claims can harm local practices, erode trust, and perpetuate inequities. To achieve significant reductions in emissions, it is typically advised that organisations focus on improving energy efficiency, adopting renewable energy sources, and implementing other mitigation strategies before resorting to purchasing quotas or offsets. Authentic efforts should prioritise transparency, community engagement, and consideration for local knowledge. Good intentions in one location cannot remedy harm caused in another.

Steering away from greenwashing

The Norwegian Guide against Greenwashing from early 2020 focuses on misleading marketing. Merely making statements about a company's commitment to nature, ethical trade, or sustainability without demonstrating actual efforts in these realms, or lacking supporting evidence, does not qualify as authentic sustainability work. (Skift – Næringslivets klimaledere, n.d.). Understanding how contributions to the SDGs in the audiovisual industry can be implemented and communicated without being perceived as greenwashing is crucial in greening the industry. The guide highly recommends that this kind of communication be avoided or performed with caution. The guide, produced by Skift – Climate Business Leaders, Zero, Future in our Hands and WWF Norway, applies 17 SDGs and emphasises the importance of communicating impact together with action.

Sustainable development of the audiovisual industry

To enhance transparency and accountability regarding environmentally conscious behaviour and sustainability mandates in the audiovisual industry, acquire an in-depth comprehension of sustainability concerns and circularity initiatives. Understanding these issues is essential to ensuring that ecological obligations are met responsibly.

In 1972, the report *The Limits to Growth* (Meadows et al., 1972), commissioned by the Club of Rome, concluded that if growth trends at the time continue unchanged, the limits to growth on our planet will be reached around 2072. Twenty years later, the Union of Concerned Scientists issued a "Warning to Humanity" signed by about 1,500 scientists. The warning highlighted the risk of a biospheric crisis if industrialisation is not significantly reduced. In 2017, over 15,000 scientists signed an updated version of the warning. These warnings highlight the need to re-evaluate our current economic model and shift our focal point towards a circular economy with a regenerative growth model that gives back to the planet more than it takes (Williston, 2019). The term "sustainable development" was used in 1980 in the first international document on living resource conservation: IUCN report *World Conservation Strategy: Living Resources for Sustainable Development*. This report proposed to stimulate a more focused approach to managing living resources and provide policy guidance on implementing this. The report influenced the Brundtland Report in 1987, also known as "Our Common Future", which defines sustainable development as "development that meets the needs of the present without compromising the ability of future generations to meet their own needs" (Brundtland, 1987, p. 41).

In 1992, total 178 countries responded to the warning from the Union of Concerned Scientists and adopted Agenda 21 to build a global partnership for sustainable development. The initiative aimed at improving human lives while safeguarding the environment, leading to the Millennium Development Goals (MDGs) in 1995 to address critical global issues, including poverty, hunger, education, gender equality, and environmental sustainability. In 2000, the SDGs replaced the MDGs. The SDGs include 17 goals, 169 targets, and 232 indicators to measure progress towards sustainability by 2030. The SDGs were designed for governments (Henriksson & Weiderman, 2020), and it falls on the industry to implement them and track progress.

As businesses have become more aware of their impact on society and the environment, the concept of corporate social responsibility (CSR) has gained prominence. While media companies, such as Banijay and FremantleMedia, have made meaningful contributions to society, it is important to note that such actions alone may not fulfil their CSR obligations. Actual CSR reporting should focus on systemic transformations in how businesses operate and their motivation to do so. CSR initiatives prevent negative societal impacts like corruption, poor working conditions, and insufficient environmental protection. This involves not only how companies spend their money but also how they earn it (Beschorner, 2012).

Implementing sustainable practices in the audiovisual industry

The audiovisual industry has been implementing sustainable practices since 2010. The Producers Guild of America Foundation's Green Production Guide (GPG) is an industry toolkit that provides a checklist for Production Environmental Actions (PEACH) and a *PEAR*. GPG also offers a resource library with helpful visuals for sustainable best practices for the production office, stage, and location managers (Sustainable Production Alliance, n.d.).

2011 BAFTA founded the British Screen Industry Organisation for Environmental Sustainability, *Albert* (www.wearealbert.org, n.d.). The organisation offers a production handbook, a creative guide, case studies and articles, a carbon calculator, a carbon action plan for certification, and free online training for the industry. Public Broadcasters NRK in Norway and YLE in Finland were among the users of *Albert*'s resources in 2021. In 2019, one of the initial circular initiatives in the Nordic countries was published, the Ekosetti guidebook, a green production guide originating in Finland. It provides some primary steps in reducing and recycling waste concerning props and set production. It also suggests ways to minimise emissions during travel and advocates influencing equipment suppliers towards a more sustainable business culture. Resilient and flexible supply chains are mentioned in SDG 9 (Industry, Innovation and Infrastructure), SDG 12, and SDG 17 (Partnerships for the Goals). The Organisation for Economic Co-operation and Development (OECD) has released a policy toolkit designed to facilitate the construction of resilient supply chains that can be accessed at https://www.oecd.org/en/topics/resilient-supply-chains.html.

In 2020, the CineRegio Green members, a subgroup for Green Filming of CineRegio, of 28 European film funds, including FilmCamp and Filminvest in Norway, released a manifesto advocating environmentally responsible filming practices. This manifesto raises awareness and encourages climate-friendly measures in film and television production and financing (Cine Regio, 2020).

In 2020, the European Union assisted an international team from Norway, Sweden, Finland, and Russia in launching a project called Green Ice Camera. The team developed the Action Planner to help media producers plan and adapt their productions mindful of the Barents region's fragile ecosystems and local communities.

Highlighting the need for systemic change, the status reports entitled *Green Matters: Environmental Sustainability and Film Production: An Overview of Current Practice* (2020a), published by the British Film Institute (BFI) and *A Screen New Deal: A Route Map to Sustainable Film Production* (2020b) offer recommendations for utilising material reuse networks, adopting novel transportation systems, and reducing energy consumption.

To promote sustainable practices in the art and cultural sector in Norway, a roadmap outlining ten basic principles for sustainable practices was published (Grønt veikart, 2021). In the summer of 2022, the Norwegian Opera & Ballet, Øyafestivalen, Strix TV, and CICERO joined forces to launch the Green Producers Tool, supported by the Research Council of Norway. The tool is designed to assist producers and purchasers of cultural productions in the Nordics in measuring and reducing their emissions. In Sweden, five film funds have committed to using the "Hållbar Film" tool (Pham, 2022) to promote sustainable productions. This tool utilises SDG-based questions to simplify sustainability efforts.

The role of SMEs in achieving SDGs and reducing CO_2 emissions

Norway's SMEs make up 99% of all enterprises in the country and generate 44% of its value (NHO, n.d.; OECD, 2017). Increasingly recognised worldwide as vital actors in the fight against climate change, SMEs have a key role in achieving the SDGs (Koirala, 2018; Searcy, 2022). However, evidence of SMEs contribution to the UN Agenda 2030 remains scarce (Roxas & Coetzer, 2012; O'Donohue & Torugsa, 2015; Del Giudice et al., 2017; Pomare, 2018), why it is important to investigate the sustainable practices adopted by SMEs in Norway's audiovisual industry.

The situation for SMEs is multifaceted. On the one hand, SMEs may struggle to implement sustainability strategies without support from their leaders and parent organisations. Scarce resources, a shortage of relevant skills, and uncertain access to financing can delay progress on social and environmental issues (Del Giudice et al., 2017; Flagstad et al., 2021). Small organisations may additionally find the sustainability reporting process too costly and time-consuming. There is also a risk of misrepresenting emissions data, and focusing solely on CO_2 reduction may divert attention from other significant environmental concerns.

On the other hand, SMEs have a unique opportunity to contribute to the SDGs. Their ability to adapt, innovate, and engage local employees in green initiatives is often more effective than larger organisations (Shevchenko et al., 2016). Sustainability reporting can benefit small organisations in several ways, including improved resource management, enhanced reputation, access to funding and investors, regulatory compliance, market differentiation, stakeholder engagement, and long-term business resilience (Riedl & Smeets, 2017; Hartzmark & Sussman, 2019; UNCTAD, 2019). These benefits can help small organisations overcome concerns about the costs and time associated with sustainability reporting and encourage them to participate. For a more in-depth analysis of the obstacles and enablers of climate change adaptation for SMEs, please refer to Schaer and Kuruppu (2018).

Rebuild in a new direction

It is no longer a question of whether to implement sustainable practices. The focus now is on how to do it fast. If humans continue to emit 40 billion tons of carbon dioxide each year, we will reach our planetary boundaries before 2030. Emitting carbon emissions with the carbon already overheating the planet is causing severe changes in climate patterns, ecosystems, and sea levels. When our planet's boundaries reach their tipping points, it is too late for amendment. Nations and industries must come together in the battle against climate change before our planet's limits are pushed too far. The audiovisual industry consumes a significant amount of energy, particularly during production. To put this into perspective, a day of shooting a major motion picture can consume as much energy as a small town does in a week.

Greenhouse gas emissions, primarily from energy consumption and transportation in the audiovisual industry, must be reduced by half each decade until 2050, equating to 6%–7% annually. Such measures are essential to secure a sustainable future for humans and to limit global warming to 1.5°C. (IPCC, 2018) A circular economy and phasing out fossil fuels will help reduce air pollution, slow ocean acidification, and reduce pressure on biodiversity (Meadows et al., 1972; Clay, 2021), and are crucial to achieving net zero by 2050 (Maxwell & Miller, 2012; Carbon Trust, 2021; European Commission, 2021b).

Transparency in the audiovisual industry is essential for promoting sustainable practices, achieved through clear sustainability reports and publicly shared information. Reliable digital data and documents are necessary for accountability, tracking progress on SDGs, and achieving openness, while weak recordkeeping hinders the monitoring of progress (Lemieux, 2020). The audiovisual industry must adapt and transform to meet changing demands, embrace new strategies, understand the lifecycle of the production (Brunklaus & Eriksson, 2015) and collaborate to reduce CO_2 emissions, provide healthy food, and design products that recover raw materials. By leveraging circularity, state-of-the-art technologies, and fresh business models, the industry can unlock its potential and increase resilience and sustainability while remaining flexible to market trends and customer preferences. Achieving the SDGs requires decisive engagement from audiovisual organisations, industry associations, regulatory bodies, and other relevant entities to revolutionise the audiovisual landscape (Guterres, 2022; Betti & Hughes, 2023).

The Corporate Sustainability Reporting Directive and Scope 3 emissions

Broadcasters, large companies, and listed SMEs within the EU must soon consider indirect emissions (Scope 3) as they comply with the new CSRD. Subsidiaries will be exempt from the sustainability reporting requirements if included in the parent company's consolidated annual report. Regardless of perspective, all production companies that distribute their production to a public broadcaster or have an owner who does so need to monitor their CO_2 emissions since public broadcasters will be required to report on full scope 1, 2, and 3 GHG emissions.

This also means that indirect emissions, such as streaming and virtual production (VP), which, according to Heidsiek (2021), consume significant amounts of energy, requiring data processing and storage, should be considered when calculating the total carbon footprint of production. Technical devices used in these processes also generate emissions. Neglecting indirect emissions can result in underestimating the carbon footprint and missing opportunities to improve sustainability (Bhatia, 2011). In Norway, the Ministry of Environment has approved two collective compliance schemes, Norsirk and RENAS, that cover 94% of the European Directive Waste Electrical and Electronic Equipment (WEEE) for collection and recycling, relevant to Scope 3.

The CSRD, together with the Norwegian Openness Act, may help achieve transparent sustainable development. The CSRD replaces the Non-financial Reporting Directive (NFRD) in January 2024 and supports the European Green Deal's goal of achieving zero net greenhouse gas emissions by 2050. The Norwegian Openness Act promotes corporate social responsibility by providing a framework for reliable digital data and documents. It enables stakeholders to hold businesses responsible for their actions while promoting ethical standards.

The study of influences on sustainability practices in the Norwegian audiovisual industry

This research aims to understand sustainability practices in NAV-SMEs by examining whether and how they communicate their progress towards sustainable development. The study was conducted through a document analysis, which assessed the communicated engagement towards sustainable development, SDG implementation, and carbon footprint monitoring, as published on the selected company websites and annual reports. The research gathered the latest information about the company's sustainability efforts, including its environmental and social initiatives, by looking for specific projects, targets, and metrics demonstrating a commitment to sustainable practices. By gathering and analysing this data, we can understand how SMEs practice sustainable development cost- and time-efficiently without extensive fieldwork.

After examining the company's platforms, a thorough evaluation was conducted to assess the quality and quantity of the data provided. This involved analysing the company's certifications and standards. The study cross-compared the selected NAV-SMEs and their parent companies to identify the commonalities and differences in their sustainability practices. It identified whether the NAV-SMEs had quantified and reported their CO_2e footprints and whether they were taking proactive steps towards achieving the SDGs. No similar research has been carried out in Norway previously.

Two measures of sustainability activities were considered to fill a gap concerning what we know today about NAV-SME's mediation of and commitment to reporting CO_2e footprint and implementation of the 17 SDGs adopted by the General Assembly.

The study involved a document analysis of the web pages and annual reports of 21 NAV-SMEs, selected based on their staff size, ranging from 10 to 230 employees, and their European ownership structure. The parent companies were chosen according to their ranking among the top 30 European players in the audiovisual industry, published by the European Audiovisual Observatory (2022). The criteria considered to decide their suitability were revenue, TV audience share, and the number of fictional TV programmes produced.

The selected 21 NAV-SMEs are subsidiaries of the five major parent companies: ITV Studios, ViacomCBS, NENT Group, Fremantle, and Banijay. These companies' vast resources and extensive reach significantly influence the Norwegian media landscape.

About the Norwegian SMEs and their international connections

Transparency in corporate practices involves sharing information about a company's management, financial performance, operations, and governance with its stakeholders. Being transparent means being honest and upfront about how your business operates from the beginning to the end. This involves revealing your entire supply chain, from pre-production to distribution, and being transparent about the company's social and environmental impact through sustainability reports, environmental impact assessments, and other disclosure forms.

Canal Digital and Viasat, subsidiaries of NENT Group, merged and became Allente in 2020. Allente, one of the 21 Norwegian subsidiaries in this study, communicates social and environmental engagement on its web page with informative text about international human rights, environmental protection, ethical guidelines, diversity, equality, and the inclusive workplace. When producing products like decoders, antennas, etc., they assess the environmental impact of the production, and they participate in organised recycling systems for WEEE (waste electrical and electronic equipment) in the Nordic countries (Allente, n.d.), all of them necessary steps towards approaching environmental severe work.

In 2009, Rubicon TV, owned by Banijay, was instructed to explore various ideas for shows focusing on environmental preservation, but the effort was not fruitful. As Lars Hognestad, former producer and director of several comedy productions for NRK, TV 2, and TV Norge, CEO of Rubicon TV at the time, clarified: "Making entertainment of such themes easily turns into moralising" (Bakøy & Schanke Sundet, 2017, p. 7). Hognestad's idea of producing environmental content was perhaps a decade too early for the audiovisual industry in Norway. In 2018, he shifted his focus to the sustainable digital infrastructure sector, which he considers more future-oriented (Hauger, 2018). Twelve years later, during the 2021 COP26 summit, ITV and ViacomCBS, along with ten other broadcasters and streamers, made a significant commitment to the Climate Content Pledge. This pledge aims to use its content to help audiences understand the consequences of tackling climate change while inspiring and educating them about sustainable alternatives. Industry leaders from BBC, Channel 4, ITV, Sky, and STV emphasised the importance of reflecting the realities of climate change in content to ensure its relevance and appeal to audiences (Albert, 2021; ITV, 2021).

There is a growing expectation among consumers, investors, and regulatory bodies for companies to be transparent about their environmental performance and to take proactive steps to address sustainability challenges (Riedl & Smeets, 2017; Hartzmark & Sussman, 2019). In recent years, companies like Patagonia, IKEA and Unilever have significantly improved their transparency and environmental responsibility practices, gaining recognition for their commendable dedication to transparency and sustainable practices. These businesses have gone beyond the norm to incorporate eco-friendly materials such as organic cotton and recycled materials. Furthermore, they have made significant efforts to embrace fair trade principles. By being transparent about their operations and actively improving their sustainability practices, these companies have reduced their environmental footprint and appealed to consumers by increasing their pursuit of ethical and sustainable products. Their commitment to sustainability is a testament to the positive impact of adopting responsible business practices.

Current reporting of CO_2e footprint

Although measuring and reporting CO_2 emissions is debatable, developed countries must update the United Nations on their emissions and removals under the United Nations Framework Convention on Climate Change (UNFCCC). This process can ensure compliance with regulations and promote collaboration. Ultimately, these efforts can drive the adoption of better practices that minimise greenhouse gas emissions and lessen the impact of climate change, but we need to act decisively and united.

The industry perceives CO_2 emissions from transporting crew, cast, and equipment to shooting locations, substantial electricity consumption for lighting, air conditioning, operating equipment in studios, and using diesel-powered generators on-location shoots as primary CO_2 polluters. Additionally, waste, special effects, and pyrotechnics can release significant amounts of methane, carbon dioxide, and other greenhouse gases (ViacomCBS, 2019; Grassman & Gouttefarde, 2020; ITV, 2021; NENT Group, 2021a). The CO_2e is reported to be rising due to the increased media consumption through streaming platforms (European Commission, 2020a; Statista, 2020).

Mastiff and Nordisk Film TV Norway, two of Banijay's subsidiaries included in this study, have proclaimed the Green Producers Club membership and will measure productions with the Green Producers Tool in 2023 (Green Producers Club, n.d.). Mastiff has also published a climate report, expressing a desire to increase the number of environmentally friendly suppliers (Mastiff, 2023), following the Eco-Lighthouse requirements (eco-lighthouse.org). Nordisk Film TV Norway has yet to publish its environmental report, which means that the effectiveness of its environmental work cannot be verified. Apart from this statement, no other mention of their sustainability engagement was found on the company's web pages in 2021.

Current ways of implementation of the United Nations' 17 Sustainability Development Goals

The responsibility for implementing the SDGs rests with the government of each member state and, in principle, with all the rest of us who live and work there. Norway has made progress in achieving the SDGs, but much work remains to ensure the country's full realisation, particularly in implementing and performing the SDGs. The European SDG index reveals that Norway still has a long way to go regarding two key areas: responsible consumption and production (SDG 12) and climate action (SDG 13), where "major challenges remain" (Ministry of Local Government and Modernisation, 2021; Lafortune et al., 2021). These two key areas are highlighted in four of the five parent companies' reports in this study (Table 3.2).

The 17 SDGs are supported by 169 targets and 232 indicators. Target 12.6 encourages companies to integrate sustainability information into their reporting cycle, and 12.8 states that by 2030, people everywhere should have relevant information and awareness about sustainable development and lifestyles in harmony with nature.

Innovative, bold, and tough decisions are needed to transform and develop the audiovisual industry to meet the SDGs and the challenge of operationalising them.

According to the European Film Commissions Network (European Film Commission Network, n.d.), many European countries are now creating incentives to implement best practices related to the SDGs. For those seeking production grants, there is a need to improve the industry's environmental reporting, both regarding collecting consistent and reliable empirical data to streamline the reporting mechanisms and to avoid distortion of competition, as some countries will have more demanding or restrictive environmental standards than others (Grassman & Goutefarde, 2020). The *Filmförderungsgesetz* (Film Support Act – FFG) in Germany introduced ecological requirements for film productions in January 2022. These new measures aim to protect the environment by granting project film funding and reference film funding only if adequate steps are taken to ensure ecological sustainability during production. Additionally, producers are required to use a CO_2e calculator to determine the greenhouse gas emissions caused by the production of their films (Etteldorf, 2022).

In Norway, a call to report climate efforts and transparent business management concerning the SDGs was introduced to the film industry in the spring of 2021 when the Norwegian Film Institute (NFI) announced a new rule regarding production subsidies. According to this rule, companies applying for production subsidies must provide their environmental profile, a plan for environmental measures during production, and a report detailing the environmental measures they have already implemented (Norsk Filminstitutt, n.d.).

While the SDGs provide a framework for what needs to be achieved globally, the self-regulating business model of CSR (corporate social responsibility) allows individual businesses to contribute to these goals. CSR extends beyond legal mandates, where companies voluntarily embrace ethical, sustainable, and responsible business practices to create value for consumers, shareholders, employees, and society.

CSR reports detail the company's sustainability initiatives, environmental performance, and community engagement efforts. NENT Group, for example, emphasises safe and fair working environments throughout the value chain in its annual report (2021a), promoting SDG 8. NENT Group's business ethics programme focuses on business ethics risks such as corruption, competition law, data protection, and sanctions, correlating with SDG 8 and SDG 16. They also take tangible measures to reduce waste (SDG 12) and maximise resource efficiency (SDG 8). NENT Group and ITV Studios have committed to creating more resilient and flexible supply chains to meet consumers' ever-evolving expectations of sustainable practices (ITV, 2021; NENT Group, 2021a).

Results: document study analysis

The primary discovery made in this study is that the analysed NAV-SMEs published little or no communication about sustainable development on their web pages. Moreover, the result contradicts the sustainability policy of the parent companies and raises uncertainty about the progress of the sustainable development of SMEs in Norway.

Current state of sustainability practices in the selected SMEs and their parent companies

The international sustainability reports published in 2020–2021 by four of the five parent companies in this study provide insight into the company's social and environmental work and their contributions to achieving the SDGs. The organisations report the company's actions to reduce CO_2e, if and how they work to affect suppliers and their use of certifications and standards. Three of the four reports analysed mention reducing Scope 1 (direct emissions from owned or controlled sources like vehicles and fuel use), Scope 2 (indirect emissions like electricity, steam, heating, and cooling), and Scope 3 emissions (indirect emissions occurring in upstream and downstream activities in the supply chain) and at least two parent companies communicate development opportunities to affect suppliers in their value chain.

ITV Studios and NENT Group, two of the major players in the European audiovisual industry, are firmly committed to achieving a net-zero carbon emission status, significantly reducing waste, and addressing the issue of raw material scarcity. By assessing and reporting the identified financial and non-financial risks related to sustainability issues in their annual reports, they can make informed decisions and mitigate potential negative impacts (Creative Europe Media, 2022; Guterres, 2022). ITV Studio has set a target to ensure that all suppliers with high environmental risks meet their sustainability criteria by 2025. They are working closely with each supplier to help them improve their impact by 2030. ITV launched a new Supplier Code of Conduct in 2021 to streamline this process, enhancing its supplier selection and due diligence processes by monitoring social and environmental factors (ITV, 2021).

NENT Group

NENT Group (rebranded to Viaplay Group in May 2022), the parent company to Canal Digital and Viasat in Norway, is a broadcasting, streaming, and content production company committed to the Science Based Targets Initiative to align its greenhouse gas emissions targets with the objectives of the Paris Agreement. NENT is a Swedish media company with a focus mainly on the Nordic market, a signatory of the UN Global Compact, a member of the UN Sustainable Development Goals Media Compact Initiative, a contributor to the Responsible Media Forum and an endorser of the UN Global Compacts Women's Empowerment Principles. NENT Group supports 8 of the 17 SDGs (see Table 3.2), and annual and sustainability reports have been published since 2018. The company communicates that its sustainability strategy is integrated into the overall business strategy and aligned with its purpose, values, and culture. However, the report does not state whether the subsidiaries Canal Digital and Viasat are included (NENT Group, 2021a).

ITV Studios

ITV Studios is a British multinational media and entertainment company. While no environmental or social reports were found for the Norwegian department of ITV Studios Norway AS, ITV Studios began doing Climate Scenario Analysis in 2020 to understand better how the changing climate could impact their business. The goal is to achieve net zero carbon and zero waste and develop sustainable culture and sourcing by 2030, reducing emissions by 10% annually. ITV's strategy is removing all single-use plastics from its operations, productions, and supply chain (ITV, 2020).

Technical innovation and collaboration, such as remote production, cloud-based solutions and virtual studios, is something ITV will focus on in the coming years, says Phil Holdgate, appointed Head of Production Sustainability at ITV. ITV has 12 green teams in the UK, the Netherlands, and the US, which nurture a culture of sustainability and generate green initiatives across the organisation. The UK report says the company will be 100% *Albert-certified* and trained by 2030 (Chapman, 2020; ITV, 2021).

Banijay

Mastiff AS and Nordisk Film TV Norway, owned by Banijay, are both members of the Norwegian Green Producers Club and have presently dedicated staff responsible for working with environmental sustainability in the business. Both companies had, in 2021, an Eco-Lighthouse certification, which is a Norwegian environmental management certification scheme (Stiftelsen Miljøfyrtårn, 2020). On the other hand, the international owner, Banijay, has not published a social or environmental report on their website. However, a 25-page Code of Conduct is published with an assurance that Banijay is taking serious steps to reduce the overall environmental impact and strive for net zero. According to the guidelines in the Norwegian

Greenwashing poster (https://www.gronnvasking.no/en), it is unclear which areas Banijay is taking action in and what their plans are. This makes it hard to consider it as valid environmental work. Banijay claims to educate audiences to drive change but offers no examples or evidence to support this assertion.

ViacomCBS

ViacomCBS Networks International, a unit of ViacomCBS Inc., broadcasts and publishes billboards and television, with production primarily in the United States. Nickelodeon, MTV, Paramount Network, Paramount +, and Comedy Central are part of its portfolio for the Nordic countries. None of the Norwegian subsidiaries communicated or published a social or environmental report by 2020.

In 2019, ViacomCBS and Paramount started decreasing their environmental impact by advising 20 productions to follow the Green Production Guide and publishing their first Environmental, Social, and Governance (ESG) report explaining the management and administration of actions. They also engaged with suppliers to increase transparency into Scope 3 emissions and set goals for the future (Sustainable Production Alliance, n.d.; ViacomCBS, 2019).

Fremantle

Fremantle is a British multinational media and entertainment company, part of the RTL Group, owned by the German media conglomerate Bertelsmann, and parent company to FremantleMedia Norge AS, Strix TV, Monster AS, One Big Happy Family, and Novemberfilm, also included in this study.

Fremantle's contribution to Climate Action (SDG 13) is to use the *Albert* calculator for its productions and businesses worldwide to further reduce its carbon dioxide emissions, aiming to institute precise measures to reduce the carbon footprint of film and television productions from 2020 to 2023 (RTL Group, 2020; Bertelsmann, 2021a). Follow-up measures are being defined in 2021 at both the group and divisional levels to further develop corporate responsibility at Bertelsmann (Bertelsmann, 2021b). The claim on Bertelsmann's webpage that its businesses contribute to five key SDGs (Bertelsmann, n.d.), does not align with Fremantle's chosen SDGs, highlighting a discrepancy between the parent company's assertions and the subsidiary's actual sustainability priorities.

In a podcast interview with the managing director and producer of FremantleMedia Norway AS, Petter Testmann-Koch (Rosvoll, 2021), awareness about sustainability issues appears important. However, there is uncertainty about how to approach it. The *Albert* calculator is used as a guiding tool in *Maskorama*, produced for NRK in 2021, as a pilot production (Rushprint, 2021; Jerijervi, 2022). The result will provide input on the needed changes, source sorting, and conscious use of batteries, equipment, and transport. Due to a lack of knowledge regarding environmental certification for equipment, Fremantle in Norway is not presently considering this when buying or renting equipment. The communicated environmental work can be considered a first step towards sustainability practices.

However, verifying their environmental work's effectiveness is impossible without a published report, actions, and a reduction plan for emissions.

Strix TV AS produced *Farmen kjendis* in Norway in 2022 for the commercial channel TV2, recording emissions using the Green Producer Tool as one solitary first step to include environmental work. Managing director Jørgen Hermansen believes that reuse and energy efficiency will make production cheaper in the long run and sees the costs of working with emissions as an investment. As part of the production's commitment to the environment, charging stations for electric cars are installed, and they encourage crew members to use bicycles and organise carpooling. They also encourage suppliers to use electric vans. Several buildings used in production are planned to be reused in the show's next season. Energy use in transport, purchasing, and waste management is logged (Bjørhovde & Veberg, 2021).

CO_2 emissions in selected parent companies

A review of the international corporations gives an impression of the organisations' footprint in relation to the number of programming hours (Banijay, n.d.-b; Fremantle, n.d.; ITV Studios, n.d.; NENT Group, 2021b), shown in Table 3.1, together with examples of their contributions to the SDGs shown in Table 3.2. The carbon calculator developed by Albert states that an average hour of TV production generates 5.7 tonnes of carbon dioxide equivalent (CO2e) (Priestley, 2022; www.wearealbert.org). This definition estimates the environmental impact of programming hours across reviewed organisations.

Assessing SDG implementation and sustainability reporting

This section presents an overview of implemented SDGs in the five international media groups examined during 2020/21. Furthermore, it investigates whether the subsidiaries have implemented and communicated the SDGs and whether the actions taken can be verified according to the greenwashing poster. In summary, SDG 5 (gender equality), SDG 12 (responsible consumption and production), SDG and 13 (climate action) were mentioned in four of the owner companies' annual environmental or social reports, data shown in Table 3.2. Banijay is omitted since no published report was found.

Table 3.2 presents an overview of the SDGs chosen by the international owner companies. Subsidiaries that did not communicate social and/or

Table 3.1 Parent organisation's footprint in relation to the number of programming hours as identified by the current study on selected cases

Parent company	*Hours of programming*	*t CO2e*
Banijay	<150,000	866,400
ITV Studios	<90,000	513,000
Fremantle	<40,000	228,000
ViacomCBS	<30,000	171,000
NENT	<30,000	171,000

Table 3.2 Reported SDGs mentioned by the SME's parent companies, as identified by the current study on selected cases

Sustainability goal	*ITV Studios*	*Viacom CBS*	*NENT Group*	*Bertelsmann*
SDG 1 NO POVERTY	x			
SDG 2 ZERO HUNGER	x			
SDG 3 GOOD HEALTH & WELL-BEEING	x		x	x
SDG 4 QUALITY EDUCATION	x	x		x
SDG 5 GENDER EQUALITY	x	x	x	x
SDG 6 CLEAN WATER AND SANITATION				
SDG 7 AFFORDABLE & CLEAN ENERGY	x	x		
SDG 8 DECENT WORK & ECONOMIC GROWTH		x	x	x
SDG 9 INDUSTRY, INNOVATION & INFRASTRUCTURE				
SDG 10 REDUCED INEQUALITIES	x	x	x	
SDG 11 SUSTAINABLE CITIES & COMMUNITIES				
SDG 12 RESPONSIBLE CONSUMPTION & PRODUCTION	x	x	x	x
SDG 13 CLIMATE ACTION	x	x	x	x
SDG 14 LIFE BELOW WATER				
SDG 15 LIFE ON LAND				
SDG 16 PEACE, JUSTICE & STRONG INSTITUTIONS			x	
SDG 17 PARTNERSHIPS FOR THE GOALS			x	

environmental actions and/or reports are not mentioned in this review but are shown in Table 3.3.

Based on the lack of published reports or statements on the 21 national companies' websites, the results show that the SDGs described and published at the international group level cannot be confirmed as implemented in their subsidiaries in Norway. Banijay is not included in this analysis since neither a CSR nor environmental report were published.

Table 3.3 Published social or environmental activities and/or reports in Norwegian SMEs, as identified by the current study on selected cases

International owner	*Norwegian company*	*Published environmental report*	*Mention standards and certifications*	*Communicated solitary actions*	*Valid*
Fremantle Media (RTL Group, Bertelsmann,)	(1) FremantleMedia Norge AS (2) Strix TV Monster Novemberfilm Miso Film One Big Happy Family Rakett	Not found 2021	(1) Albert Carbon Calculator (2) Green Producers Club	Yes (1 and 2)	(1) No (2) No
ITV Studios	ITV Studios Norway	Not found 2021	No	No	Not relevant
Banijay, EndemolShine Group	(3) Mastiff (4) Nordisk Film TV Norway Rubicon TV (2020)	(3) Published 2021	(3) Miljøfyrtorn (2020+2023) (3) Green Producers Club (4) Miljøfyrtorn (2019) (4) Green Producers Club	Yes – at the international level	(3) Yes (4) No
Nordic Entertainment Group (NENT), rebranded as Viaplay Group	TV3 Viaplay Viafree (5)Viasat (allente) TV6	Not published 2021	(5) Allente Supply Chain Sustainability Policy	(5) Yes	(5) No
ViacomCBS	Nickelodeon MTV Paramount Network Paramount +, Comedy Central	Not found 2021	Green Production Guide	No	Not relevant

None of the analysed production companies in Norway report that they relate to the SDGs, and only 5 out of 21 production companies mention certification, standards, or environmental engagement on their web pages or in published articles. Three selected SMEs and one parent company, Banijay, mention that they believe our planet is important and are taking the necessary steps to reduce their carbon footprint and overall environmental impact. Without backing information or published sustainability reports, activities like this do not count as valid according to the Norwegian Guide Against Greenwashing (Skift – Næringslivets klimaledere, n.d.), data shown in Table 3.3, and guidelines discussed in the subsection, *Steering Away from Greenwashing*.

Discussion

It is reasonable that, despite a willingness to engage with sustainable practices, NAV-SMEs may face communication barriers due to lack of knowledge and limited resources, including inadequate infrastructure, staffing and finances. This emphasises the need to improve industry skills and knowledge, increase transparency and communication, and take relevant actions towards sustainable development. Cross-industry collaborations and systems thinking are crucial to address complex challenges like sustainable development and climate change.

Systems thinking in a circular economy

Systems thinking considers the whole ecosystem, viewing the organisation and its environment as interconnected and interdependent. Sharing sustainability practices, emissions reports, and actions taken to implement SDGs can help the audiovisual industry practice a circular economy with a holistic perspective to identify unintended consequences.

Systems thinking view an organisation and its environment as interconnected rather than isolated, with a holistic perspective that can identify ripple effects and unintended consequences of sustainable practices.

To promote a sustainable and circular economy, where materials never become waste and nature is regenerated, it is essential to utilise incentives to address market failures and encourage the transition. Systems thinking suggests that effecting change in a system necessitates the identification of all system players, understanding the relationships between them, and assessing the impact of these relationships on the system and its external environment (Nature, 2020). Peter Senge (2006), the pioneer of "learning organisations", outlines three critical characteristics of systems thinking, essential for anyone seeking to understand complex systems and their behaviour, emphasising:

- the importance of continuous learning,
- being open to new perspectives, and
- consider multiple viewpoints when examining a phenomenon, "triangulating" the perspectives.

Leveraging circulatory principles alongside systems thinking allows us to create more robust, sustainable, and interconnected solutions for our planet's future. Considering the interconnected web of factors contributing to emissions, adapting systems thinking will help us achieve sustainable practices. For a company's sustainability efforts to have a meaningful impact, they must be incorporated into a comprehensive strategy rather than restricted to isolated actions (Rodriguez & Ricart, 1997). This entails taking responsibility for the environmental and social consequences of the company's actions, such as investigating the impact on health and diversity (both on and off-screen) and on sensitive natural areas and communicating the measures that will be taken to prevent such harm.

Numerous production companies have already adopted system thinking practices on a smaller scale, such as repurposing set materials, eating healthy, and routinely donating excess food to promote circularity and environmental responsibility. Eco-labelling mechanisms for equipment, soundstage facilities, and studios in the industry are also topics of the sustainable practice discussions (ITV, 2021; NENT Group, 2021a; Iraldo et al., 2020).

Strategies like transitioning to renewable energy, using energy-efficient equipment, promoting sustainable transportation, and raising awareness among professionals are being implemented, and the COVID-19 pandemic accelerated innovation in the film and TV industry, leading to the adaptation of new ways of working. Remote production, IP-based solutions, and video conferencing tools have become more prevalent. These changes have enhanced transformations in content production, editing, and distribution, positively impacting the industry. According to Ecoprod Coordinator Alissa Aubenque in France, the industry is shifting from an individualistic approach to a more systemic change (Heidsiek, 2021).

However, it is difficult to determine the level of engagement or how the Norwegian audiovisual industry works towards implementing the SDGs, as there is a lack of communication regarding sustainable practices and reporting. Therefore, it is essential to encourage and facilitate transparent reporting of sustainability practices and SDG implementation in a structured manner, from the international corporate group level to the national organising units, to enable better understanding and collaboration towards achieving a circular economy in the audiovisual industry.

Building trust and long-term value

Transparency is an important aspect of building trust and ensuring accountability in companies. It promotes ethical conduct and holds companies responsible for their actions. By adopting proactive measures to minimise social and environmental impact, companies can establish trust with stakeholders, enhance reputation, and create long-term value for their businesses (Borglund et al., 2017; Miles & Covin, 2000, pp. 299–311).

Since the beginning of the twenty-first century, there has been growing interest in investing in companies and funds with a trustful social and environmental impact (Bauer et al., 2005; Dorfleitner et al., 2015). Incorporating the SDGs into production strategies can benefit leaders, including increased knowledge, skills, and perspective on the circular economy (United Nations, 2020; European Commission, 2021b). This, in turn, can lead to informed and effective decision-making regarding attracting top talent, retaining loyal customers, and establishing a relevant and forward-thinking brand reputation (Henriksson & Weidman, 2020; ITV, 2020). Raising awareness, facilitating informed decision-making, and encouraging innovation can ultimately provide a competitive edge and improve profitability (Surroca et al., 2010; Miralles-Quirós et al., 2019; UNCTAD, 2019).

The industry should report transparently on the entire company's emission sources and environmental and climate impacts with increased pressure on Scope 3 subcontractors to avoid making false claims about the environmental footprint (greenwashing).

Furthermore, the decision-makers and investors might be missing detailed and comprehensive information on the impact of the industry for two reasons: reporting from NAV-SMEs is not included in the international owners' environmental reports and the overall impact of the audiovisual industry, especially with the fact that the manufacturing of technical products, devices and other technical products used to view the produced content, is typically not included in CO_2e calculations applied in the industry. Both corporate and government policies could reap benefits from improved data and streamlining of holistic reporting, for instance, to avoid distortion of competition when funding co-production in Europe.

A unified green standard for sustainable audiovisual production

Regarding motivation or incentives to act, the commitment from top management is essential in any learning and improvement process (Rodriguez & Ricart, 1997; Epstein & Roy, 1998). Companies that are leaders in corporate transparency and environmental responsibility have robust sustainability programmes. They conduct regular assessments of their environmental impact, set targets for reducing emissions and waste, and engage with stakeholders to gather feedback and input on their sustainability efforts. Published sustainable development strategies or annual sustainability reports are effective ways for customers, investors, and the company to monitor progress towards objectives and goals regarding environmental, social, and economic concerns (Riedl & Smeets, 2017; Hartzmark & Sussman, 2019).

A precise policy with clear guidelines and goals should define responsibilities and tools supporting good follow-up and reporting routines. Organisations committed to sustainability can use the SDG compass to formulate a sustainability strategy and the Global Reporting Initiative (GRI) standards to report on their impacts related to the economy, environment, and people. (Bernard, Abdelgadir, & Belkhir, 2015). The sustainability management system for the film industry BS 8909 (British Standards Institution, 2011), is a Plan-Do-Check-Act cycle, meeting established regulations and standards (Kääpä, 2018). Other certification schemes and internationally agreed-upon standards is ISO 14000 (environmental management) and ISO 26000 that can guide the integration of sustainability into a business, securing environmental work for audiovisual productions' life cycle analysis and environmental labelling.

Table 3.4 The three-pillar strategy, by Lucia Recalde (European Commission)

Think Green: EXCHANGE and LEARN	*Film Green: MEASURE and COLLABORATE*	*Be green: Incentives CHANGE*
Stakeholder dialogue	Data collection on industry practices	Support tools that help introduce new business models
Train Professionals	Harmonization of data – CO_2 calculation – green labels – standards	Introducing sustainability into award criteria for project selection
Raise awareness and promote good practices	Set up key performance indicators (KPI)	Spotlight on sustainable work, practices, and stories

Due to investor and financier demands, the audiovisual industry faces increased inquiry around environmental practices, reporting, and sustainable production. This shift is expected to significantly impact small businesses in the industry, potentially limiting their ability to secure financing from regional and national sources and participate in international co-productions.

However, it is essential to acknowledge that the media industry may have some resistance to political conditions that restrict the freedom of capital owners. Editorial freedom is almost sacred and of utmost importance for solving societal tasks. While control from authorities is often viewed as unnatural and dictatorial, editorial limitations based on market research and audience preferences are generally considered more acceptable (Gripsrud, 2015). This could make knowledge about audience perception of green productions relevant to accelerate the transition needed.

June 2021 European Green Deal and the Creative Europe MEDIA programme gathered the first stakeholder meeting *Media and Audio-visual Action Plan: Towards a climate-neutral audiovisual sector*, to initiate the phrasing of a unified green European Standard for sustainable Audiovisual Production and Distribution, presenting greening as a business opportunity for the industry (European Commission, 2021a). In the meeting, Lucia Recalde presented the three-pillar strategy shown in Table 3.4 (Recalde, 2021):

A second meeting took place in Berlin in 2022, where members agreed that changing mindsets on screen is valuable, engaging the crew is essential, and "sustainability has to be a norm" (European Commission, 2022a). However, the network believes there is insufficient data to make informed decisions on what areas the industry contributes the most to climate change. To help collect data, a primary plug-in tool will be developed that can be integrated into existing CO_2e calculators, focusing on accommodation, transport, energy, catering, and set construction (Creative Europe Media, 2022).

The ongoing dialogue regarding the importance of a uniform green European standard for sustainable audiovisual production and distribution (European Commission, 2020a, 2020b, 2022a) is vital for thinking and acting transparently and interconnectedly.

Prospective trajectories in ecomedia research

The results of this study have provided valuable insights into NAV-SME's communicated commitment to sustainable development, the implementation of the SDGs, and the measurement and reporting of the generated CO_2 footprints. The findings underscore the importance of transparency and accountability in achieving SDGs and highlight the need for further research into effective strategies for reducing carbon footprints and promoting sustainable practices in the audiovisual industry.

Further research would be relevant to gain insight into the ongoing sustainability practices of SMEs in the audiovisual industry by observing the micro-level actions undertaken by managers and how these actions contribute to sustainable development in the industry. Subsequent research should conduct qualitative studies in the proposed relationships to closely examine the work going on and at what level the subsidiaries are involved when mediating social and environmental work at the international corporate level.

It would be relevant to perform qualitative, in-depth interviews with both international and national leaders and producers to gain a deeper understanding of what prevents international companies from including their subsidiaries in their reporting, as well as get the producers' take on the fact that the measurements they register at present, may not be visible in the organisation. Furthermore, it is relevant to investigate the published reports further and carefully examine implemented measures and actions. Forced Labour (SDG 5 and SDG 8) is one area to study, in relation to the Norwegian Openness Act, considering cotton, garments, props, set construction materials, vehicles, cleaning, security, and construction with higher risk for modern slavery and labour exploitation (www.globalslaveryindex.org; STV, 2022).

A follow-up study between 2020 and today is needed to review NAV-SME's sustainability commitments and analyse their evolution comprehensively. Conducting follow-up research can help identify and manage environmental, social, and governance (ESG) risks, which can have significant financial and reputational impacts. Regular reviews can increase confidence among stakeholders, including investors, customers, and employees, by demonstrating the company's commitment to sustainability.

This chapter highlights the need for including affiliated NAV-SMEs in the environmental and social analysis in the reporting from the corporate groups. By having the top international management presenting and introducing social and environmental policies in their national subsidiaries, the credibility of the internationally published reports increases and lowers the risks (Dun & Bradstreet, 2022), and there would likely be a much higher possibility to attract investors (British Standards Institution, 2011; Riedl & Smeets, 2017; Hartzmark & Sussman, 2019; UNCTAD, 2019). This may, in turn, help the subsidiaries implement new and necessary work methods, which, as a result, affect the opportunity for NAV-SMEs to contribute to the SDGs, subsequently affecting Norway's overall contribution to the SDGs.

Conclusion

The study's primary objective was to assess the communication of commitment to sustainable development, implementation of the SDGs, and monitoring and reporting of carbon footprint by NAV-SMEs. The study showed that despite the political goals of their parent companies, NAV-SMEs communicate insufficient sustainable development and carbon footprint management. This shortcoming is concerning, as small and medium-sized enterprises (SMEs) are pivotal in advancing the Sustainable Development Goals (SDGs). Through their capacity for innovation, job creation, and income generation, SMEs significantly contribute to the transition toward a sustainable and equitable future. (Koirala, 2018; Searcy, 2022).

In addition, the study addresses the environmental impacts associated with the production of films and television programs. Notably, transportation, electricity, fuel, housing, travel, and waste were identified as having the most substantial environmental impact in 2021. The chapter highlights the importance of transparency and responsibility in adopting sustainable practices. It calls for the implementation of the SDGs and the necessity for monitoring and reporting CO2 emissions, enabling the industry to learn from one another in a timely manner. Overall, the study's findings shed light on the status of communicated sustainable development activities in NAV-SMEs and their contribution to sustainable development and the SDGs, addressing SMEs' adoption of sustainable practices in Norway's audiovisual industry.

References

AV Data 4 Europe. (n.d.). *Key data*. AV Data 4 Europe. https://avdata4europe.eu/key-data/ [Accessed 2024-10-26].

Babun, T., & Holmqvist, S. (2018). *An SME-Heavy Sector*. AV Data 4 Europe. https://avdata4europe.eu/key-data/.

Allente. (n.d.). *Bærekraft*. https://www.allente.no/om-oss/barekraft/ [Accessed 2021-04-21].

Bakøy, E., & Schanke Sundet, V. (2017). Remember, it's just television. *Journal of European Television History & Culture*, *6*, 1–12. https://mediarep.org/server/api/core/bitstreams/356f9638-bda8-4eb0-a9ce-c41487faeb38/content.

Banijay (n.d.-a). *Nordics*. https://www.banijay.com/companies/territories/nordics/ [Accessed 2020-10-29].

Banijay Group (n.d.-b). *Banijay*. https://www.banijay.com/ [Accessed 2023-01-29].

Bhatia, P. (2011). *The greenhouse gas protocol: Scope 3 standard*. World Resources Institute and World Business Council for Sustainable Development. https://ghgprotocol.org/sites/default/files/standards_supporting/Chapter1.pdf

Bauer, R., Koedijk, K., & Otten, R. (2005). International evidence on ethical mutual fund performance and investment style. *Journal of Banking & Finance*, *29*(7), 1751–1767. https://doi.org/10.1016/j.jbankfin.2004.06.035.

Bennett, J. (2010). *Vibrant Matter: A Political Ecology of Things*. Duke University Press.

Bernard, S., Abdelgadir, S., & Belkhir, L. (2015). Does GRI reporting impact environmental sustainability? An industry-specific analysis of CO**2** emissions performance between reporting and non-reporting companies. *Journal of Sustainable Development*, *8*(9), 190–205.

Bertelsmann (2021a). *Climate Neutrality 2030 - How Far Along Is Bertelsmann?* https://www.bertelsmann.com/corporate-responsibility/engagement/project/climate-neutrality-2030-how-far-along-is-bertelsmann.jsp.

Bertelsmann (2021b). Bertelsmann Executive Board decides on further development of Corporate Responsibility. https://www.bertelsmann.com/corporate-responsibility/engagement/project/bertelsmann-executive-board-decides-on-further-development-of-corporate-responsibility.jsp [Accessed 2021-04-21].

Bertelsmann (n.d.). *United Nations Sustainable Development Goals*. https://www.bertelsmann.com/corporate-responsibility/reporting/united-nations-sustainable-development-goals.jsp.

Beschorner, T. (2012). What Is Corporate Social Responsibility (CSR)? [Video]. https://youtu.be/E0NkGtNU_9w [Accessed 2019-09-15].

Betti, F., & Hughes, K. (2023). Here's How We Can Turn More Industries into Circular Economies [Video]. World Economic Forum. https://www.weforum.org/agenda/2023/01/industry-circular-economy-change/ [Accessed 2023-01-29].

Bjørhovde, H., & Veberg, A. (2021). Hvor mye skader en TV-produksjon klimaet? Nå får vi svaret. *Aftenposten*, June 18, p. 46.

Borglund, T., De Geer, H., Sweet, S., Frostenson, M., Lerpold, L., Nordbrand, S., Sjöström, E., & Windell, K. (2017). *CSR och hållbart företagande*. Andra upplagan Stockholm: Sanoma utbildning

British Film Institute (2020a). *Green Matters Environmental Sustainability and Film Production: An Overview of Current Practice*. https://core-cms.bfi.org.uk/media/1717/download.

British Film Institute (2020b). *A Screen New Deal - A Route Map to Sustainable Film Production*. https://core-cms.bfi.org.uk/media/2940/download.

British Standards Institution. (2011). *BS 8909:2011 Specification for a sustainability management system for film*. BSI. https://knowledge.bsigroup.com/products/specification-for-a-sustainability-management-system-for-film?version=standard

Brundtland, G. H. (1987). *Our Common Future: Report of the World Commission on Environment and Development*. Oxford: Oxford University Press.

Brunklaus, B., & Eriksson, M. (2015). *Miljöpåverkan av filmproduktion, modell och metod för beräkning med hjälp av livscykelanalys* (Report no. 2015:17). Gothenburg: Chalmers University of Technology.

Chapman, S. (2020). ITV commits to science-based emissions targets. *Sustainability Magazine*. https://sustainabilitymag.com/esg/itv-commits-science-based-emissions-targets [Accessed 2020-06-18].

Cine Regio (2020). *Green Report 2020 on Sustainability in the European Regions*. Brussels: Cine Regio. https://www.cineregio.org/dyn/files/pdf_download/11-file/CineRegio_GreenReport2020_25022020_SinglePages.pdf.

Clay, J. (2021). *Breaking Boundaries: The Science of Our Planet* [Film]. Silverback Films & Indikate Productions.

Cottle, S. (2003). *Media Organisation and Production* (Media in focus). London: SAGE Publications Ltd.

Creative Europe Media (2022). *European Film Forum: Towards a Climate-Neutral Audiovisual Sector*. Berlin. https://digital-strategy.ec.europa.eu/en/library/european-film-forum-towards-climate-neutral-audiovisual-sector.

Cubitt, S. (01 Jan. 2005). *EcoMedia*. Leiden, The Netherlands: Brill. https://doi.org/10.1163/9789004454910

Del Giudice, M., Khan, Z., De Silva, M., Scuotto, V., Caputo, F., & Carayannis, E. (2017). The microlevel actions undertaken by owner-managers in improving the sustainability practices of cultural and creative small and medium enterprises: A United Kingdom–Italy comparison. *Journal of Organizational Behavior*, *38*(9), 1396–1414. https://doi.org/10.1002/job.2237.

Directive (EU) 2022/2464 of the European Parliament and of the Council (2022). The Corporate Sustainability Reporting Directive. EUR-Lex. https://eur-lex.europa.eu/legal-content/EN/TXT/?uri=CELEX%3A32022L2464

Dorfleitner, G., Halbritter, G., & Nguyen, M. (2015). Measuring the level and risk of corporate responsibility – An empirical comparison of different ESG rating approaches. *Journal of Asset Management*, *16*(7), 450–466. https://doi.org/10.1057/jam.2015.31.

Dun & Bradstreet. (2022). *2022 Environmental, Social & Governance (ESG) Report*. https://www.dnb.com/content/dam/english/dnb-data-insight/Dun_&_Bradstreet_Global_ESG_Report_2022.pdf

Epstein, M., & Roy, M.-J. (1998). Managing corporate environmental performance: A multinational perspective. *European Management Journal*, *16*(3), 284–296. https://doi.org/10.1016/S0263-2373(98)00005-X.

Etteldorf, C. (2022). New German film support act enters into force on 1 January 2022. Institute of European Media Law. European Audiovisual Observatory. https://merlin.obs.coe.int/article/9409.

European Commission (2020a). Europe's Media in the Digital Decade: An Action Plan to Support Recovery and Transformation (p. 13). https://eur-lex.europa.eu/legal-content/EN/TXT/?uri=CELEX%3A52020DC0784.

European Commission. (2020b). *A new Circular Economy Action Plan: For a cleaner and more competitive Europe* (COM/2020/98 final). (p. 4). EUR-Lex. https://eur-lex.europa.eu/legal-content/EN/ALL/?uri=COM:2020:98:FIN

European Commission (2021a). "Common Statement": Towards a Unified Measurement Methodology of CO_2 Emissions in the European Audiovisual Sector. https://digital-strategy.ec.europa.eu/en/news/common-statement-towards-unifiedmeasurement-methodology-co2-emissions-european-audiovisual-sector.

European Commission. (2021b). *Horizon Europe strategic plan 2021-2024*. Publications Office of the European Union. https://doi.org/10.2777/794570.

European Commission (2022a). *Common statement towards a unified measurement methodology for CO2 emissions in the European audiovisual sector*. Digital Strategy. https://digital-strategy.ec.europa.eu/en/news/common-statement-towards-unified-measurement-methodology-co2-emissions-european-audiovisual-sector [Accessed 2022-12-01].

European Commission (2022b). *Recovery and Resilience Scoreboard*. https://ec.europa.eu/economy_finance/recovery-and-resilience-scoreboard/assets/thematic_analysis/scoreboard_thematic_analysis_culture.pdf [Accesses 2022-08-01].

European Commission (n.d.). *A European Green Deal*. Digital Strategy. https://commission.europa.eu/strategy-and-policy/priorities-2019-2024/european-green-deal_en.

European Film Commissions Network (n.d.). *Green filming*. EUFCN. https://eufcn.com/green-filming/. [Accessed 2023-03-27].

Flagstad, I., Johnsen, S., & Rydstedt, L. (2021). The process of establishing a green climate: Face-to-face interaction between leaders and employees in the microsystem. *The Journal of Values-Based Leadership*, *14*(1). https://doi.org/10.22543/0733.141.1343.

Fremantle (n.d.). *Distribution*. Fremantle. https://fremantle.com/distribution/.

Fritsche, R. (2020). *A Study in Green*. Trollhättan: Film i Väst.

Grassman, P., & Gouttefarde, M. (2020). *Greening the European Audiovisual Industry*. European Union. https://digital-strategy.ec.europa.eu/en/library/greening-european-audiovisual-industry.

Green Producers Club (n.d.). *Green Producers Club.* https://www.greenproducers.club/ [Accessed 2023-01-28].

Gripsrud, J. (2015). *Mediekultur, mediesamfunn*. 5. utg. Oslo: Universitetsforlaget.

Grønt veikart (2021). https://www.xn--grntveikart-hgb.no/.

Guterres, A. (2022). *We Need All Hands on Deck for Faster, Bolder Climate Action*. United Nations [Video]. https://youtu.be/7WCXFoDsjcQ.

Hartzmark, S. M., & Sussman, A. B. (2019). *Do investors value sustainability? A natural experiment examining ranking and fund flows*. Journal of Finance, 74(6), 2789-2837. https://doi.org/10.1111/jofi.12841

Hauger, K. K. (2018*). Har jobbet med «alt» av norske komikere – nå sier han farvel til tv-bransjen.* Kampagne. https://kampanje.com/jobb/2018/11/har-jobbet-med-det-som-er-av-norske-komikere--na-sier-han-takk-og-farvel-til-tv-bransjen/.

Heidsiek, B. (2014). An important incentive: The Flanders Audiovisual Fund in Belgium is asking producers for a carbon footprint. Cineropa. https://cineuropa.org/en/newsdetail/252782/.

Heidsiek, B. (2021). At Cannes, new innovations for green production in the spotlight. Cineuropa. https://www.cineuropa.org/en/newsdetail/408044/.

Henriksson, H., & Weidman, E. (2020). *Sustainability Leadership, a Swedish Approach to Transforming Your Company, Your Industry and the World*. Cham: Palgrave Macmillan.

Intergovernmental Panel on Climate Change (IPCC). (2018). *Global warming of 1.5°C: An IPCC special report on the impacts of global warming of 1.5°C above pre-industrial levels and related global greenhouse gas emission pathways, in the context of strengthening the global response to the threat of climate change, sustainable development, and efforts to eradicate poverty*. https://www.ipcc.ch/report/sr15/

Iraldo, F., Griesshammer, R., & Kahlenborn, W. (2020). The future of ecolabels. *International Journal of Life Cycle Assessment*, *25*, 833–839. https://doi.org/10.1007/s11367-020-01741-9.

ITV (2020). ITV Social Purpose Report 2020 (p. 3). https://www.itvmedia.co.uk/news-and-resources/itv-social-purpose-impact-report-2020-shaping-culture-for-good.

ITV (2021). *ITV Social Purpose Report 2021*. https://d3sebdkplhxau9.cloudfront.net/6916/4796/2459/ITV_Social_Purpose_Report_2021.pdf.

ITV Studios (n.d.). *Who we are*. ITV Studios. https://www.itvstudios.com/#who-we-are.

Jerijervi, D. R. (2022). Fremantle slår sammen selskaper: - Vil gi oss enda mer styrke. *Kampanje*. https://kampanje.com/medier/2022/09/fremantle-slar-sammen-selskaper---vil-gi-oss-enda-mer-styrke/.

Kääpä, P. (2018). *Environmental Management of the Media*. New York: Taylor & Francis.

Kardosa, M. (2012). The relationship between entrepreneurship, innovation and sustainable development: Research on European Union countries. *Procedia Economics and Finance*, *3*, 1030–1035.

Koirala, S. (2018). SMEs: Key Drivers of Green and Inclusive Growth. Environment Directorate, OECD. https://www.oecd.org/greengrowth/GGSD_2018_SME%20Issue%20Paper_WEB.pdf.

Koirala, S. (2019). *SMEs: Key Drivers of Green and Inclusive Growth* (OECD Green Growth Papers, No. 2019/03). Paris: OECD Publishing. https://doi.org/10.1787/8a51fc0c-en.

Lafortune, G., Cortés Puch, M., Mosnier, A., Fuller, G., Diaz, M., Riccaboni, A., Kloke-Lesch, A., Zachariadis, T., Carli, E., & Oger, A. (2021). *Europe Sustainable Development Report*

2021: Transforming the European Union to Achieve the Sustainable Development Goals. SDSN, SDSN Europe and IEEP. France: Paris.

Le Gallou, M. (2022). *The EU Could be about to Take a Giant Step against Carbon-Neutral Greenwashing*. Euractiv. https://www.euractiv.com/section/climate-environment/opinion/the-eu-could-be-about-to-take-a-giant-step-against-carbon-neutral-greenwashing/.

Lemieux, V. (2020). Transparency in the 21st century: The role of records in achieving public access to information, protecting fundamental freedoms and monitoring sustainable development. In A. Thurston (Ed.), *A Matter of Trust: Building Integrity into Data, Statistics and Records to Support the Achievement of the Sustainable Development Goals* (pp. 173–188). University of London Press. https://www.jstor.org/stable/j.ctv14t45v5.16.

Mastiff (2023). *Innrapportering for 2021*. https://mastiff.no/wp-content/uploads/Miljorapport-2021-Mastiff-AS-Miljofyrtarn.pdf.

Maxwell, R., & Miller, T. (2012). *Greening the Media*. Oxford: Oxford University Press.

Meadows, D. H., Meadows, D. L., Randers, J., & Behrens III, W. W. (1972). The *Limits to Growth; A Report for the Club of Rome's Project on the Predicament of Mankind*. New York: Universe Books.

Miles, M. P., & Covin, J. G. (2000). Environmental marketing: A source of reputational, competitive, and financial advantage. *Journal of Business Ethics*, *23*(3), 299–311. https://doi.org/10.1023/a:1006214509281.

Miralles-Quirós, M. M., Miralles-Quirós, J. L., & Redondo-Hernández, J. (2019). The impact of environmental, social, and governance performance on stock prices: Evidence from the banking industry. *Corporate Social Responsibility and Environmental Management*, *26*, 1446–1456. Nature (2020). Imagine a world without hunger, then make it happen with systems thinking. *Nature*, *577*(7790), 293–294. https://doi.org/10.1038/d41586-020-00086-5.

NENT Group (2021a). *2021 Annual & Sustainability Report*. https://www.viaplaygroup.com/reports-presentations/nent-group-publishes-2021-annual-sustainability-report-and-new-sustainability.

NENT Group (2021b). NENT Group Closes Sale of 12 Production Labels to Fremantle. https://www.viaplaygroup.com/sites/default/files/pr/202109298509-1.pdf.

Næringslivets Hovedorganisasjon (NHO). (n.d.). *Små og mellomstore bedrifter (SMB)*. https://www.nho.no/tema/sma-og-mellomstore-bedrifter/. [Accessed 2023-01-29].

Nordisk Banijay (n.d.). *Om selskapet*. https://nordiskbanijay.no/om-oss/.

Norsk filminstitutt. (n.d.). *Produksjon av spillefilm etter konsulentvurdering*. https://www.nfi.no/tilskudd/produksjon/produksjon-av-spillefilm-etter-konsulentvurdering

Norsk Filminstitutt (n.d.). *Produksjon av dokumentarserie etter konsulentvurdering*. https://www.nfi.no/tilskudd/produksjon/produksjon-av-dokumentarserie-etter-konsulentvurdering.

NOU 2023:15 (2023). *Bærekraftsrapportering — Gjennomføring av direktivet om bærekraftsrapportering* (CSRD). https://www.regjeringen.no/no/dokumenter/nou-2023-15/id2977731/ [Accessed 2023-12-29].

O'Donohue, W., & Torugsa, N. (2015). The moderating effect of "Green" HRM on the association between proactive environmental management and financial performance in small firms. *The International Journal of Human Resource Management*, *27*(2), 239–261.

OECD. (2017). *Meeting of the OECD Council at Ministerial Level: Enhancing the Contributions of SMEs in a Global and Digitalised Economy*. https://one.oecd.org/document/C/MIN(2017)8/en/pdf.

Olsberg, J., & Barnes, A. (2014). *Impact Analysis of Fiscal Incentive Schemes Supporting Film and Audiovisual Production in Europe*. European Audiovisual Observatory.

https://rm.coe.int/impact-analysis-of-fiscal-incentive-schemes-supporting-film-and-audiov/16808e4506.

Pham, A. (2022). *Swedish Regional Funds Launch Sustainability Digital Tool Hållbar Film*. Nordisk Film & TV Fond. https://nordiskfilmogtvfond.com/news/stories/swedish-regional-funds-launch-sustainability-digital-tool-hallbar-film.

Pomare, C. (2018). A Multiple Framework Approach to Sustainable Development Goals (SDGs) and Entrepreneurship. In N. Apostolopoulos, H. Al-Dajani, D. Holt, P. Jones, & R. Newbery (Eds.), *Entrepreneurship and the Sustainable Development Goals* (Contemporary Issues in Entrepreneurship Research, Vol. 8, pp. 11–31). Emerald Publishing Limited. https://doi.org/10.1108/S2040-724620180000008006

Priestley, J. (2022). *Albert: Average Hour of TV Contributes 5.7t CO2e per Hour*. https://www.tvbeurope.com/production-post/albert-average-hour-of-tv-contributes-5-7t-co2e-per-hour.

Recalde, L. (2021). *Think Green, Film Green, Watch Green* [Presentation]. Sustainability Summit. European Commission. https://tech.ebu.ch/publications/think-green-film-green-watch-green.

Revell, A., Stokes, D., & Chen, H. (2010). Small businesses and the environment: Turning over a new leaf? *Business Strategy and the Environment*, *19*(5), 273–288. https://doi.org/https://doi.org/10.1002/bse.628.

Riedl, A., & Smeets, P. (2017). Why do investors hold socially responsible mutual funds? *Journal of Finance*, *72*(6), 2505–2550. https://doi.org/10.1111/jofi.12547.

Rodriguez, M., & Ricart, J. (1997). *A Model for Strategic Positioning and Performance Improvement* (IESE Research Papers 335). IESE Business School.

Rosvoll, A. (2021). *Bærekraft i medieproduksjon*. Ndla. https://ndla.no/nb/subject:1:ca0f428c-d59a-4836-83be83cbc3191a23/topic:f8032384-f0cc-4db0-8349-084f4f8ea521/topic:6aebd0f0-d5f9-4888-85a4-554b99b92cfe/resource:cf3ed92d-2931-44bc-ba5f-915d9c517f0e/15891 [Accessed 2022-12-01].

Roxas, B., & Coetzer, A. (2012). Institutional environment, managerial attitudes and environmental sustainability orientation of small firms. *Journal of Business Ethics*, *111*(4), 461–476.

RTL Group (2020). *Fremantle Aims to Reduce CO2 Emissions from TV Production*. https://www.bertelsmann.com/corporate-responsibility/projects-worldwide/project/fremantle-aims-to-reduce-co2-emissions-from-tv-production.jsp.

Rushprint (2021). NRK vil innta lederrolle i bransjens grønne skifte. *Rushprint*. https://rushprint.no/2021/04/nrk-vil-innta-lederrolle-i-bransjens-gronne-skifte/.

Schaer, C., & Kuruppu, N. (2018). Private-Sector Action in Adaptation: Perspectives on the Role of Micro, Small and Medium Size Enterprises. https://unepccc.org/publications/private-sector-action-in-adaptation-perspectives-on-the-role-of-micro-small-and-medium-size-enterprises/.

Searcy, C. (2022). *Implementing the Sustainable Development Goals: Six Steps for Small- and Medium-Sized Enterprises*. CPA. https://www.cpacanada.ca/en/business-and-accounting-resources/management-accounting/organizational-performance-measurement/publications/management-accounting-guidelines-mags/performance-management-measurement/sustainable-development-goals-guideline-case-study [Accessed 2023-01-29].

Senge, P. M. (2006). *The Fifth Discipline: The Art and Practice of the Learning Organization*. New York: Random House.

Shevchenko, A., Lévesque, M., & Pagell, M. (2016). Why firms delay reaching true sustainability. *Journal of Management Studies*, *53*(5), 911–935. https://doi.org/10.1111/joms.12199.

Skift – Næringslivets klimaledere. (n.d.). *Guide against greenwashing.* https://gronnvasking.no/en

Spangler, T. (2021). Hollywood studios release carbon-emissions report, showing wide variance among productions (EXCLUSIVE). *Variety*. https://variety.com/2021/film/news/sustainable-production-alliance-carbon-emissions-report-1234942580/.

Statista (2020). Video Streaming (SVoD), Worldwide. https://www.statista.com/outlook/206/100/video-streaming--svod-/worldwide.

Stiftelsen Miljøfyrtårn (2020). Mastiff ønsker samarbeid med bransjen om grønnere TV-produksjoner. https://www.miljofyrtarn.no/mastiff-onsker-samarbeid-med-bransjen-om-gronnere-tv-produksjoner/.

STV Group (2022). Modern Slavery and Human Trafficking Statement 2022. https://www.stvplc.tv/media/zsrezogi/modern-slavery-statement-2022-approved-13-december-2022.pdf.

Surroca, J., Tribó, J. A., & Waddock, S. (2010). Corporate responsibility and financial performance: The role of intangible resources. *Strategic Management Journal*, *31*(5), 463–490. https://doi.org/10.1002/smj.820.

Sustainable Production Alliance. (n.d.). *Green Production Guide.* https://www.greenproductionguide.com/

Sustainable Production Alliance & Producers Guild of America Foundation. (2021). *Production Environmental Accounting Report (PEAR)*. Green Production Guide. https://greenproductionguide.com/wp-content/uploads/2021/04/SPA-Carbon-Emissions-Report.pdf

The Carbon Trust (2021). *Carbon Impact of Video Streaming*. London. https://www.viaplaygroup.com/sites/default/files/carbon-impact-of-video-streaming-1.pdf.

UNCTAD (2019). *Guidance on Core Indicators for Entity Reporting on the Contribution towards the Implementation of the Sustainable Development Goals*. United Nations Publication. https://unctad.org/publication/guidance-core-indicators-entity-reporting-contribution-towards-implementation.

United Nations (2020). *Raising Awareness and Assessing Sustainability Literacy on SDG 7*. https://sustainabledevelopment.un.org/sdinaction/hesi/literacy.

Viacom CBS (2019). *Action: Environmental, Social, and Governance Report*. https://www.paramount.com/files/documents/ViacomCBS_ESG_Report_2019_2020-1.pdf.

Victory, J. (2015) Green shoots: Environmental sustainability and contemporary film production. *Studies in Arts and Humanities*, *1*(1), 54–68. https://doi.org/10.18193/sah.v1i1.6.

Ministry of Local Government and Modernisation. (2021). *Voluntary National Review 2021 Norway: Report on the Implementation of the 2030 Agenda for Sustainable Development*. United Nations. https://sustainabledevelopment.un.org/content/documents/28233Voluntary_National_Review_2021_Norway.

Wearealbert (2021). *Creating a Sustainable Future. Annual Report 2021*. https://wearealbert.org/wp-content/uploads/2023/01/albert-AR-2021_Finalv2.pdf.

Williston, B. (2019). *The Ethics of Climate Change: An Introduction*. Routledge. London.

Wu, A., Matutu, B., & Helsing, D. (2017). *Environmental Issues and Management Opportunities for the Southern Swedish Film Industry*. [Master's Thesis, International Institute for Industrial Environmental Economics (IIIEE)].

Part 2

Consumption

4 Who can stop the greenwashing[1]

Ingun Grimstad Klepp and Ingrid Haugsrud

Consumers neither want nor can take responsibility for distinguishing between green marketing and greenwashing (Heidenstrøm et al., 2021). This is the conclusion of a recent study of Norwegian consumers' opinions and understandings of green marketing of clothing and cosmetics. To take responsibility, the consumers must be able to trust marketing based on green claims (Berg, 2020) which, especially related to clothing, is far from reality (Heidenstrøm et al., 2021).

In stark contrast to these findings, the European Union points to the consumer as the key factor in its Green Deal ("A European Green Deal", n.d.) and the much-awaited transition. Through their choices in the marketplace, consumers are assigned a significant role in the green transition, and this is further reinforced in the EU strategy for Sustainable textiles, launched in 2022 with measures such as the Product Environmental Footprint (PEF) and a digital product passport (Directorate-General for Environment, 2022). In the Proposal for an EU directive on Green Claims from March 2023, it is taken for granted that "consumers want to be better informed on the environmental impacts of their consumption" and green marketing is seen as a vital part of "the green transition" (EC, 2024). The proposal doesn't discuss the border between greenwashing and other green marketing, besides the issue of trustworthy documentation. Likewise, it doesn't discuss the problem of more marketing in a situation of overproduction (Klepp et al., 2023). The textile industry's eagerness to appear environmentally friendly and sustainable using text and images has escalated. Studies of such marketing show that the amount of greenwashing is formidable (Changing Markets Foundation, 2021; Kassatly & Baumann-Pauly, 2021; Kassatly & Baumann-Pauly, 2022). The textile industry's environmental impact has not been reduced, but the amount of so-called sustainable collections or green collections has, however, increased (Changing Markets Foundation, 2021). With this backdrop, it is timely to ask: *Who can stop greenwashing?* In our context, this is limited to greenwashing of clothing and other textiles.

In this chapter, we will highlight a specific case to discuss this. The Norwegian Consumer Agency (NCA) issued a ruling in 2022 aimed at the Norwegian outdoor brand Norrøna that stated:

> The Higg MSI data did not constitute sufficient documentation for the claims made by the Norwegian trader in their marketing. The NCA concluded that

DOI: 10.4324/9781003392705-7

> the trader's use of Higg MSI data in marketing was misleading, and therefore prohibited under the Norwegian Marketing Control Act.

This warning will in the following be referred to as "the ruling". We will discuss what greenwashing is, based on this case, however, a good starting point can be the Norwegian Guide against Greenwashing's definition:

> Greenwashing is a form of misleading marketing or communication, where a product, service or company is presented as "better" in respect to climate change, the environment or animal and human rights issues, without proper documentation to back this claim.[2]

We will utilise the documents the NCA has made public (Norwegian Consumer Authority, 2022a, 2022b; Norwegian Consumer Authority & Netherlands Authority for Consumers and Markets, 2022), alongside looking at their participation in Sustainable Apparel Coalition (SAC)'s annual meeting (Sustainable Apparel Coalition, 2022a) and articles and press coverage, to discuss the case. All the actors' websites have also been explored, as well as previous research. Finally, we will build on our own experience and insights gained through having had a role in the case from the very beginning up until now, where we convey the experiences from our standpoint. In presenting the case, we will emphasise the actors and their roles.

The actors

NGO: Naturvernforbundet (friends of the Earth Norway)

Naturvernforbundet (Friends of the Earth Norway) is a non-governmental organisation (NGO). According to themselves, they are an organisation with

> over 37,000 members in more than 100 local groups, working to solve environmental issues both locally and globally. Our main goal is to protect the nature and environment so that human activity does not exceed the tolerance limits of our planet. We are engaged in a wide range of issues in environmental and nature conservation, but work specifically with the areas conservation, climate change, energy and transportation.
>
> (Naturvernforbundet, 2022)

Textiles have not been an important focus area, but are part of their work on consumption, which advisor and project leader Janne Melbye Gillgren was responsible for. She was the one who set the ruling in motion on behalf of her organisation, by filing a complaint against Norrøna and following up on this complaint with the Norwegian Consumer Authority (NCA).

Governance: Norwegian Consumer Authority

The NCA describes itself in this way:

> The Consumer Authority [...] is a public enforcement authority. We work to make markets easier and safer for consumers. The Consumer Authority prevents and stops illegal marketing, unfair contract terms and other forms of illegal commercial practices targeted to consumers. We achieve this by offering guidance and entering into dialogue with traders, by effective use of economic sanctions and through information. We also work to protect the rights of the consumers and to ensure that consumers may take informed decisions.
>
> (Norwegian Consumer Authority, 2023)

Central in their work, is following up on the Marketing Control Act:

> It regulates how the Consumer Authority operates, and is the most important law we enforce. In addition to this, we ensure that traders comply with other parts of consumer protection legislation such as the Cancellation act, the Financial Services Act and several other laws.
>
> When traders infringe the Marketing Control Act, the Cancellation Act, the Financial Agreements Act or other pieces of legislation that the CA enforces, the CA may prohibit this conduct (MCA § 40) and impose administrative fines (MCA §§ 42 and 43). Natural or legal person [sic] that are accessories to infringements, may also be the subject of decisions by the CA. The CAs decisions may be appealed to the Market Council (MCA § 37).
>
> (Norwegian Consumer Authority, 2023)

It is important to note that the NCA not only are mandated to state their opinions but also have legal instruments that can force market actors to follow their ruling, by imposing fines and other measures. They also have a more active role in their ability to make rulings than similar governing bodies in other countries.

Assistant Director Tonje H. Drevland was responsible for the case on behalf of the NCA and is therefore an important part of this case. "The ruling" is presented as follows by the NCA:

> In the spring of 2022, the Norwegian Consumer Authority (NCA) investigated a Norwegian clothing company's use of the Higg MSI tool in marketing towards consumers.
>
> Higg MSI is a tool developed by the Sustainable Apparel Coalition (SAC) as a part of the Higg Index. The Higg MSI measures certain environmental impacts of materials used in garment production. The SAC allows traders to use the Higg MSI to present information about the environmental impacts of materials used in textiles to consumers.

> The NCA found that the Higg MSI data did not constitute sufficient documentation for the claims made by the Norwegian trader in their marketing. The NCA concluded that the trader's use of Higg MSI data in marketing was misleading, and therefore prohibited under the Norwegian Marketing Control Act, which is based on the EU Unfair Commercial Practices Directive (UCPD).
>
> This conclusion could be seen as a warning to other traders operating in the EU/EEA area, as the NCA found that the use of Higg MSI data in marketing towards consumers in general could easily be misleading.
>
> (Norwegian Consumer Authority, 2022a)

The NCA has for a long time provided general guidance on the use of environmental claims in marketing. As a result of the ruling, the SAC did, however, ask for more specific guidance. This resulted in "GUIDANCE TO THE SUSTAINABLE APPAREL COALITION ENVIRONMENTAL CLAIMS IN MARKETING TOWARDS CONSUMERS BASED ON THE HIGG MSI" – written in collaboration with the Netherlands Authority for Consumers and Markets (the ACM) (2022a).

For the ruling, the NCA's argumentation is both clear and challenging. This was presented in letters, on webpages, in the aforementioned guidance, in lectures, and in the SAC's annual conference for the textile industry. Here, Drevland's message is particularly clear:

> I want H&M, Inditex, all large players to take a step back and realize that the steps they are taking internally may feel [like a great cost] to them but remember to look at it from the other side, from the environmental perspective.[3]
>
> (2022a)

She also stressed that "wrong information is worse than no information".

Her message and the documents from this case can be summarised as follows:

- Environmental benefit claims must be substantiated, and true, and cannot be misleading.
- Environmental benefit claims must be backed by relevant documentation.

The critique from the NCA on the use of the Higg MSI or rather the Higg Index Sustainability Profile is as follows:

- Global averages are not product-specific.
- The LCA data that backs the global averages and the Higg MSI is outdated.
- In addition, the LCAs underpinning the claims were not intended for the comparisons that were made.

Brand: Norrøna

It was Norrøna who, according to the NCA, had breached the Marketing Control Act in the case we are discussing. Norrøna is a family-owned Norwegian clothing brand founded in 1929. The company is one of Norway's leading outdoor brands and specialises in textiles and accessories for skiing, snowboarding, mountaineering, surfing, downhill biking, hunting, and outdoor life. Through its 37 stores, the company has operations in Norway, Finland, Sweden, Switzerland, France, and the USA. Today, the company is run by the family's fourth generation, with Jørgen Jørgensen as the chief executive officer. It is a well-established company, esteemed for its quality equipment well-suited for the Norwegian outdoor life. They have an ambitious roadmap with plans for their sustainability work towards 2029 (Norrøna, 2023), and there is nothing that suggests that they are worse greenwashers than anyone else.

In 2021, Norrøna piloted the Higg Index Sustainability Profile in Norway, a consumer-facing label claiming that an organic cotton t-shirt in one of their collections was "more sustainable" than a conventional cotton t-shirt. The label used data based on the Higg MSI (see below). Faced with the NCA's ruling, their initial response was to become defensive. "We do not want to mislead consumers in any way, but on the contrary ensure as good information as possible about the products that may be purchased" (our translation), Norrøna's marketing director Martin Lien, replied in an email to Norway's public broadcaster, NRK (Aasen, 2022). Still, they acknowledge that the data about cotton production is not perfect, but that it "is the best information currently available". This is an argument we will return to. Later, CEO Jørgensen adopted a humbler attitude and emphasised that he and the industry as a whole have something to learn. In the SAC annual meeting, Norrøna's Director of Innovation and Sustainability Brad Boren was equally humble (Sustainable Apparel Coalition, 2022a).

However, the ruling is not only about Norrøna per se. The NCA also sent a warning to the Swedish fast fashion actor H&M, in case they considered using the Higg Index Sustainability Profile in marketing in Norway, as well as a letter to the SAC telling them to inform all their members about the ruling, and what consequences similar claims on the market in Norway could trigger. In addition, they informed other consumer authorities in the EU/EEA about the decision and issued a general warning to "other traders operating in the EU/EEA area" (Norwegian Consumer Authority, 2022a). However, it did not stop with this. NCA started a coordinated action from the Consumer Protection Cooperation Network (CPC), coordinated by the European Commission and led by four consumer protection authorities from Germany, Denmark, Norway, and Sweden against Zalando. According to a press release from the EU from February 2024, Zalando will remove all their misleading environmental claims from their website (EC, 2024). Thus, a large international player has been forced to follow "the ruling".

The industry organisations SAC and TE, and their tools

The SAC is, according to their description, "a global, multi-stakeholder non-profit alliance for the consumer goods industry" which "seeks to lead the industry toward a shared vision of sustainability". They represent about half of the global apparel and footwear industry, and in 2011 they launched the Higg Index that "enables" brands retailers, and manufacturers from the apparel, and footwear industry to measure, improve and share their social and environmental performance via a common "sustainability language" (The Sustainable Apparel Coalition, 2023). The Textile Exchange (TE) is an NGO that initially had organic cotton as its focus and has since branched out to manage several other labelling schemes. They engage businesses as members, as these are looking for certification schemes. The TE has recently launched a Climate+ strategy, which aims for a reduction in GHG emissions through the TE's Preferred Fibre and Material Matrix (PFMM). The strategy has the Higg MSI as its baseline, at least this was noted in all slides presenting the strategy until recently. Based on TE's "preferred" fibres, which once again have the MSI as the baseline, any improvement will – according to TE – be part of the needed reduction in greenhouse gas emissions (Textile Exchange, 2023a).

The SAC is one of the parties in this case because, as the NCA writes, they are: "the owner of the Higg MSI and have contributed to the documentation and answers given by Norrøna in the case" (Norwegian Consumer Authority, 2022b). On May 5, 2022, the NCA also had a meeting with the SAC regarding the documentation underlying the consumer-facing claims.

"The *Higg* Materials Sustainability Index (*Higg* MSI) is the apparel industry's most trusted tool to measure and score the environmental impacts of materials", according to the SAC (Sustainable Apparel Coalition, 2023b). Before Higg became a privately owned, for-profit company, the MSI tool was open to scrutiny. The underlying data has since been behind a paywall, but after receiving criticism for this, the SAC has opened for those who register with them. Still, it is somewhat unclear how much of the underlying data that can be addressed (Kassatly & Baumann-Pauly, 2022; Klepp et al., 2022). The SAC is therefore responsible, together with Norrøna, and Norrøna turned to the SAC for help when they needed documentation for the claims put forward relating to the organic cotton t-shirt. The SAC also reacted quickly to the charges, by taking down the label with immediate effect, thus impacting H&M's and Zalando's marketing (Tobiasson, 2022).

The SAC issued a response to the NCA ruling, stating that they will launch a third-party expert review of the Higg MSI and collaborate with the NCA on how to present information to consumers (Sustainable Apparel Coalition, 2022b), and in 2023 KPMG did publish a report, but this did not answer the main question whether the data was suited for consumer-facing information or not (KPMG, 2023). Recently, the SAC has rebranded the Higg Index as Worldly and changed its name to Cascale. Apparel insider writes that this "will be viewed by many as an attempt to distance both organisations from the bad press and negativity associated with their previous incarnations" (Matthews, 2024).

The NCA's strong criticism of the Higg Index Sustainability Profile was particularly serious as the SAC and their work with the Higg have been central to the development in the early stages of the EU's planned anti-greenwashing weapon, the PEF. The PEF is, according to the SAC,

> a Life Cycle Assessment (LCA) based method to quantify the relevant environmental impacts of products (goods or services). It builds on existing

> approaches and international standards, and is part of the "Single Market for Green Products Initiative" that is initiated by the European Commission.
>
> The aim of the PEF is to create a common language and method for calculating a product's environmental footprint, which is the foundation for a set of specific rules. These rules are called the Product Environmental Footprint Category Rules (PEFCR), and are a common approach across the EU, normally created at an industry level.
>
> (Sustainable Apparel Coalition, 2023a)

Later, the controversy opened up an ask for new studies on several textile materials. The SAC is also a member of the Policy Hub. Prior Chair of the Policy Hub Baptiste Carriere-Pradal is now Chair of the Technical Secretariat of the Apparel EU PEF on behalf of the SAC. The secretariat voting members are dominated by the industry, and the SAC members have a majority of the vote (PEF Apparel and Footwear, 2023). The data and the studies that underpin the Higg MSI are to a large extent the same data and studies that are being used in the development of the PEFCR. The European Commission's Joint Research Centre has been tasked with verifying the scientific robustness of the database. Obtaining new Life Cycle Assessments (LCA) suitable for comparison is both challenging and expensive. It becomes even more difficult if global averages cannot be used, which is the mainstay of the LCA-based Higg MSI. Another problem is that parts of the tool are behind a paywall and therefore unavailable to consumers and for documentation.

Press and research

During the SAC's annual conference in 2022, Tonje Drevland started her contribution by stating that the NCA and other consumer authorities had been following the textile industry for several years (Sustainable Apparel Coalition, 2022a). When a complaint was filed by Friends of the Earth Norway, they chose to pursue the case because the complaint referred to scientific papers that questioned the Higg MSI data. This gave research and critical journalism an important role in unpacking the issue.

Both Tone Skårdal Tobiasson and Ingun Grimstad Klepp have been among journalists and researchers pointing to limitations in Higg MSI in scientific articles and op-eds (Klepp & Tobiasson, 2022; Klepp et al., 2017; Tobiasson & Klepp, 2021; Tobiasson et al., 2021). They have also been featured in countless debates on radio, TV, and online events, conferences, workshops, and webinars about the subject. Tobiasson, Klepp, and others knew that the SAC and Higg (now Worldly) were not able to document their claims. It is in general not illegal to lie or to misinform unless you are under oath. Using false claims in marketing, on the other hand, is illegal in Norway. Therefore, Klepp and Tobiasson were on the lookout for companies that not only used the Higg MSI internally but also took the step of fronting this in marketing. In the spring of 2021, Norrøna did exactly this in Norway. This was widely reported in the international press as an important step for Higg and for the companies that were first movers (Glover, 2021). Klepp and Tobiasson were therefore well prepared to help, first through informal meetings with Friends of the Earth Norway, and then with the NCA. The main goal was to document the weaknesses in the Higg Index Sustainability Profile claims and to find relevant research and other resources that countered the claims. Most notable was the work of Veronica Bates Kassatly, an independent analyst and consultant who has authored several white papers with Dorothée Baumann-Pauly: The Great Green Washing Machine: Part 1 and more importantly Part 2: The Use and Misuse of Sustainability Metrics in Fashion (2021, 2022). Worth mentioning is also her significant contributions related to cotton and other fibres, and how the incorrect claims and misuse of LCA data abound (Kassatly & Baumann-Pauly, 2022). Another important contribution is the report *Cotton: A Case Study in Misinformation* (2021) which is cited in the ruling (Norwegian Consumer Authority & Netherlands Authority for Consumers and Markets, 2022). Later an even more comprehensive report was published (Kassatly & Townsend, 2024).

The literature related to clothing and the environment is dominated by the textile industry itself, both in influencing what is discussed and through the production of "truths" (Austgulen, 2016). This is often based on reports – in many cases commissioned by the industry and rarely based on peer-reviewed research. Therefore, it is important to note that there are several academic research papers discussing the Higg MSI. One of these concluded the following in 2019:

> This paper has highlighted a series of issues with the Higg MSI that relate to inconsistencies with the international guidelines and best practice for LCA, specifically with reference to fabrics made from natural fibre types. When considered collectively, we conclude that the Higg MSI is not suitable for public disclosure or comparative assertions, and has limited capability in its present form to enable the textile industry or interested stakeholders to compare different fabric types, or reliably choose between fabric types with confidence that this will result in lower impacts to the environment.
>
> (Watson & Wiedemann, 2019)

In other words, both academic research and critical journalism have pointed out serious weaknesses in the Higg MSI in general, and the claims surrounding cotton in particular. It is also evident that research and critical journalism played a role in documenting the controversies and providing the necessary information to the consumer authorities.

Consumers

Whether the consumers have a role in the ruling can be debated, however, this is all fundamentally about consumers. Marketing, including green marketing claims and certainly greenwashing, would be pointless if the marketers did not believe that consumers could be guided or misled into favouring and thus buying more of something (deemed "greener") than of something else.

Furthermore, the legislation that enabled halting Norrøna's Higg Index Sustainability Profile marketing is based on protecting consumers. The policy surrounding green marketing claims and any investment in official labelling schemes (such as the Nordic Swan Ecolabel)[4] is founded on a way of thinking where the consumer's choices are influenced in a sustainable direction through marketing that puts forward some products as "greener" than others. This way of thinking can in practice have several weaknesses.

Firstly, this presupposes that the consumers are influenced by green claims and further, that they can distinguish between green marketing and greenwashing. There is little evidence to support this (Heidenstrøm et al., 2021). The report by Heidenstrøm et al. about consumers' perception of green marketing found that consumers were unable to distinguish between greenwashing and green marketing, and they did not have sufficient knowledge to navigate claims regarding materials or even distinguish them (2021). In general, trust in marketing is low. The trust in the authorities, however, is high (Heidenstrøm et al., 2021). Moreover, consumers believe that it is the authorities who are responsible for regulating the market and exposing greenwashers (Heidenstrøm et al., 2021). A survey conducted by the business organisation Norwegian Fashion and Textile Agenda (NF&TA), supports the findings of Heidenstrøm et al.'s (2021) report. Only 32% of respondents were concerned with sustainability when shopping for clothing, and they navigated the market in a variety of ways (Nyhaug, 2020). A similar survey was carried out by the Nordic Swan Ecolabel in 2022, showing that 7 of out 10 consumers believe that companies often exaggerate the sustainability claims of their products. Additionally, only 1 in 5 believe that the authorities and companies are doing enough to transition into more sustainable production and consumption (Nordic Swan Ecolabel, 2022).

Another issue is the idea that consumers, through «green purchasing», can contribute to a reduction in greenhouse gas and environmental impacts, rather than addressing the volumes as the underlying issue. A recent article about Norwegian consumers shows that "believing that fibres of any kind are sustainable negatively affects consumption reduction. An explanation for this could be that if the fibres used to produce clothing are considered sustainable, reducing consumption is not necessary" (Sigaard & Laitala, 2023, p. 17). For green marketing and green claims to contribute to reducing environmental impact, the difference between the products must be substantial and the marketing must be based on correct and irrefutable data. In the case of clothing, the use phase is crucial – and using garments for a long time has consequences for the total environmental impact per use (Klepp et al., 2020; Watson & Wiedemann, 2019).

Finding clothes that fit the individual's body, tastes and needs is difficult. Buying clothes that have a less environmental impact will be yet another factor to take into consideration and can easily contribute to other criteria being superseded thus leading to unsatisfactory purchases. This could potentially increase the environmental impact, as garments may need to be replaced more often, or not cover the consumers' needs to the same extent. This aspect of green claims is, as far as we know, little researched, but there are examples of this in the previously mentioned report, showing that consumers feel that the challenge of trying to find something that fits their bodies and their lives is already more than enough (Heidenstrøm et al., 2021).

For green claims to have a positive effect on environmental issues overall, several factors must therefore be in place. The differences between the products must be significantly larger than the negative effect that marketing certain products as greener than others has. As far as we know, there is a lack of critical research on the effects of green claims on clothing towards consumers, and of course also on the difference between products for this to be possible to know. What we do know is that this remains a theoretical question, all the while clothing consumers neither trust the marketing nor their ability to assess this.

The discussion: who could and can

There are two business players central to the ruling, Norrøna and the SAC, representing the majority of all textile-related businesses in the world. Could they have stopped the greenwashing that was happening through the adoption of the Higg Index Sustainability Profile? The answer is "yes". There was more than enough evidence showing that the Higg MSI claims could not be verified. There is no reason to underestimate the SAC – they have the resources to know what they are doing. It is another matter with Norrøna. In the panel debate during the SAC conference in 2022, Brad Boren from Norrøna emphasised that they are a small player and that they wished to learn (Sustainable Apparel Coalition, 2022a). The NCA supported him and Drevland said that it was the large and global actors who should take on the biggest responsibility. Even so, Norrøna had invested in the Higg tool and chose to market their organic cotton t-shirt with figures that at that time had long since been debunked (Kassatly, 2020). It would not have taken many Google searches to find that the information given by Higg, and the data on cotton in particular, were disputed. Therefore, we conclude that the industry, including Norrøna and the SAC, indeed could stop the greenwashing that they perpetuated if it was important to them.

In the narrative of the ruling, it is the NCA and Friends of the Earth Norway that had the greatest means and willingness to prevent greenwashing. Furthermore, the NCA had power through the Marketing Control Act to enforce a ruling. Still, the NCA could not have done this on their own. Other actors were involved, such as NGOs, critical journalism, and research. Nevertheless, we will discuss the matter a little more closely. What are the limits to the NCA's possibilities to stop greenwashing?

It seems that they do this in two slightly different ways: one way is through an actual complaint made by an outside actor and the second is through appealing to the industry to take a step back and examine their actions, seen through the eyes of the consumers and through considering what this means for the environment. Is it conceivable that the companies' disposition to greenwash can be halted by asking them to rethink the importance of what they are doing? Or is it simply that the repercussions, i.e., the ruling and the threat of fines, were what caused the dramatic aftermath of the NCA's ruling, the taking down of the Higg Index Sustainability Profile?

The quality of the data used as a basis for the green claims was essential in the ruling. The following debate (Britten, 2022; Glover, 2022) has subsequently raged between those who claim that the existing LCA data is so flawed as to be unusable and those who argue that, while imperfect, it is better than nothing and needs to be improved, not scrapped. The last argument presupposes that companies and labelling schemes must engage in green marketing, even if factual knowledge of the product's environmental impact is lacking. Do they believe that they must carry out green marketing even when it is not based on relevant data? In that case, pious exhortations are unlikely to have any effect, but it would be an idea to investigate where this thought originates and how it can be challenged. Should not only greenwashing but also green marketing, in general, be combatted?

The EU's ambitious textile strategy points in the opposite direction. Here, the emphasis is on information to consumers about the product's environmental impact. However, the questions surrounding data are not only whether they are up-to-date and comparable but also related to the use of global averages. If, as the NCA's ruling argues, they do not address the specific product and in turn are not relevant for the consumer, or if there are no significant differences between products, then would the PEF also not easily be perpetuating greenwashing? In the annexes to the guidance, it is highlighted that: "If expert studies give rise to significant disagreement or doubt over environmental impacts, the trader should refrain from the claim altogether" (Norwegian Consumer Authority & Netherlands Authority for Consumers and Markets, 2022). There are such disagreements, and it applies to both the Higg MSI and the PEF – but could it have consequences for the PEF? In this scheme, the database and thinking originate mainly from the SAC and the Higg MSI, which again is based on the LCA's global average logic. The PEF is less so than the Higg MSI, a simplification of the LCAs, but in both cases, the data represent different parameters and the documentation is faulty and contested, another major point in the guidance provided by the NCA and their Dutch counterpart (2022). The systems involved as such are complex and thus more difficult to understand for all of us, which opens the question of their use or even their right to exist.

Nemes et al. (2022) question what makes a certification scheme greenwashing. This is an important question because it concerns the possibility of halting the PEF. The NCA's ruling stated that the Higg Index Sustainability Profile was greenwashing if the use of the scheme was consumer-facing. In contrast, their authority had no means to say anything about the tool as such. Therefore, it can still be used business to business (B2B). If we take consumers' opinions seriously, incorrect green claims will not have a large impact, considering that most people do not factor in such information in their decision-making process (Heidenstrøm et al., 2021). On the other hand, the same information used B2B could be particularly harmful because it is to a greater extent used as a basis for decisions – which, in turn, affects the consumers' options and the downstream producers. It is also possible that the power of consumer authorities, and especially the NCA, shown in the ruling, is easily pulverised if the communicator of the unreliable information is no longer the company itself, or industry organisations such as the SAC, but authorities such as the EU, through tools like the PEF.

This perspective is important, and it got a lot of attention in the international press in the aftermath of the ruling. Articles with headlines like "EU PEF tool's regulations in question now after Higg's MSI" stating that "a group of 12 organisations have expressed their concerns over the EU Commission's plans to use Product Environment

Footprint category rules (PEF-CR) 'as a standalone method' for communicating green claims in apparel and footwear" (Safaya, 2022) or "After Higg Came Under Fire for Greenwashing, Now This One's in the Hot Seat, Too" (Chua, 2022). A powerful tool for scrutiny, like the PEF, might just as well be a powerful greenwashing tool – if the knowledge it is based on is insufficiently documented, outdated, contested, or irrelevant, to mention some of the criticisms against the Higg MSI. Thus, the power of the NCA and other consumer authorities to halt greenwashing might be short-lived, and as soon as the EU implements the PEF, their strength might be limited. This indicates that it is urgent to follow up. The SAC themselves have called for speeding up the PEF process, and one can wonder why (Martin, 2022).

It will become more difficult to stop greenwashing based on a lack of documentation if this is hidden in the PEF system. Finding the numbers behind the score will demand a lot of detective work from consumers and others. It will perhaps become even more important to establish what *is* essential and relevant information for consumers. Political decisions about the pace of GHG reduction and other impact categories could have been used as a basis. Reductions of less than 25% will unlikely be significant if the target is a 50% reduction by 2030, or as TE states, 45% (Textile Exchange, 2023b). An investigation into the potential negative effects of labelling schemes (including the PEF) through increased sales is also urgent. Such research can be utilised in discussing the necessary environmental improvements to negate the effect of increased green claims that the PEF might be perpetuating or otherwise lead to.

Conclusion: not alone

This chapter concludes that both the textile industry and the consumer authorities can stop greenwashing. However, the lack of serious industry initiatives addressing this indicates that there is a lack of will. The consumer authorities, however, have both the ability and the will to stop greenwashing through the Marketing Control Act. However, they depend on support from other actors, such as NGOs, research, and critical journalism. Nevertheless, the discussion shows that their power may be weakened through an over-national labelling scheme which further obscures the documentation for environmental claims. It is conceivable that the criticism against the Higg MSI will affect the PEF and contribute to the scheme being either postponed, rejected, or possibly improved. We hope that the consumer authorities will continue to use the power they have while they have it, as we see in the Zalando case. Halting or changing the PEF is primarily a political issue. The prospects for research and critical journalism to develop knowledge about greenwashing also depend on the policy, and not least, what is considered essential and relevant for consumers.

Notes

1 Acknowledgements: the chapter is supported by the research projects *Wasted Textiles* funded by The Norwegian Research Council and *Grønt eller grønnvasket?* Funded by the Norwegian Ministry of Children and Families.

2 Grønnvaskingsplakaten/Guide against Greenwashing: https://gronnvasking.no/en/home/.
3 https://www.youtube.com/watch?v=f5dcHKwRTZM.
4 https://svanemerket.no/en/.

References

A European Green Deal (n.d.). Retrieved from https://ec.europa.eu/info/strategy/priorities-2019-2024/european-green-deal_en.

Aasen, K. R. (2022). Villeder forbrukere om miljøvennlige klær. *NRK*. Retrieved from https://www.nrk.no/norge/forbrukertilsynet-mener-norrona-bryter-loven-1.16003658.

Austgulen, M. H. (2016). Environmentally sustainable textile consumption—What characterizes the political textile consumers? *Journal of Consumer Policy*, *39*(4), 441–466. doi:10.1007/s10603-015-9305-5.

Berg, L. (2020). *Tillit og forbrukerforhold i EU28 og Norge – Resultater fra EU-kommisjonenes Consumer Conditions Scoreboard*. Retrieved from https://hdl.handle.net/20.500.12199/3123.

Britten, F. (2022, 28.06.2022). Fashion brands pause use of sustainability index tool over greenwashing claims. *The Guardian*. Retrieved from https://www.theguardian.com/fashion/2022/jun/28/fashion-brands-pause-use-of-sustainability-index-tool-over-greenwashing-claims.

Changing Markets Foundation. (2021). *Fossil fashion: The hidden reliance of fast fashion on fossil fuels*. Retrieved from https://changingmarkets.org/wp-content/uploads/2021/01/FOSSIL-FASHION_Web-compressed.pdf.

Chua, J. M. (2022). After Higg came under fire for greenwashing, now this one's in the hot seat, too. *Sourcing Journal*. Retrieved from https://sourcingjournal.com/sustainability/sustainability-news/product-environmental-footprint-eu-pef-greenwashing-microplastics-fast-fashion-384780/.

Directorate-General for Environment. (2022). *EU strategy for sustainable and circular textiles*. Retrieved from Brussels: https://environment.ec.europa.eu/publications/textiles-strategy_en.

EC. (2024). Zalando commits to provide clearer information for consumer following EU action [Press release].

Glover, S. (2021, 27.05.2021). Higg impact data to be shared with consumers. *Ecotextile news*. Retrieved from https://www.ecotextile.com/2021052727850/labels-legislation-news/higg-impact-data-to-be-shared-with-consumers.html.

Glover, S. (2022). LCAs in sustainability data - Ask the experts. *Ecotextile News*. Retrieved from https://www.ecotextile.com/2022100729922/features/lcas-in-sustainability-data-ask-the-experts.html.

Heidenstrøm, N., Haugsrud, I., Hebrok, M., & Throne-Holst, H. (2021). *"Hvorfor kan ikke bare alle produkter være bærekraftige?" Hvordan forbrukere oppfatter og påvirkes av markedsføring med bærekraftpåstander* (16). Retrieved from https://oda.oslomet.no/oda-xmlui/handle/11250/2838317.

Kassatly, V. B. (2020). The use and misuse of LCAs. *Apparel Insider (14)*. Retrieved from https://www.veronicabateskassatly.com/read/lca-misuse.

Kassatly, V. B., & Baumann-Pauly, D. (2021). *The great greenwashing machine part 1: Back to the roots of sustainability*. Retrieved from: https://gcbhr.org/backoffice/resources/reportfinal72dpi2.pdf.

Kassatly, V. B., & Baumann-Pauly, D. (2022). *The great green washing machine part 2: The use and misuse of sustainability metrics in fashion*. Retrieved from: https://gcbhr.org/backoffice/resources/great-green-washing-machine-report-part-2final.pdf.

Kassatly, V. B., & Baumann-Pauly, D. (2022). *The rise of life cycle analysis and the fall of sustainability - Illustrations from the apparel and leather sector*. Retrieved from Geneva Center for Business & Human Rights: https://gcbhr.org/insights/2022/07/the-rise-of-life-cycle-analysis-and-the-fall-of-sustainability-illustrations-from-the-apparel-and-leather-sector.

Kassatly, V. B., & Townsend, T. (2024). *European Union ecodesign for sustainable products regulation: Summary of inconsistencies and potential deficiencies*. Retrieved from https://www.crdc.com.au/publications/ESPR-critique.

Klepp, I. G., & Tobiasson, T. (2022). *Local, slow and sustainable fashion fibres: Wool as a fabric for change*. Cham: Palgrave MacMillan.

Klepp, I. G., Laitala, K., & Berg, L. L. (2023). Consumption research Norway's feedback on the proposal for a directive on substantiation and communication of explicit environmental claims. https://clothingresearch.oslomet.no.

Klepp, I. G., Laitala, K., & Wiedemann, S. (2020). Clothing lifespans: What should be measured and how. *Sustainability*, *12*(15), 6219. doi:10.3390/su12156219.

Klepp, I. G., Laitala, K., Haugrønning, V., Sigaard, A. S., & Tobiasson, T. S. (2022). The fate of natural fibres in environmental evaluations: A question of volume. In I. G. Klepp, & T. S. Tobiasson (Eds.), *Local, slow and sustainable fashion: Wool as a fabric for change* (pp. 35–59). Cham: Springer International Publishing.

Klepp, I. G., Tobiasson, T. S., & Laitala, K. (2017). Why cotton as linen? The use of wool in beds in Norway. *Textile-Cloth and Culture*, *15*(1), 68–85. doi:10.1080/14759756.2016.1212887.

KPMG. (2023). *Technical review of the Higg MSI and Higg PM tools*. Retrieved from https://cascale.org/wp-content/uploads/2023/10/KPMG-Report-Higg-Product-Tools-Review.pdf.

Martin, A. (2022). Why we believe the European Commission should be fully committed to the PEF. Retrieved from https://apparelcoalition.org/why-we-believe-the-european-commission-should-be-fully-committed-to-the-pef/.

Matthews, B. (2024). Sustainable apparel coalition rebrands as cascale. *Apparel Insider*. Retrieved from https://apparelinsider.com/sustainable-apparel-coalition-rebrands-as-cascale/.

Naturvernforbundet. (2022). About Naturvernforbundet. Retrieved from www.naturvernforbundet.no.

Nemes, N., Scanlan, S. J., Smith, P., Smith, T., Aronczyk, M., Hill, S., … Stabinsky, D. (2022). An integrated framework to assess greenwashing. *Sustainability*, *14*(8), 4431. Retrieved from https://www.mdpi.com/2071-1050/14/8/4431.

Nordic Swan Ecolabel. (2022). *Nordic consumer sustainability index*. Retrieved from https://svanemerket.no/content/uploads/2022/11/Nordic-Consumer-Sustainability-Index-2022_frokostseminar-Norge.pdf.

Norrøna. (2023). Norrøna responsibility roadmap 2029. Retrieved from https://www.norrona.com/en-GB/about-norrona/responsibility/roadmap-2029/.

Norwegian Consumer Authority, & Netherlands Authority for Consumers and Markets. (2022). Guidance to the Sustainable Apparel Coalition. Retrieved from: https://www.forbrukertilsynet.no/wp-content/uploads/2022/10/nca-and-acm-joint-guidance-environmental-claims-based-on-higg-msi.pdf.

Norwegian Consumer Authority. (2022a). Consumer authorities issue guidance on environmental claims to the textile industry. Retrieved from https://www.forbrukertilsynet.no/eng-articles/consumer-authorities-issue-guidance-on-environmental-claims-to-the-textile-industry.

Norwegian Consumer Authority. (2022b). *Misleading marketing of organic cotton garments using Higg MSI data - Liability as an accessory*. Retrieved from https://www.forbrukertilsynet.no/wp-content/uploads/2022/06/sac-misleading-marketing-of-organic-cotton-garments-using-higg-msi-data-liability-as-an-accessory.pdf.

Norwegian Consumer Authority. (2023). The Consumer Authority. Retrieved from https://www.forbrukertilsynet.no/english.

Nyhaug, O. P. (2020). *Tekstilaksjonen: Bærekraftige holdninger og handlinger 2020*.

PEF Apparel and Footwear. (2023). Members of the Technical Secretariat. Retrieved from https://pefapparelandfootwear.eu/who-is-involved/#members.

Safaya, S. (2022, 2.11.2022). EU PEF tool's regulations in question now after Higg's MSI. *Just-style.com*. Retrieved from https://www.just-style.com/news/eu-pef-tools-regulations-in-question-now-after-higgs-msi/.

Sigaard, A. S., & Laitala, K. (2023). Natural and sustainable? Consumers' textile fiber preferences. *Fibers*, *11*(2). doi:10.3390/fib11020012.

Sustainable Apparel Coalition (Writer). (2022a). *Challenges & opportunities for standardizing eco-labelling*. Sustainable Apparel Coalition.

Sustainable Apparel Coalition. (2022b). Press release: SAC response to the guidance document from the Norwegian and Dutch consumer authorities. Retrieved from https://apparelcoalition.org/press-releases/sac-response-guidance-document-norwegian-dutch-consumer-authorities/.

Sustainable Apparel Coalition. (2023a). About PEF. Retrieved from https://apparelcoalition.org/about-pef/.

Sustainable Apparel Coalition. (2023b). Make better choices at every stage of a product's development. Retrieved from https://apparelcoalition.org/higg-product-tools/.

Textile Exchange. (2023a). About. Retrieved from https://textileexchange.org/about/.

Textile Exchange. (2023b). Climate+ guides the fashion, textile, and apparel industry towards a shared goal. Retrieved from https://textileexchange.org/climate-vision/.

The Sustainable Apparel Coalition. (2023). The Sustainable Apparel Coalition. Retrieved from https://apparelcoalition.org/the-sac/.

Tobiasson, T. (2022). A volatile labelling landscape: The future for consumer-facing green claims. *Wool2Yarn*.

Tobiasson, T. S., & Klepp, I. G. (2021). EU truer bunaden. *Nettavisen*. Retrieved from https://www.nettavisen.no/norsk-debatt/eu-truer-bunaden/o/5-95-317395.

Tobiasson, T. S., Klepp, I. G., & Grøva, L. (2021). Ny regjering gir 1–0 til norsk ull - i EU er det knockout. *Nationen*. Retrieved from https://www.nationen.no/motkultur/kronikk/ny-regjering-gir-1-0-til-norsk-ull-i-eu-derimot-er-det-knock-out/.

Watson, K. J., & Wiedemann, S. G. (2019). Review of methodological choices in LCA-based textile and apparel rating tools: Key issues and recommendations relating to assessment of fabrics made from natural fibre types. *Sustainability*, *11*(14), 3846. doi:10.3390/su11143846.

5 Future of sustainable fashion communications

From marketing messages to the mediation of mutable meanings

Rachel Matthews and Tiziana Ferrero-Regis

Introduction

Marketing and communication are failing to support an ecological and just transition in fashion. High levels of fashion consumption, driven by marketing activities and growth-focused business models in fashion, sit at odds with the calls for this industry to transition to sustainable and responsible practices. The contradiction has seen the rise of "greenwashing" and "social washing", and the proliferation of fashion marketing messages that over-simplify or co-opt aspects of sustainable fashion to manage this disconnection. Consumers who are seeking information are confused, mistrustful, or simply don't understand the complexity of messaging in much marketing and promotion of sustainable fashion (Turunen & Halme, 2021). As such a comprehensive and realistic roadmap for a sustainable fashion system remains elusive.

This chapter examines the strategies of three fashion brands (Ganni, Bode, and A.BCH) who each take different approaches to communicate the meaning of sustainable fashion for their brands. Analysis of their branded social media accounts and website content reveals the benefits and limitations of their methods. Through this investigation, the chapter critically reimagines an alternative function for marketing of sustainable fashion, better suited to supporting an ecological and just transition. It argues that the interconnected and dynamic nature of today's communication landscape can be better exploited for slower forms of storytelling centred on practices instead of products, and proposes a framework for building social media content as product *anatomy* extending and deepening an understanding of a garment's attributes that constitute sustainability.

Communications and mediation of fashion through online channels have power, they form an essential linkage in the fashion system that helps build connection between producers and consumers (Crewe, 2013) and fashion marketing channels occupy valuable spaces capable of shaping mindsets and behaviours (Moeran, 2006; Matthews, 2015). To hasten an ecological and just transition, we need fashion communications to develop new approaches to effectively promote the sustainable potential of fashion – a challenge that requires a cultural shift in marketing to avoid simply commodifying sustainability in an unsustainable fashion system, or as Blühdorn frames it "sustaining the unsustainable" (2011, 36). The chapter sets

DOI: 10.4324/9781003392705-8

out a new direction for narrative creation in fashion communications by asking the question: Is it possible to rebalance and reconcile two systems, fashion and marketing, both based on growth, with the industry's central concerns with sustainability?

Sustainable fashion is not a singular or stable concept (Fletcher, 2013). It is a "tricky" expression (Payne & Ferrero-Regis, 2019, 180) because the very meaning of fashion – continuous change predicated on newness – negates the possibility of sustaining sustainability. Fashion that is slow, upcycled, recycled, circular, vintage, repurposed, designed for disassembly, designed for durability, modular, ethically or responsibly produced, biodegradable as well as digital clothing and those made of biomaterials are all badged as sustainable fashion. However, these alternative fashion practices often fall in the category of greenwashing, with little evidence of carbon emission reduction, neutrality or positivity. In this light, the European Union is updating existing rules regarding claims of sustainability, requesting transparency and verifiability about impact (European Parliament, 2024). Communication of sustainability becomes thus pivotal to changes in consumer behaviour, and consequently to systems change. The three case studies – Ganni, Bode, and A.BCH – have been selected because they offer different approaches to sustainable fashion, and occupy different market levels. Further, the difference in their geographical location, scale, and approach to production and distribution provides insights into the contexts from which their brand communications emerge. As these case studies demonstrate, for fashion brands working with a sustainable ethos, their specific take on sustainability is also a crucial part of the brands' identity and differentiation.

The aim of this study is not to dictate a new sustainable fashion communication regime or offer a correct way to market a sustainable fashion product; rather identify methods and practices that open space for alternative and nuanced perspectives on fashion's evolving relationships with sustainability, shifting marketing to an informative function instead of a rapid-fire form of promotion. In doing so, the chapter proposes a notion of responsible fashion marketing that makes sustainability more visible, understandable, and actionable, to foster the formation of new cultural capital in sustainable fashion.

Literature review

Socio-materiality as theoretical framing

The study adopts a socio-material perspective to examine the marketing and communications of sustainable fashion. This approach has its roots in Science and Technology Studies (STS) and Actor-Network Theory (ANT) (Latour, 1987, 2005). Although there are differing perspectives on socio-materiality, they share common themes. Socio-material approaches focus on materials as being dynamic and entangled with human activity. All socio-material objects are heterogeneous assemblages, and they consider all things (human, non-human, knowledge, technology, systems) that become linked in webs of activity to generate knowledge decentring predominance of the human agency (Fenwick et al., 2015). Socio-material perspectives examine whole systems; they do not seek to separate out human relations from stuff (material objects), rather they help us recognise how connections and understanding are enhanced and deepened by our relations with the stuff / objects. These perspectives accept the fundamental uncertainty, fluidity, and messiness of everyday life (Orlikowski, 2007). From this viewpoint, socio-materiality allows analysis of the disparate elements that converge in promotions and activities designed to create meaning and engagement with objects (Hipfl, 2018). For example, through a convergence of various elements, a white t-shirt with a printed slogan can be a political statement, a design classic or a wardrobe basic – each with different associations and price tags.

In the study of sustainable fashion communication, the tracing of actants drawn together in branded social media feeds (combinations of word and images, people, places and spaces where objects are depicted as well as the interactivity of shoppable images, hashtags, links) become associated and entangled to create meaning. The meaning and influence are not uncovered in one hero image, the converging elements enliven each other collectively building knowledge as a composite construct (Moura & Bispo, 2019).

There are multiple and mutable concepts of sustainability in fashion, as mentioned. The attributes that make a garment sustainable are held in the choice of materials or in the decisions of the designer. The sustainability of a garment can be constituted variously across its lifecycle – creative and commercial decisions from its inception, concepts of sustainable design (from zero-waste, to modular, to DFD), selection of makers and how they are valued, business decisions based on environmental and social "costs" as well as how it is used and cared for. As such, there is a diversity of entities that converge in networks and assemblages that generate knowledge across its production, distribution, and consumption. As Entwistle notes:

> While fashion appears to us – in shops, in our wardrobes and so on ready-made and finished, it is the end produce of complex interventions into the natural world, and entangled into network of actors around the globe, human and non-human (from water and chemicals to grow cotton at one end of the process, through to hangers and other devices to display clothing.
>
> (2019, 272)

Further, Entwistle suggests the actor-networks that are assembled and reassembled in fashion can be usefully applied to "connect up nature-culture" in fashion, including its environmental entanglements (282, 2019).

In this investigation, socio-materiality helps to illuminate alternative practices suitable to communicate the complexity in making a fashion product sustainable. Lury (2009) suggests the *brand as an assemblage* and *brand as new media object* in her study of business operations in the twenty-first century. Brands demonstrate mutable fluid qualities that are in flux and changed by new associations via entities such as events or collaborations and this socio-material approach has supported case study analysis here. The theoretical framework also complements

Lusty's (2021) assessment of fashion's future terrain through the lens of critical fashion studies. Here she identifies how fashion, as both an industry and an everyday aesthetic practice, intersects with some of today's most critical issues, including sustainability, globalisation, decolonisation as well as consumption practices (816). Through fashion's engagement with these issues, there has been a marked "ethical turn" generating practices that display new levels of respect and empathy towards people, the planet, animals, and products of fashion. This new ethical attitude in fashion has revealed unforeseen entanglements of social, material, and environmental issues – "the ethical turn has taken fashion into new and productive networks of knowledge and everyday assemblages" (Lusty, 2021, 818). Thus, we need to recraft fashion narratives to support brands and micro-businesses to better communicate the complex process of building sustainability into their product and evolve genuine mediation strategies to promote consumer understanding.

Fashion and sustainability

Philosophically, fashion is predicated on continuous change, newness, and storytelling. With the exponential growth of fast fashion from the 1990s, change and newness have resulted in overproduction and multiplication of similar products in infinite variations: a summer dress, offered in many styles, colours, prints, lengths, and materials. Within such a system, this summer dress can be promoted as sustainable because of the materials selected for its production, yet being offered through many drops in global retail. Initiatives at the polar ends of the fashion supply chain (production and consumption) are continuously developed to change a fashion paradigm built on constant change and economic growth. Design-led strategies that keep materials in circulation as long as possible, or post-consumer textile waste recovery schemes are solutions that have increasingly been implemented in the fashion industry. In addition, measures to address textile waste at local community level, and niche initiatives by bigger luxury brands, have been implemented, but they are limited in their ability to subvert the global fashion system.

The generation of this type of sustainable fashion, a "quick fix" (Farley et al., 2015), leads to the phenomenon of greenwashing, and rebound effects creating "paradoxical outcomes" (Olson, 2022, 396) of "sustainable" products whose environmental benefits remain uncertain. Zink and Geyer (2017) add that the existence of parallel – sustainable – products in the market can easily be integrated by consumers within their buying routines and everyday life, only creating more choice for consumers. At best, niche sustainable fashion products risk becoming part of the accumulation of primary and secondary products that increase consumption and waste (Zink & Geyer, 2017). Recently, Bel Jacobs noted sustainability in fashion is "still stuck in the pilot phase" (in Cernansky, 2022). Despite the growth of alternative materials and clothing resale, sustainable ways to "do" fashion are still peripheral, in a system refusing to make deeper and necessary changes. Whitney McGuire (in Cernansky, 2022), a co-founder of community consultant group Sustainable Brooklyn, points out that brands' superficial attempts to resolve problems are causing the emergence of what McGuire calls "cause-related marketing" around sustainable products.

The circular economy and its discontents

The discursive space emerging for sustainability, through a growth in practices, scholarship, reports, and business consultancy unfolds in semiotic fields that are constantly renegotiated and reconstituted. The result is that through the mediatic dilution of its meaning, sustainability has become a slippery term, a buzzword shared among businesses and organisations as diverse as investment companies such as Goldman Sachs, non-governmental agencies, activist groups, luxury brands, the World Trade Organisation and the UN. The circular economy (CE) model, sustainability's implementation framework for the transition to a clean fashion industry, has become a concept that is presented as particularly effective in advancing a complete change of the traditional linear model of production and consumption. However, with zero-waste at its centre, and the focus on creating a better environment, circularity is still seen as part of a growth economic model.

Critiquing the CE, and implicitly the broad understanding of sustainability, Norris (2017, 2) asserts that "CE modelling tends to include people simply as product users in a system of material flows governed by large brands". Echoing Norris (2017), Niinimäki et al.'s (2020) analysis of the environmental impact of the fashion industry rests firmly on solutions such as slowing the industry through "decreasing clothing purchases and increasing garment lifetimes" (1). When analysing fashion and sustainability marketing, these critiques and reflexions must better recognise the need for brands' storytelling that proposes ways to do more with less products. The demand for increased transparency and accountability has resulted in company policies such as Corporate Social Responsibility (CSR). However, Sailer et al. (2022) maintain that CSR may signal companies' intentions to deal with ethical and environmental obligations, not necessarily implementing them.

Fletcher and Tham's (2019) discuss the infrastructure that sits around fashion production, identifying six landscapes that will help drive necessary change in knowledge, skills and mindsets of fashion in production and consumption. One of these directions is language: new communication for fashion. Fletcher and Tham contend that language is created through the interconnection of communication, thinking and doing, stating that it is a means through which thoughts and actions become visible, thinkable, do-able and discursive (2019, 52). Further, in this language landscape, Fletcher and Tham argue that a broader range of expression around sustainability must emerge, to open more tangible visions of what fashion and sustainability can look like. Through this work, we can find communication practices that focus on a deeper and more respectful understandings in fashion, those that facilitate collaboration rather than reinforcing problematic binaries such as producer-consumer, fast-slow, good-bad. In a similar way to the notion of "the ethical turn" in fashion (Lusty, 2021), Fletcher and Tham ask if it is possible to consider the ethics of language and mediation in sustainability as part of the transformation in fashion and beyond (2019, 58). Rethinking the mediated experiences of fashion suited to this era of increasing social and environmental precarity, common themes of respect, consideration, and empathy emerge in relation to people and the planet and entangled in fashion products themselves (Arthur, 2023). Daniel Miller

(2001, 230) uses the term "respectful encounter" when he discusses the important role of both consumption and materialism (or a devotion to objects) in society. He observes that our connection to objects is not separate from our relations with people, but inherent in our social relations. In its haste, contemporary fashion marketing ensures our encounters with fashion and clothing are fast and superficial. The possibility of respectful encounters with sustainable fashion as an alternative approach in marketing is developed below as a means to mediate its meaning.

Mediatisation of fashion sustainability

The integration of digital communication has meant that fashion is now visible almost instantaneously as new trends, drops and mini trends are released. Rocamora (2016) notes the centrality of media in processes of social and cultural transformation and of fashion in particular. Increasingly, practices of production and consumption are articulated on digital media (Rocamora, 2016), transforming the way in which brands communicate visually with a growing focus on the product's immaterial aspects. Semprini (2012, 36) calls this shift "dematerialization of products", which tend to be increasingly "light", for example light-weight fabrics, as well as influencing stories, that become a progressively mediatic phenomenon or performance. Immateriality as well as differences in language used to reveal different brand positions when narrating sustainability is explored below.

With its 1,158 billion active users (Statista, 2020), Instagram (IG) offers a unique opportunity for lifestyle brands to create storytelling and narratives about their products. The platform is predominantly used by young consumers, with people between 18 and 34 as the most frequent users (Statista, 2021). Kusumasondjaja (2020, 15) reports that "more than 95m photos are shared on Instagram daily". This content overload "consumes" messages (Semprini, 2012, 35), diminishing their capacity to produce and hold signification. They are quick and throw-away snippets of communication designed to aid rapid decision-making by consumers based on wants. Likewise, with the operations in fast fashion, there is overproduction and overconsumption of superficial fashion media messages moving quickly through channels designed for rapid replenishment.

The risk here is that brands trivialise their communication of sustainability, and thus they turn increasingly to the spectacular, the performance, collaborations with other niche brands, influencers, and celebrities to compete for attention. These fashion marketing methods do not provide opportunities for respectful understanding fashion items (Rose, 2013). Speed and reach are of the essence (Paulicelli et al., 2021) with little time or space devoted to "getting to know you" in brands' encounters. Fashion and its promotion on IG have collapsed the distance between marketing messages and purchasing fashion (Rocamora, 2018). Networked channels, mobile apps, and platform functionality have evolved to be instantly shoppable. To support the acceleration of consumption and gratification, increasingly rapid delivery operations have developed for online purchases (Berg et al., 2018). To achieve its design-production processes, fast fashion is mediated and consumed rapidly – whether the product has been produced sustainably or not. For sustainability in fashion to be authentically mediated, it requires the telling of stories and content that draws upon both material-immaterial values that converge in sustainable fashion products. These types of stories have longer tails, that require a reconsideration of content creation that unpacks how a garment becomes sustainable and remains sustainable through the reconceptualisation of practices of caring, maintaining, and styling through activation with other garments in the wardrobe. The goal is to achieve garment longevity as a critical property of sustainability (Niinimäki, 2024).

Research design

Mediating meaning in sustainable fashion

The dimensions of mediation (in Figure 5.1) set out a framework to consider how marketing content on social media can attempt to facilitate comprehensive encounters with products. This is a complex socio-material interaction, as such the sub-sections of the framework aim to reveal an assemblage of resources, technologies, entities, and people involved in making fashion sustainable. Through separating the various perspectives, it invites content creators to work more closely with those designing and making the products, informing themselves about the product's anatomy and life story, to provide a deeper appreciation of its sustainable attributes. Through networked and relational means, extended and interlinked product narratives can expose dimensions of sustainability within a garment's "life story"; the networked conditions of digital media allow links, handles, and tags to connect consumer-users to other sites of knowledge and third-party verifications. This situates the material object in a complex web of its relations with planet, people, and prosperity where consumer-users can use multiple elements to form an overall perception (Singer et al., 2023, 357) of sustainability. The intention is to counter the disconnect with actual garments created by the continuous stream of digital communications focused only on aesthetics. Communication strategies and narratives of fashion cannot remain fast and superficial; the physical object needs to exist as comprehensively on the internet as it does in reality. The framework prompts ways to extend and celebrate multiple product attributes, enabling a more holistic understanding through its entanglements of materials, technology, matter, and meaning (Orlikowski & Scott, 2016).

The dimensions of the framework resemble familiar topics and tropes in existing fashion marketing and propose using the familiar as a portal into deeper excavations that expose decisions and details that usually remain hidden. Restrictions in space and speed on social media often curtail product information, whilst hasty scrappy content fails to fully convey the sustainable credentials of the product. Marketers need to rethink the digital feed, not simply use the space for brief branded updates. It is an interface where they, together with the consumer-users, can connect over a shared interest in the garment, and negotiate responsibilities of guiding/cycling it throughout the economy (Fletcher, 2013).

Figure 5.1 Dimensions of mediation for sustainable fashion (2023). (*Rachel Matthews.*)

The framework uses individual lenses (see Figure 5.1) to examine sustainability thematically.

These allow sustainable values, decisions, and actions underpinning a brand's enactment of sustainability to be more comprehensively surveyed.

1 Aesthetics

Sustainable fashion needs to be aesthetically compelling, to displace non-sustainable fashion and to negate the rebound effect of sustainable fashion merely being an additional available product (Zink & Geyer, 2017). Further, brand identity needs to remain clear. However, content designed to tell the life story of a garment can use garment aesthetics, something that often first attracts the consumer, to elucidate the decisions taken by the designer. Garment aesthetics are the result of the design process. This presents an opportunity to justify why the brand has designed this product in this way – designed for durability, disassembly, or waste mitigation? Deeper considerations that hold the potential to change the way consumers-users view the design features of a product.

2 Materials

Crafting messages that evoke the sensory benefits of fabric help address consumer-user questions their interest in wearing the garment – elevating and celebrating its materiality through the screen. Content that offers a deeper understanding of the tactile qualities of the garment can also explain why certain materials have been selected. Fabric selection, much like discussion of garment aesthetics, allows brands to articulate their understanding of the socio-ecological benefits of using certain materials (including research they have done to inform sourcing and supply chain decisions). Information about the sustainable credentials of materials, if conveyed, is often technical or scientific making it rather abstract or unverifiable. Here marketers can need to assist consumer-users to understand how fabric choices help the garment to perform well over its lifetime, include proof points, and promote this as part of its value.

3 Labour and labour relations

Mediating the meaning of sustainable fashion needs to highlight garment makers, or risk being seen to interpret sustainability as simply an environmental concern, ignoring the social dimensions. Spotlighting "who made" the garment means special skills and time involved in making a well-crafted product become valued and visible, creating space in the fashion discourse to note importance of artisans, craftspeople, and traditional skills. People and labour humanise the product; including them and their skills not only provides transparency of the supply chain but also allows brands to demonstrate their values, especially towards issues of social sustainability of fashion.

4 Transparency

A respectful encounter needs to instil trust in the brand and the product and transparency is the means of reassurance. This means content needs to be clear, relevant, and accessible as well as verifiable across all dimensions of mediation (design, labour, etc.). It is the responsibility of the brand and their marketers to provide evidence that backs their claims of sustainability – proof points. Many countries are now legislating the way product information needs to be communicated, with companies required to present supporting scientific evidence to validate their claims (McKinsey & Co., 2023). Proof points can take various forms but will require underlying research informing the brand's decision-making – a form of content requiring new literacies in sustainable fashion communications. These (legally enforceable) narratives need to convey relevant data, evaluation, and measurement processes in accessible and relatable ways for consumer-users.

5 Environmental Impact

The environmental impact of the product needs to be understood across the entire product life cycle (or life story), with the brand taking responsibility for its footprint from inception, through production, its use stage as well as end of life or afterlife stewardship. Content setting out the environmental impact of a single product offers a way to talk about the specific impacts in granular detail. It can provide garment specific guidance on topics such as durability and repairs, laundry and garment care and end of life solutions for the garment. Providing guidance on how to ensure the durability of the garment, so it can be kept in use for longer, can assist in slowing down production and consumption (Niinimäki et al., 2020). However, it is important to highlight that the real impact is in the volume of products, unsold inventory, often ending in incineration, and the volume of product returned.

6 Business Operations

Business models and operational matters also offer a lens to better understand the sustainability of fashion – and a significant opportunity to change existing sales-focused narratives. Business models are rarely explicitly discussed, rather they emerge in fashion marketing through content focused on price and product discounts, new collections, and their convenient distribution – even for sustainably produced garments. This creates conflict and contradiction in brand messages – promoting compulsive consumption of sustainable products. Business content in the product life story needs to connect with sustainability, articulating values-driven business initiatives. For example, promoting of broader notions of value (rather than dollar value) could help consumer-users better comprehend "fair pricing" for sustainability or quantify "costs" in terms of natural and social resources (Thorpe, 2015). This type of narrative then reinforces the decision-making processes revealed in other aspects of content, such as material selection and labour.

Methods

This research utilises a qualitative-quantitative methodology, employing a layered semiotic approach to analyse images, context, and text (Barthes, 1991; Semprini, 2012). Barthes (1991) has proposed a way for reading written fashion in magazines that generates "what is fashionable and what is not" (Rocamora, 2015, 132). Semprini uses semiotics combined with socio-cultural and historical contexts, with the ambition of providing a theoretical and epistemological analysis of brand identity and communication. Contexts have also been examined through grey literature and an interview with the founder of A.BCH, Courtney Holm. Despite approaching Bode and Ganni, it was not possible to obtain direct information. This represents a limitation of this study.

Figure 5.2 demonstrates the layered and systematic approach to the semiotic analysis of brands and their messages. This analytical structure has been adapted to investigate communication of sustainability narratives in IG. Our findings have followed Semprini's (2012) indication of what he calls "wordly figures" (95) or fundamental categories to avoid the infinite multiplication of variation or surface classifications. Therefore, we refer to Themes as content; Spaces as the depiction of the world of the brand; Style as aesthetics; Actors as in labour relationships; and Rhetoric as the values that emerge to the surface of posts.

In addition to Semprini's (2012) categories adapted in this analysis, further visual and textual analysis found parallel, yet distinct dimensions used to constitute sustainability in fashion: materials, environmental impact, transparency, and business models. These elements were identified through both visual mapping and textual analysis; however, the semiotic and socio-material framing of this project ensures that these entities are also seen in relation to one another, converging. The findings set out below piece together image, text, and context in combination with various converging elements in messages about the brands, their products, and their conceptions of sustainability in fashion. The findings have been used to craft an analytical framework – dimensions for mediating meaning in sustainable fashion.

Instagram (IG) posts of three fashion brands were collected in the months of October and November 2022. The three brands, Ganni, Bode, and Melbourne's

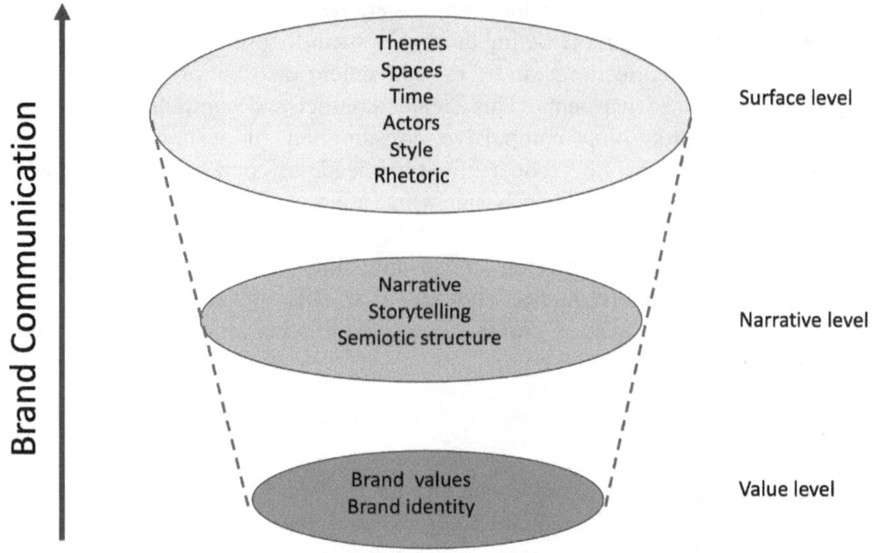

Figure 5.2 The layered structure of brand communication. (Adapted from Semprini, 2012). (*Tiziana Ferrero-Regis*.)

A.BCH were chosen as they represent three approaches to sustainable fashion, as it emerges from their digital communications, and from media discourses and brand values as communicated through their websites and the press. These brands represent three business levels: Ganni is based in Copenhagen and is a global vertically integrated brand; Bode is an American independent family-owned designer brand, and A.BCH is an Australian local micro brand/studio that, as they declare, is the first in Australia to employ circularity in their practices. We collected a total of 160 posts manually, with a focus on brands' communication of sustainability messages, and not on consumers' engagement, although differences in numbers of "likes" was noted, where "like" signifies a form of quick and superficial engagement. Key words related to sustainability were identified from scholarly and grey literature (see Table 5.1) to which other recurrent key words in the brands' posts were added. The brands' websites were also surveyed to assess the narratives developed on their IG accounts against the information emerging from their other online presence.

Images and texts were analysed together, as we paid particular attention to the coherence of the message delivered through visual and textual means. Experimental mood boards (or visual assemblages) which grouped types of images were created as a method to track and physically document elements that feature and reoccur in the brands' messaging (see Figure 5.3). This approach to mapping and visualising findings from media analysis aligns with methods used in critical cartography and visual research methods (Cosgrove, 1999; Butler-Kisber & Poldman, 2010). Reassembling images taken from IG feeds allowed a non-linear reading of the images. Analysis through visual mapping has the capacity to go beyond the

Table 5.1 A breakdown of the most recurrent key words in IG texts (*Rachel Matthews and Tiziana Ferrero-Regis)*

Key words	*Ganni*	*Ganni Lab*	*Bode*	*A.BCH*	*Total*
Animal	0	5	0	0	5
Applique	0	0	4	0	4
Biological	0	14	0	1	15
Bode	0	0	27	0	27
Carbon	0	7	0	0	7
Certified	0	16	0	0	16
Circular	0	0	0	9	9
Collaborate/tion	5	6	0	0	11
Customised	0	0	0	1	1
Embroidery	0	0	4	0	4
Environment	0	16	0	0	16
Exclusive	9	6	0	0	15
Fabric	0	13	0	0	13
Fibre	0	0	0	2	2
Folk	0	0	3	0	12
Forever	4	0	0	0	4
Ganni	136	55	0	0	191
Hand (made)	0	0	12	0	12
Icon	5	0	0	0	5
Impact	0	8	0	0	8
Materials	0	7	0	1	8
Nature	0	0	0	2	2
Off-cuts	0	0	0	1	1
One-of-a-kind	0	0	3	0	3
Organic	0	7	0	0	7
Origin	0	0	6	0	6
Plastic	0	0	0	1	1
Recycled	14	6	0	3	23
Responsible	0	11	0	0	11
Social	0	8	0	0	8
Tencel	0	0	0	2	2
Undyed	0	0	0	1	9
Unsustainable	0	0	0	1	1
Waste	0	0	0	3	3
Wool	5	0	0	0	5

Source: (Rachel Matthews and Tiziana Ferrero-Regis)

superficial or immediately visible to reveal greater intent in structures and patterns (Corner, 1999, 213). Through this part of the analysis, brand identity and aesthetics were revealed, confirmed, and/or contested through repeated visual tropes used to present products, people, and places of the brand (Table 5.1). Themes, spaces, actors, style, and rhetoric are comprehensive of many ways in which fashion is presented, allowing coherence and consistency with socio-material perspectives and theory. The two data analysis approaches (visual mapping and text analysis) were initiated independently but became integrated through iterative and relational analysis techniques. Together the authors examined emerging and accumulating

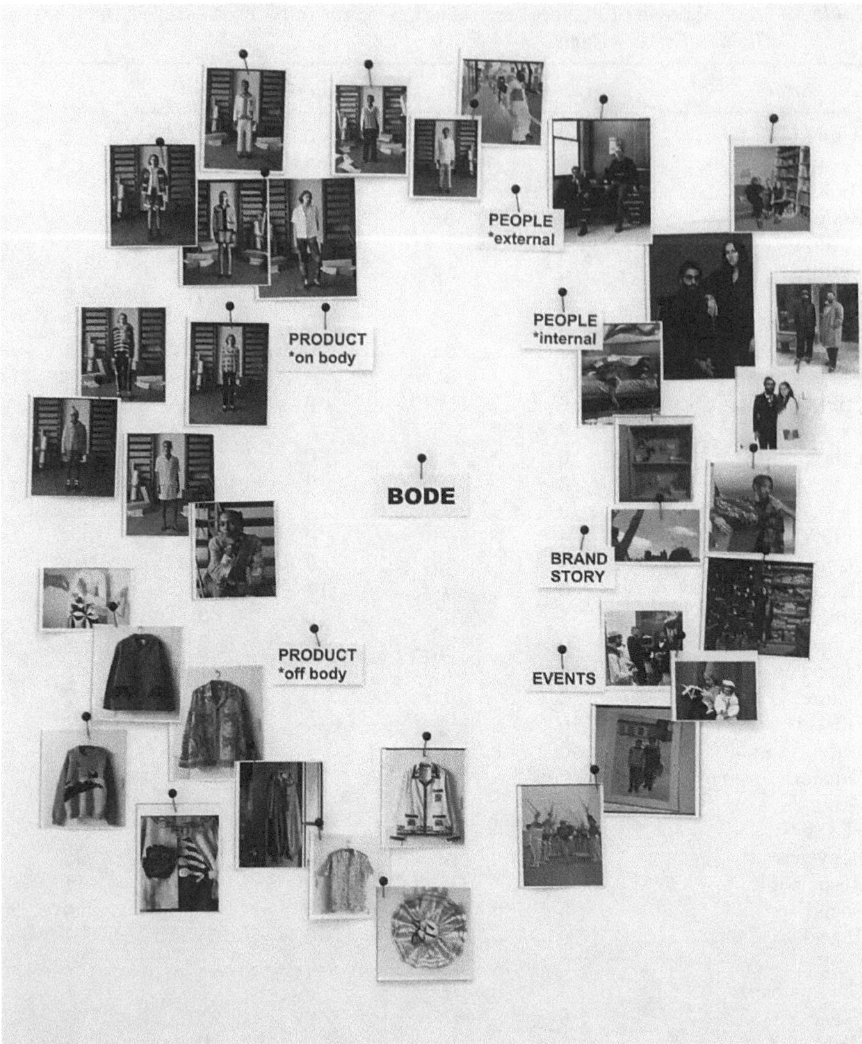

Figure 5.3 Visual assemblage – visual mapping of Bode IG feed (1 October 2022–30 November 2022). (*Rachel Matthews*.)

data sets comparing notes on new patterns and interconnections as a means of sense-checking the themes that emerged.

Case studies

The three fashion brands were chosen for their business size, market level, and for their geographical location and reach. How a fashion brand enacts sustainability is difficult to perceive simply through its marketing. In addition, the explicit use of the word "sustainability" in communications has become a contested term, often provoking scrutiny and criticism of brands (Robertson, 2018) – neither Ganni, Bode, or A.BCH want to declare themselves as such; however, A.BCH self-proclaims circularity. Each of the three brands are perceived to utilise responsible fashion practices. The differing notions of how sustainability was constituted by each brand on social media is analysed below with a brief profile of the brands.

Ganni

Ganni is a Danish ready-to-wear label originally founded as a cashmere brand in 1999, but it has evolved since 2009 when Ditte Refstrup (the creative director) and husband Nicholaj took over. Two factors were fundamental to the brand's growth. The first is the use of local influencers on their social media. The second is Ganni's location in Copenhagen, a city that rose to "style centre" from the 1980s (Beard, 2011), and thus taking advantage of the growth of creative enterprises and new generations of creative workers. Currently the brand is sold in over 600 luxury stores world-wide and operates 24 of its own concept stores. Ganni makes a pertinent contribution to this study as in 2018 they were accused of greenwashing, and in 2019 of social-washing (Gayle, 2019). They have subsequently adopted a range of strategies to address the criticism. Significantly, they countered the claims by stating explicitly that they were not a sustainable brand, rather they have worked to become a more responsible version of themselves since 2013, implicitly recognising a transitional path to sustainability. Further, in an article on the *Business of Fashion*, they acknowledged their short-comings and highlighted the challenges of marketing contemporary fashion to an engaged and critical consumer (Khan, 2020).

In 2020, the brand launched an additional IG account @GanniLab (alongside @Ganni), to provide transparency on their responsible strategies. The content on these two different accounts reveals a clear divide between the marketing of Ganni's fashion products and the brand's sustainability communication. @Ganni contains conventional fashion content – photoshoots, flat product lays, and reposts of stylish young women wearing Ganni products. In contrast, @Gannilab posts details of fibre and fabric production, aspects of their supply chain and collaborations and partnerships with third parties. Over the two-month duration of the study, there were only two cross-postings between these IG accounts. The brand has built a detailed "responsibility" tab on the Ganni website that includes annual responsibility reports, stated goals, action plans, and details of progress towards these outcomes. Ganni emphasises its production of new garments using new biomaterial and recycled fibres and makes visible their connection with people in their supply chain. They partner with third-parties such as Provenance (for supply chain traceability) or Mylo (for fabric innovations) and have B Corp status. In 2023, Ganni participated in Copenhagen Fashion Week, the first requiring participating brands to abide by their Sustainable Requirements Framework (mainly based on fabric choice).

Bode

Bode is an independent menswear label founded in 2016 by Emily Adams Bode Aujla Since its inception, the brand has won many accolades including winning the Woolmark Prize and CFDA American Menswear Designer of the Year 2022. Stocked in 120 stores worldwide with two flagship stores in the USA as well as a tailoring shop, Bode's perspective on sustainability and fashion came originally from making one-of-a-kind pieces from vintage deadstock and antique textiles. To scale, the business is now made up of 30%–40% one-of-a-kind pieces with the remaining of 600 styles offered made from new textiles that have been reproduced, replicating traditional printing and hand-embroidery techniques in vintage textiles (Wray, 2019). Central to the appeal of Bode's products is their connection to historical narratives, heritage, and craftspeople – in particular those of America's history of crafting such as quilting and rituals of garment personalisation such as senior cords. In a 2020 *Esquire* magazine article, the brand's founder Aujla was asked about fashion and its sustainability, she dismissed sustainability as a "marketing ploy" (Flammia, 2020). However, she describes her products as "love letters to the past" (Wray, 2019) and employs upcycling, waste-reduction methods, and slow fashion practices. Prior to 2023, Bode had not worked to a traditional delivery schedule, but has subsequently entered a period of growth, adding a range of womenswear and sportswear to their product offering and have aligned these collections to seasonal delivery dates.

A.BCH

A.BCH was an independent fashion label founded by Cortney Holm in Melbourne, Australia, in 2017. It has been described as Australia's first fully circular fashion label, promoting circularity through its design process and business operations. The label manufactures locally, and its products are accredited by Ethical Clothing Australia (ECA). Eschewing wholesale or use of stockists, the business sells direct to consumers through its website and by appointment at their Circular Fashion Studio in Melbourne. Holm describes her approach as hyper-transparent and hyper-local, noting that they also need to be "part of each customer transaction to follow through with care instructions, repairs and our recycling take back program" (Bailey, 2020). The A.BCH website demonstrates this hyper-transparency with pages that detail all the materials they use (and don't use), with comprehensive garment life-cycle guides including end of life solutions; every garment is able to be either composted or recycled. In addition to the product ranges, information that supports consumer-users to make informed choices throughout the garment's life (such as laundering instructions) is available on the website. A.BCH offers 18 garment categories across men, women, gender-neutral and accessories, with rental options. There is also A.BCH Red Line that sells limited editions or one-of-a-kind garments developed by experimenting with waste reduction techniques. In 2020, Holm won the Australian Fashion Laureate award for Sustainable Innovation. Unlike Ganni and Bode, A.BCH does not avoid using the word sustainable, rather they proudly state that they make every step of their garments circular journey as visible and as sustainable as they can be (A.BCH website, n.d.). In 2023, Courtney Holm announced the launch of Circular Sourcing, a digital platform for the circulation of high-quality surplus fabric and deadstock – a venture supported by a grant from local government (Australianfashioncouncil.com, 2023). In 2024, Holm announced A.BCH will no longer produce any new clothing, but would remain dedicated to advancing circularity (ABCH.world.com).

Findings

Thematic analysis revealed fundamental differences in the way in which the three brands communicate their sustainability. There are some striking observations in the use of words by the three brands. Ganni's posting is above all self-referential, with 136 mentions of the brand name within their text. The second most occurring keyword is "recycled", revealing their key strategy for sustainability is through materials, with five mentions of "wool". Ganni also uses language by proxi, for example words such as "forever" (4), to infer longevity of clothing as a form of sustainable consumption, and "exclusive" (9) meaning small production runs and thus elimination of overproduction and waste. In contrast, A.BCH's most used key words refer openly to sustainability, with circular mentioned nine times. Bode's most recurrent keyword refers to hand-made, reflecting their commitment to exclusive and unique products.

Aesthetics

Bode's version of sustainability (as "love letters to the past") is captured in their consistent vintage, nostalgic, sepia-tinted aesthetics on IG. Figure 5.4 reflects the brand's visual identity, depicting a timeless genderless figure. The aesthetics of the space are difficult to date, adding to the sense of timelessness. Across IG, Bode brand aesthetic allows people of any gender to see themselves in Bode's world. Product shots make up most of the imagery, but intermingled are images that relate to Bode's Aujla's personal memories and family history such as old photos or toys that she has kept from childhood.

Ganni's aesthetics across both IG accounts and the website has the look of a young contemporary fashion brand, built on a cult-like community of followers. Overall, there is a strong graphic language that uses choppy collages of products with text and pops of neon pinks and greens. The people depicted in Ganni's posts and website are young creative women, posing or enjoying themselves at events. There are also multiple images of their products and accessories styled as flat lays, in a cool urban Scandi-chic or mid-century modern interior (see Figure 5.5). Ganni's world has a clear fashion aesthetic on @ganni. On @gannilab, the same graphic style is used in the visuals, with much more text. The images are of new materials, products, or supply chain locations. The overall aesthetic result is that of a young, global brand built on trends.

Figure 5.4 An example of Bode's vintage sepia-hued aesthetic. (*Rachel Matthews.*)

In contrast to Ganni, A.BCH's aesthetics only really emerges from their website, where clean layout with minimal use of graphics communicates brand identity as fashion capable of restraint. The brand's use of images on social media lack the visual consistency of the website. On IG, A.BCH uses neutral colours, grey, natural colour of spun cotton, and black, focussing more on the message of basic clothes. A consistent aesthetics of fashionability emerges from seven posts from A.BCH's participation in 2022 Melbourne Fashion Week. Holm (2023) underlines that this was part of a strategy to be seen, raising brand awareness for future applications for government funding (see Figure 5.6). Seven images out 35 present clothing in outdoors, with green and earthy terracotta colours in evidence.

Transparency

As discussed, Ganni has created two IG accounts and a website separating out the fashion and shopping content from content that provides transparency on their business operations. On the website, there are pages dedicated to steps taken to become B Corp certified. On @Gannilab, most posts focused on demonstrating transparency within the early tiers of the supply chain with content of people, locations or linking to third party certifications and verifications. The visibility of their manufacturing bases (in locations such as Portugal and Turkey) reveals Ganni's

Figure 5.5 Ganni's brand identity is revealed through their references to Nordic aesthetics. (*Rachel Matthews.*)

globally dispersed supply chain and business operations, something evident on @Ganni by posts on new stores openings in Seoul, Hong Kong, and Shanghai that occurred during the two months of the study.

A.BCH has dedicated most of their website to demonstrating the work undertaken to be a circular fashion brand, providing granular detail on their local supply chain operations. Its posts on IG attempt to bring some backstory to the product, but the messages are compromised by uninspiring images of clothing hanging on racks with limited supporting text. Holm (2023) is aware of the minimal approach of her IG account and has consciously chosen to focus on highlighting practices of circularity: recycled cotton yarn; upcycled second-hand clothing; alterations. The places where this becomes evident are in IG posts and videos capturing Holm working in her studio or promoting events and workshops where people are invited into the space.

Labour

Ganni separates labour involved in the garment production process and the product. @ganni details the creative labour of the brand's creative director and collaboration with others such as artists and illustrators, but does not mention the

Figure 5.6 A.BCH used backdrops of the city to confer a cool and modern aesthetics to the clothes during Melbourne Fashion Week 2022. (*Tiziana Ferrero-Regis.*)

makers involved in the production phase of the fashion supply chain, while the garment manufacturers (and their factories) are profiled and visible on @gannilab. The makers in Bode's supply chain are not visible in images, but craftspeople are referred to in garment descriptions. Bode's founder, Aujla features in several posts, often with her partner or other "friends" of the brand. A.BCH proudly describes its local supply chain and ECA accreditation and posts images of Courtney Holm with the makers working in the studio. These messages are most clearly conveyed on the website.

Materials

@Gannilab focuses on new fabric innovations, recycled and reclaimed materials including traceable denim, and a user guide about how to care for clothes. Material innovation is the central focus of the brand's responsible messaging; however, analysis of the website reveals fabric innovations are only used in a small fraction of Ganni products. Ganni names new biomaterials they are trialling quoting trade names (Mylo, Pyratex) and highlights some renewable energy used in textile manufacturing (see Figure 5.7). This limited notion of sustainability is predicated on "new" textiles – although named these are not explained, making it difficult to understand the real benefits of their use. This narrative based on alternative materials side-steps issues of over-production and textile waste.

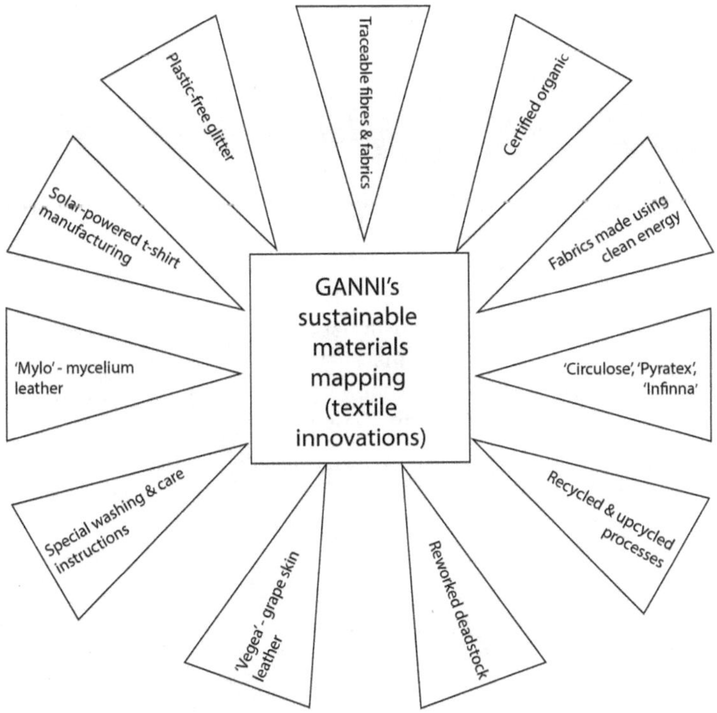

Figure 5.7 Mapping materials in sustainable fashion marketing – Ganni (2023). (*Rachel Matthews.*)

Both United Nations and the European Community want to reduce textile waste through durable clothing (Zero Waste Europe, 2023), and thus prioritise reuse, repair and remanufacture to decrease the production of new clothing. Marketing ways to do more with less new clothing provides a way to support this change across the entire value chain.

Fabrics are central in the way sustainability is constituted in Bode's content on social media (see Figure 5.8); however, they focus on traditional textiles and craftsmanship. The preservation of vintage textiles, haptic childhood memories, and material souvenirs of American traditions is inferred in the content, through reference to textile history and making processes in text. In several articles Ajula describes their extensive archive of vintage quilts and American textiles as inspiration; however very few products are made from any salvaged materials, most are described as "faithful reproductions" of original nineteenth-century garments, for example. The production of the replicas are described as created by artisans or craftspeople in various locations (in the USA and also India), but with little information on the production of fibres / fabric of the replicas or preservation of heritage craft skills.

A.BCH's constitution of sustainability is based on circularity where the preservation of fibres and fabrics within the system is central. Sustainability in A.BCH

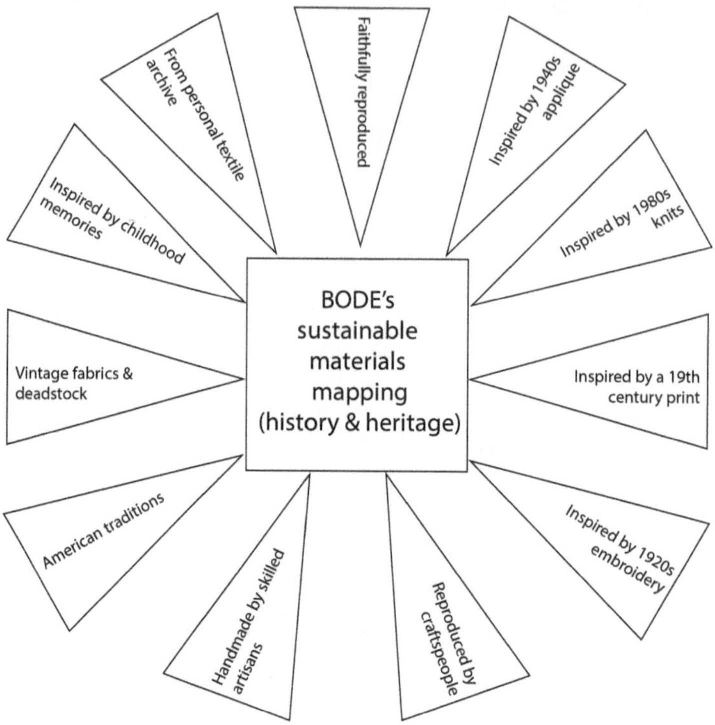

Figure 5.8 Mapping materials in sustainable fashion marketing – Bode (2023). (*Rachel Matthews.*)

content is framed within limitations such as mono materials, no dyes or finishes, restricted colour palettes, and reuse of fibres and fabrics (see Figure 5.9). This is not always evident in the visuals alone; the text details supply chain, material choices, and processes of circularity. Written descriptions of sustainable material choices and fibre types are well developed on the website, with technical information communicated in an accessible and straightforward way. Much of the discussion of materials is given a scientific rather than creative spin, described as created in the laboratory and informed by biological systems.

Environmental impact

Environmental impacts on the content are inferred through organic farming methods (e.g., in organic cotton) or through recycled fibre sourcing that has saved textile waste from landfill. On @Gannilab, there are references to reducing the environmental impact of their supply chain, through installing solar panels and carbon in-setting (which come with useful explanations). Bode's approach is to reference the preservation of vintage and rare textiles to avoid waste and limit environmental impacts but with no clear evidence. At A.BCH, the material selection is framed in

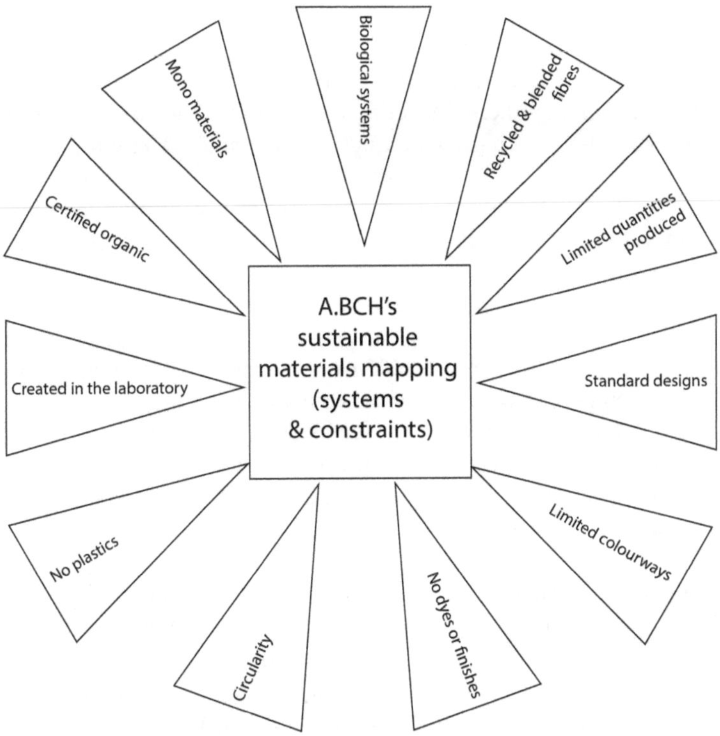

Figure 5.9 Mapping materials in sustainable fashion marketing – A.BCH (2023). (*Rachel Matthews.*)

relation to garments' lifecycle through concepts of fibre recycling at end of life or the biodegradability of the fabric, with instructions on how to compost clothing at home – a process that is reliant on the type of fibre.

Business operations

Through the communication strategies of these brand, a sense of these brands' business models and operations emerges. There is some transparency through external messages about internal operations. @gannilab reveals some of their manufacturing locations and the people who work there, whilst the announcements of new store openings on @Ganni reveal the global scale of operations. A.BCH provide what has been described as "radical transparency" (Richards, 2021) to ensure every aspect of the micro business's operations is visible. A key element is that the promotion of sales, new additions to product ranges, and showcasing seasonal collections at various fashion weeks (Bode at Paris Fashion Week and A.BCH at Melbourne Fashion Week) make it difficult to discern the sustainability of the business models of these brands; a significant contributor to the continued over-production and over-consumption of fashion.

Each of the three case studies hints at how certain content on social media and websites can be leveraged to mediate a view of fashion and sustainability, but fail to make a comprehensive case. Content needs to be more systematic (and systemic) – intentionally inter-connecting information about aesthetics (and design decisions), materials (sourcing and production implications), environmental impact of product lifecycle (pre and post-consumer care implications), labour (valuing the makers and their skills), business model (insight into values-driven, post-growth business initiatives), and transparency (visibility, verification, or proof points).

Discussion

As noted above, fast fashion is a problematic business model evident not only in design-production processes but also in the way contemporary fashion is communicated and mediated to consumers. To reconceptualise marketing for the purpose of sustainability, there is a need to see beyond the moral judgement (and implicit guilt) associated with consumption and possession of material goods. Daniel Miller urges us to resist simplifying consumption as either intrinsically good or intrinsically bad, as it is a "complex and contradictory" process (2001, 227). He asks us to acknowledge its rich symbolism and its interconnection with our social and material relations, something that highlights how acquisition involves valuing, savouring, and appreciating a range of physical attributes and emotional responses. This process requires what has been described as a "respectful encounter" (Miller, 2001, 230), signalling the need for introductions to garments to be undertaken with deeper respect, patience, and affinity to foster relationship building and care in fashion (Fletcher & Tham, 2019).

What could a respectful encounter with fashion look like? A respectful encounter necessitates a different mindset, with marketing / mediation that resembles a form of great customer service. Marketers need to anticipate the types of questions consumers might have about the product (from the tough questions about its production through to assistance with its care), with content that contains explanations and include ways to verify the answers they provide. This mindset must prioritise consumer-user concerns, demonstrating empathy with their decision-making and address the lack of trust that has emerged from greenwashing and lack of transparency (Robertson, 2018). Marketers can then establish themselves as credible experts (Nunes et al., 2021) through responsible well-informed and detailed fashion content that enables closer connection with the garment. For this to be effective, mediation practices need to shift from fast, short-term content strategies to longer-term thinking. Despite the speed of media channels and the power of algorithms, marketing professionals have the ability to reduce the number of products promoted and create space for new narratives of fashion to emerge. Further, social media can be exploited to tell more complex stories across a transmedia landscape, through interactive links, handles, and hashtags. Transmedia story-telling can assist in networked knowledge production (Hipfl, 2018), enriching ways fashion practices can be contextualised in a garment and through its use – as a composite construct (Nunes et al., 2021).

However, even by slowing and extending the nature of communications, can the marketing of sustainable fashion operate outside of capitalistic norms? Ensuring the customer is better informed before acquiring a product can rebuild trust, provide transparency, and simplify choice but does not automatically bring about sustainable outcomes. If the purpose of marketing remains to drive growth in sales of new products – regardless of whether these have been designed / produced using responsible methods, it will remain part of fashion's problem; with fashion narratives of newness, immediacy and disposability (UNEP, 2023) persisting.

Fashion marketing professionals need a new sense of purpose paired with new literacies to tell alternative fashion stories (Black, 2013; Fletcher & Tham, 2019). Current practices are underpinned by highly developed skills in narrative building, lifestyle associations and ideas of social capital – strengths that can be repurposed. If put to work to irradicate the promotion of overconsumption, marketing can drive alternative mediations of fashion based on use practices, understood, and valued as a social practice (von Busch, 2022).

However, marketers must be knowledgeable and accountable for what they say. They must be conversant with the current science, terminology, and the design, production, and business practices of responsible fashion (Arthur, 2023). They need in-depth product knowledge, across every tier of the brand's supply and value chains (including diverse usage and realistic end-of-life solutions) as well as changes to business operations that consider social and environmental impacts. Swap short-term transactional content for longer-term appreciation of fewer products, changing emphasis from shopping for aesthetic novelty to ways of unlocking the potential in product performance. This lays the groundwork for marketers to devise new communications about less fashion production and consumption, not as a deficit, but through normalising ways of extending the life of products in various ways such as styling or remodelling and advancing notions of shared product stewardship to ensure longevity.

Changing the priorities of fashion marketing from driving convenient and compulsive consumption demands an upending of existing mindsets and practices; existing fashion marketing approaches restrict understanding of and necessary behavioural change for sustainable outcomes. While sustainable fashion must deal with closing resource loops at scale, attention should be paid to *slowing* the entire system. Slowing the loop means to reduce the amount of material flowing into the economy and as marketing and communications act as a form of connective tissue in this loop, they have a role to play in ensuring material is valued for as long as possible. Sufficiency can be defined as "having enough to live well without excess" (Bocken et al., 2022) and aligns with Raworth's concept of Doughnut Economics (2017), defined as a safe operating space for humanity to thrive without exceeding planetary boundaries. Concepts of sufficiency – living well without excess – align with slowing material loops, and hence consumption of the new, but not through denial, rather reframing good lifestyle choices made over time. This sets out one means of repurposing existing marketing tropes to eliminate content designed to stimulate overconsumption and develop a longer slower discourse on fashion product use.

Limitations of the findings

The study has focused on IG for data collection and as a communication channel capable of mediating respectful encounters. The functionality of channels such as IG, Facebook, and TikTok through which most marketing materials circulate has limitations. These channels encourage quick and throw-away snippets of communication designed to aid rapid decision-making and ease of acquisition (Sailer et al., 2022). Further, the commercial mechanisms behind SEO and algorithms ultimately govern the content in users' feeds. The current configuration of IG makes it difficult to amplify brand-created content on social media, as it can be easily over-looked or diluted by "fitting in" with the channels' specifications. For more complex fashion narratives, transmedia storytelling can help to ground messages beyond social-media algorithms.

Conclusion

To gain attention, sustainable fashion brands are having to mimic established practices designed to promote fashion through aesthetic novelty – practices that become conflated with a marketing discourse of constant shopping for new things. Consumer-users make quick assumptions about the products, where potentially false or misleading inference goes unchecked. This chapter asked if we can rebalance and reconcile two systems, fashion and marketing, both based on growth, with the industry's central concerns with sustainability. For this systemic change to occur in fashion, marketing and communications must actively participate in eliminating messages of over-consumption. Marketing's function and objectives must change from rapid-fire promotions to slower forms of information and education of the customer based on acquisition, use, and disposal practices.

Simmel (2020) noted, as we become superficially connected to many products, we are deeply involved with none. Further, sustainability in fashion is complex and constituted differently in different products. Beyond driving growth, marketing is a point of connection across the entire value chain, where its communications and interactions can help present a garment in more detailed and transparent terms. This can initiate slower respectful relations and mediate sustainability as it plays out over across the product lifecycle. Further, redefining the function of fashion marketing offers a pathway towards greater accountability in claims of sustainability, whilst also making its adoption more visible, understandable, and actionable.

References

A.BCH. (n.d.). *BCH A circular fashion label.* Available at: https://abch.world/ (Accessed: 17 October 2022).

Arthur, R. (2023). *UNEP and UNFCCC The Sustainable Fashion Communication Playbook.* https://www.unep.org/resources/publication/sustainable-fashion-communication-playbook.

Australian Fashion Council. (2023). *A.BCH launch circular sourcing.* Available at: https://ausfashioncouncil.com/a-bch-launch-circular-sourcing/ (Accessed: 18 January 2024)

Bailey, I. (2020). Laureate finalist A.BCH has Created its own Seasons: Here's why. Available at: https://www.ragtrader.com.au/news/laureate-finalist-a-bch-has-created-its-own-seasons-here-s-why (Accessed: 17 October 2022)

Barthes, R. (1991 (1977)). *Image-music-text,* trans. Stephen Heath. New York: Hill and Wang.

Beard, N. (2011). "Defining the fashion city: Fashion capital or style centre?", in de Witt-Paul, A., & Crouch, M. (eds.), *Fashion Forward*. Oxford: Inter-Disciplinary Press, pp. 219–232.

Berg, A., Heyn, M., & Rolkins, F. (2018). "Faster fashion: How to shorten the apparel calendar". *McKinsey*, www.mckinsey.com, viewed 21 February 2020. https://www.mckinsey.com/industries/retail/our-insights/faster-fashion-how-to-shorten-the-apparel-calendar.

Black, S. (2013). *The Sustainable Fashion Handbook*. New York and London: Thames & Hudson.

Blühdorn, I. (2011). "The politics of unsustainability: COP15, post-ecologism, and the ecological paradox". *Organization & Environment*, 24(1), 34–53. https://doi.org/10.1177/1086026611402008.

Bocken, N. M. P., Niessen, L., & Short, S. W. (2022). "The sufficiency-based circular economy—An analysis of 150 companies [original research]". *Frontiers in Sustainability*, 3. https://doi.org/10.3389/frsus.2022.899289.

Butler-Kisber, L., & Poldman, T. (2010). "View of the power of visual approaches in qualitative inquiry: The use of collage making and concept mapping in experiential research". *Journal of Research Practice*, 6(2), 17 October. hp/jrp/article/download/197/232/197-Article%20Text-1489-2-10-20110408.pdf. Accessed 21 March 2020.

Cernansky, R. (2022). "Fashion is stuck in the pilot phase". *Vogue Business*, December 15. https://www.voguebusiness.com/sustainability/sustainable-fashion-is-stuck-in-pilot-phase.

Copenhagen Fashion Week. (2023). "Sustainability requirements". https://copenhagenfashionweek.com/sustainability-requirements.

Corner, J. (1999). "The agency of mapping: Speculation, critique and invention", in D. Cosgrove (ed.), *Mappings*. London: Reaktion, pp. 213–252.

Cosgrove, D. (1999). 'Introduction: Mapping meaning', in D. Cosgrove (ed.), *Mappings*. London: Reaktion, pp. 1–3.

Crewe, L. (2013). "When virtual and material worlds collide: Democratic fashion in the digital age". *Environment and Planning A: Economy and Space*, 45(4), 760–780.

Entwistle, J. (2019). "Actor-network-theory and fashion", in Rocamora, A., & Smelik, A. (eds.), *Thinking through Fashion: A Guide to Key Theorists*. London: Bloomsbury Visual Arts.

European Parliament. (2024). "Stopping greenwashing: How the EU regulates green claims". https://www.europarl.europa.eu/topics/en/article/20240111STO16722/stopping-greenwashing-how-the-eu-regulates-green-claims.

Farley, G. J., Hill, C., & Hill, C. (2015). *Sustainable Fashion: Past, Present and Future*. London: Bloomsbury Publishing.

Fenwick, T., Edwards, R., & Sawchuk, P. (2015). *Emerging Approaches to Educational Research: Tracing the Socio-material*. London: Routledge.

Flammia, C. (2020). Emily Adams Bode is making old things new—and unbelievably cool, Esquire, viewed 15 January 2023. https://www.esquire.com/style/mens-fashion/a30514171/emily-adams-bode-fashion-designer-artist-pro.

Fletcher, K. (2013). Sustainable *Fashion and Textiles: Design Journeys*. London: Routledge.

Fletcher, K., & Tham, M. (2019). Earth *Logic: Fashion Action Research Plan*. London: JJ Charitable Trust.

Gayle, L. (2019). "Trendy Danish fashion label GANNI is accused of using women in developing countries as 'marketing props' after featuring photos of 'poor brown' people as fashion show backdrops". *Mailonline*, 7 February. https://www.dailymail.co.uk/femail/article-6666297/Blogger-accuses-Ganni-fetishizing-women-developing-countries-Fashion-Week-show.html.

Hipfl, B. (2018). "Affect in media and communication studies: Potentials and assemblages". *Media and Communication*, 6(3), 5.

Holm, C. (2023). Interview with the authors, Melbourne, 2 February 2023.

Khan, A. (2020). "When 'Mea Culpa' is the best marketing". *Business of Fashion*, 12 October, https://www.businessoffashion.com/articles/sustainability/sustainability-marketing-transparency-ganni/.

Kusumasondjaja, S. (2020). "Exploring the role of visual aesthetics and presentation modality in luxury fashion brand communication on Instagram". *Journal of Fashion Marketing and Management: An International Journal*, 24(1), 15–31. https://doi.org/10.1108/JFMM-02-2019-0019.

Latour, B. (1987). *Science in Action: How to Follow Scientists and Engineers Through Society.* Cambridge, MA: Harvard University Press.

Latour, B. (2005). *Reassembling the Social: An Introduction to Actor-Network-Theory.* Oxford: Oxford University Press.

Lury, C. (2009). "Brand as assemblage". *Journal of Cultural Economy*, 2(1–2), 67–82.

Lusty, N. (2021). "Fashion futures and critical fashion studies". *Continuum*, 35(6). https://doi.org/10.1080/10304312.2021.1993568.

Matthews, R. (2015). "Contemporary fashion tastemakers: Starting conversations that matter". *Catwalk: The Journal of Fashion, Beauty, and Style*, 4(1), 51–70.

McKinsey & Company. (2023). *The State of Fashion 2024: Finding Pockets of Growth as Uncertainty Reigns*. New York, NY: McKinsey, McKinsey & Company.

Miller, D. (2001). "The poverty of morality". *Journal of Consumer Culture*, 1(2), 225–243.

Moeran, B. (2006). "More than just a fashion magazine". *Current Sociology*, 54(5), 725–744.

Moura, E. O. d., & Bispo, M. d. S. (2019). "Sociomateriality: Theories, methodology, and practice". *Canadian Journal of Administrative Sciences / Revue Canadienne des Sciences de l'Administration*, 37(3), 350–365.

Niinimäki, K. (2024). "Textiles and garment lifetimes", in Niinimäki, K. (ed.), *Recycling and Lifetime Management in the Textile and Fashion Sector*. Boca Raton: CRC Press, pp. 1–14.

Niinimäki, K., Peters, G., Dahlbo, H., Perry, P., Rissanen, T., & Gwilt, A. (2020). "The environmental price of fast fashion". *Nature Reviews Earth & Environment*, April 2020. https://doi.org/10.1038/s43017-020-0039-9.

Norris, L. (2017). "Urban prototypes: Growing local circular cloth economies". *Business History*. https://doi.org/10.1080/00076791.2017.1389902.

Nunes, J. C., Ordanini, A., & Giambastiani, G. (2021). 'The concept of authenticity: What it means to consumers'. *Journal of Marketing*, 85(4), 1–20.

Olson, E. L. (2022). "'Sustainable' marketing mixes and the paradoxical consequences of good intentions". *Journal of Business Research*, (150), 389–398. https://doi.org/10.1016/j.jbusres.2022.05.063.

Orlikowski, W. J. (2007). "Sociomaterial practices: Exploring technology at work". *Organization Studies*, 28(9), 1435–1448.

Orlikowski, W. J., & Scott, S. V. (2016). "Digital work: A research agenda", in Barbara Czarniawska (ed.), *A Research Agenda for Management and Organisation Studies.* Northampton MA: Edward Elgar Publishing, pp. 88–95.

Paulicelli, E., Manlow, V., & Wissinger, E. (2021). *The Routledge Companion to Fashion Studies*. London: Routledge.

Payne, A., & Ferrero-Regis, T. (2019). "Sustainable fashion in Australia: Raw fiber, fast fashion, and new localism", in Gwilt, A., Payne, A., & Ruthschilling, A. (eds.), *Global Perspectives on Sustainable Fashion*. London: Bloomsbury, pp. 180–190.

Raworth, K. (2017). *Doughnut Economics: Seven Ways to Think Like a 21st-Century Economist*. White River Junction, VT: Random House Business.

Richards, H. (2021). "Rethinking value: "radical transparency" in fashion". *Journal of Media & Cultural Studies (special issue: Fashion Futures),* 35(6), 914–929.

Robertson, M. (2018). *Communicating Sustainability*. London: Routledge.

Rocamora, A. (2016). "Mediatization and digital media in the field of fashion". *Fashion Theory*, 21(5), 505–522.

Rocamora, A. (2015). "Thinking through fashion: An introduction", in Rocamora, A., & Smelik, A. (eds.), *Thinking Through Fashion: A Guide to Key Theorists*. London: Bloomsbury Visual Arts, S.L.

Rocamora, A. (2018). "Mediatization and digital retail", in: Adam Geczy & Vicki Karaminas (eds.), *The End of Fashion*. London: Bloomsbury , pp. 99–112. ISBN 978-1-3500-4504-0

Rose, J. (2013). "Let me entertain you: The rise of branded marketing". *The Guardian*, 26 September. https://www.theguardian.com/media-network/2013/sep/26/branded-entertainment-content-marketing.

Sailer, A., Wilfing, H., & Straus, E. (2022). "Greenwashing and bluewashing in black friday-related sustainable fashion marketing on Instagram". *Sustainability*, 14(3), 1494.

Semprini, A. (2012 (1993)). *Marchi e mondi possibili: Un approccio semiotico al marketing della marca*. Milan: Franco Angeli.

Simmel, G. (2020 (1957)). "Fashion", in Malcolm Barnard (ed.), *Fashion Theory*. London: Routledge, pp. 92–101.

Singer, M. F., Callendar, C. L., Ma, X., & Tham, S. M. (2023). "Differences in perceived influencer authenticity: A comparison of Gen Z and Millennials' definitions of influencer authenticity during the de-influencer movement". *Online Media and Global Communication*, 2(3), 351–378.

Statista. (2020). "Most popular social networks worldwide as of October 2020, ranked by number of active users". https://www.statista.com/statistics/272014/global-social-networks-ranked-by-number-of-users/.

Statista. (2021). "Distribution of Instagram users worldwide as of October 2021, by age group". https://www.statista.com/statistics/325587/instagram-global-age-group/.

Thorpe, A. (2015). "Economic growth and the shape of sustainable fashion", in Fletcher, K., & Tham, M. (eds.), *Routledge Handbook of Sustainability and Fashion*. London: Routledge, pp. 64–73.

Turunen, L. M., & Halme, M. (2021). "Communicating actionable sustainability information to consumers: The Shades of Green instrument for fashion". *Journal of Cleaner Production*, 297, 126605.

Von Busch, O. (2022). '"What is to be sustained?": Perpetuating systemic injustices through sustainable fashion". *Sustainability: Science, Practice and Policy*, 18(1), 400–409.

Wray, A. (2019). *Bode is scaling through storytelling*, Vogue Business, viewed 15 January 2023, https://www.voguebusiness.com/fashion/bode-scaling-collections-through-storytelling.

Zero Waste Europe. (2023). "Threading a path: Towards waste prevention targets". https://zerowasteeurope.eu/wp-content/uploads/2023/07/Textiles-Waste-Prevention-Paper.pdf.

Zink, T., & Geyer, R. (2017). "Circular economy rebound". *Journal of Industrial Ecology*, 21(3), 593–602. https://doi.org/10.1111/jiec.12545.

Part 3

Communication

6 Creating sustainability by mythmaking

IKEA's advertising campaigns "The Trash Collection" and "The Life Collection"

Astrid Skjerven

Introduction

In an era of urgent environmental challenges, the business sector is faced with the challenge of finding new economic models. The United Nations Sustainable Development Goals (SDGs), launched in 2015 and to be achieved in 2030 (UN, no date) serve as universally accepted guidelines. International agreements and national jurisdiction directed towards companies and consumers are aiming to facilitate a transition to a circular economy. This makes branding ad customer communication an important tool. Being able to stand out as an environmental-friendly enterprise has become a vital issue and a competitive edge. However, sustainability has become a commercial commodity, and "greenwashing" is an increasing problem. At the same time, the dependence of economic growth is still prevailing. It is even stated explicitly in SDG 8 (UN, no date). In this way both public authorities and companies are facing a wicked problem.

As a leading global brand in home furnishings and the world's biggest furniture retailer, IKEA is a company whose response to the changed societal conditions, and its communication with the customers, is of vital importance. To understand the mechanisms of green commissioning, IKEA Norway's advertising campaign "The Trash Collection", and its follow-up "The Life Collection" which were explicitly directed towards the SDGs, has therefore been chosen as a case.

The chapter analyses the underlying intention of the campaign, its impact, and the role of the customers. In particular, the narrative and mythological means used to influence the consumers have been investigated.

The concept and the revised strategy

IKEA is a company that is directed towards families and life in the home. It describes itself as "a value-based company which is passionately engaged in life in the home" (IKEA, 2022). Its vision is "to create a better everyday for the many people, and this influences everything we do. From the products we make to the materials we use, the services we offer, how we live together, and the ideas we share" (IKEA, 2022). Its brand strength is exceptionally high.[1] Its reputation is

DOI: 10.4324/9781003392705-10

built on the founder Ingvar Kamprad's vision and business concept of offering products fit for a contemporary and democratic lifestyle, accessibility, rational production, and optimal exploitation of materials (Torekull, 1999). The story has been incessantly repeated by Kamprad himself and the IKEA staff and has become a narrative of mythological character, both for the customers and for the corporate culture.[2] The brand has become a symbol of the Swedish welfare state, which by its development into a global enterprise, has become accessible worldwide. The narrative has been carefully maintained and updated and is still a basis for the company's strategic choices. With its emphasis on optimal utilisation of materials, accessibility for most people, and democratic values, it has a certain affinity with the SDGs. At the same time, IKEA is dependent on economic growth within a capitalistic political system. The company needs to increase its sales figures for the product range, which consists of cheap products that often are discarded and replaced with new items within a short time. In fact, the company is infamous for its contribution to increasing consumption and a "use and discard" mentality. In the new era of a green transition, it is vital to counteract this by changes in production, retail, and market communication as well as consumer behaviour.

In 2012, three years before the SDGs were launched, IKEA started on the journey of a more circular economic model. Kamprad's narrative constituted a foundational source of inspiration. It was implemented through all the different steps of the IKEA value chain: from the sourcing of raw materials to the production and transportation of IKEA products (Edvardsson & Sebhatu, 2021). It was based on IKEA's first strategy that explicitly was directed towards issues of sustainability, the *People & Planet Positive Strategy*, which had already been launched in 2012. In 2018, as a consequence of the SDGs, a revised version was launched, where the goals had been included (IKEA, 2018). It comprised the transformation of not only the IKEA business and the industries in the IKEA value chain but also everyday life in the home for its customers (IKEA SR, 2018), by facilitating a lifestyle and identity that corresponded with the SDGs. The implementation was led by the company's ambitious CEOs and followed up by the staff. The strategy has since been reviewed annually to secure alignment with the total IKEA strategic framework and further pursued statistically in the annual *Sustainability Reports*. The strategy of 2018 signalled an ambition to transfer to a greener business model, which was strengthened in the revised strategy of 2022. It had the motto "Welcome 2030", thereby explicitly referring to the SDGs, which were going to be achieved within that year.

The brand as myth

Myths are mostly regarded as phenomena that belong to Antiquity. In our days, the term is mostly used about what is believed to be false conceptions of reality that need to be revealed and discarded. This conception has prevented a more nuanced analysis of their significance. The most influential contributor to the role of the myth in modern society is the French philosopher, Roland Barthes. In 1957, he defined a myth as a historically dependent and intentional story that converts reality into language and a system of communication (Barthes, 1957). He claimed that there exists a modern version that takes place in everyday life. Its aim is to preserve the norms and political and economic interests of the ruling class, the bourgeoisie. Historically founded stories are distorted in a way that makes them appear as evident and therefore indisputable truths: "history is converted into nature" (Barthes, 1957). The myth consumer is subjected to their imperative character and intentional force, which leaves no immediate space for doubt. The myth makers are often commercial enterprises who through their advertisements mediate narratives that express the excellence of a certain product in order to make the myth consumer purchase it (Barthes, 1957). This view has been extended and modified by the Danish-American philosopher Nina Rosenstand (1981). She agrees with Barthes that the modern, mostly commercially founded myth plays a major role in our everyday lives, in the same way as movies do. But she also claims that like in ancient times, the myth might represent an ideal truth. It is a model of the world seen from a specific attitude. This means that there is a certain discrepancy between myth and reality. Although created by and to the benefit of the myth maker, the myth consumer may also influence its grade of reality by their reaction to it, for instance, by choosing to go to the cinema to see a particular movie or purchase a product.

Although written in the last century, these interpretations display the vital importance of consumption in today's consumer culture, which can be defined as "a culture of the use and appropriation of objects or things" (Lury, 2011). One can even argue, like the art historian Hal Foster, that we live in a seamless economic system where the subject, i.e., the consumer, has been objectified and thereby made unable to make critical choices (Foster, 2002). He thereby continues the dystopic view of the consumer society as defined by the philosopher Jean Baudrillard (1996). A more pragmatic view is put forward by the sociologist Dale Southerton. He states that consumption occurs not so much for the purpose of purchasing needed objects, but to take part in meaningful societal practices and the display of lifestyles (Southerton, 2020). Contrary to Foster, he argues that consumer choices are the outcome of an individual's values and attitudes. The individual is presented as a sovereign consumer, where consumption is largely a matter of personal decision-making within commercial markets that, in turn, respond to consumer demands and provide a range of product choices from which to shape their lifestyle. To change, e.g., towards more sustainable ways of life, requires changes in the attitudes that shape, and values that frame consumer choices. This, in turn, corresponds with the role of the myth-consumer as interpreted by Rosen stand's view that the myth consumer can act within a given framework.

Transferred to our own societal situation of the SDGs and the case of IKEA, this means that what the company mediates through the myths they create through their marketing. They work as wished future realities that can only be fulfilled by the interplay between the company and its customers. The decision-makers and other staff at IKEA as well as the customers can influence the realisation of the company's vision by choosing how to react, purchase, and discard. In this way, IKEA's market communication is playing a significant role in shaping the society and its possible achievement of the SDGs.

The Trash Collection

Since the change of strategy in 2012 and revised in 2015, there has been a corresponding shift in the way of communication towards the customers. The most visible efforts are found in the annual catalogues. It displayed not only furniture in various kinds of rooms but also happy families of diverse ethnicity in their homely environment made up of IKEA objects (https://ikeamuseum.com/en, 2023). The IKEA logo was also given a less important role in the visual composition. In this way, the narrative had been made the main sales argument, displacing the brand and its products. The company thereby displayed its awareness of the importance of mediating narratives which people could make their own and thereby shape their lifestyle by purchasing IKEA products (Figure 6.1).

Figure 6.1 Front page of the IKEA catalogue 2016.

Following the strategy of its mother firm, IKEA Norway started the process of adapting to more environmental-friendly ways of running its business, led by the then CEO Clare Rodgers (2020). Like other national branches of the company, it had implemented three initiatives: an offer to buy back used products, establishing a second-hand section at the warehouses, and offering reserve parts available for internet purchase. In this way, the customers had been encouraged to make more sustainable choices.

In 2018 IKEA Norway engaged the country's biggest communication agency TRY as their main advertising partner. This signalled a shift in and a higher prioritisation of market communication. TRY's first engagement was to do a makeover of the firm's profile to display the company's environmentally friendly offers to the customers. The slogan "Welcome 2030", which explicitly referred to the time of fulfilment of the SDGs, constituted the brief for the commission (Sandø, 2023). The campaign was the result of a long discussion process between IKEA and TRY. According to TRY, the management at IKEA had little awareness of the company's bad reputation. They therefore had to convince its representatives to make a campaign that informed not only about the company's environmental offers but also the consumers' perception of it (Contagious, 2021). This reflects how attached the staff was to the IKEA narrative. The first major task TRY focused on was to develop an advertising campaign, which had its main goal "to inform about concrete measures that IKEA does to help the customers throw away less" (https://kampanje.com/reklame…). Implicitly, this meant a special focus on Goal 12, Responsible Consumption and Production, and 13 Climate Action.

In 2021, the lavish advertising campaign "The Trash Collection" was rolled out. To optimise the result, the film studio Aparent had been hired to shoot the living and still images (Kreativt Forum, 2021). The story to be told was that reuse instead of throwing away furniture would reduce the climate footprint. The production was made as a documentary, where the objects, 16 in all, were continuously filmed and photographed. The advertisements displayed the discarded products as they were found in the streets or containers and waste management facilities, accompanied by a short text that told where they were picked up, what had been done to refurbish them, and that they could be purchased in the IKEA's second-hand shops at prices lower than those of the new items. As such, the items constituted an extension of the company's sustainable product range, made available in the already-existing second-hand shops at IKEA-warehouses (Figures 6.2 and 6.3).

The campaign was highly controversial in its raw brutality, both in content and form. The worn-down furniture and its filthy surroundings were displayed in all its horror, with the soundtrack of the Joe Tex old blues hit from 1964 with the telling title "Hold on to what you got". The campaign constituted a complete break with the appealing, idyllic family interiors in bright colours, which were the well-known visual expression for IKEA. TRY describes the campaign as "disruptive" (Sandø, 2023). It resembled a film documentary. The logo was placed discretely at the bottom of the ad. The campaign signalled the company's offer to facilitate durability and reuse of their products for the customers. The daring form of the campaign was inspired by street art and on contemporary pictorial art, which often contains

Figure 6.2 IKEA's advertising campaign "The Trash Collection" 2021. (*Billy*.)

critical comments on waste. The use of an English title underlines the distance to everyday life in Norway, but also signals its global relevance. The exclusivity was further underlined by calling the objects a collection, referring to the fact that this was a selection of "one-off" objects with an individual history. The texts of the ads described their provenience, a practice that is usual for the registration of precious objects and works of art. In this way, the objects were elevated to the status of unique, highly estimated pieces that would be taken care of for generations. To the customers, it offered the opportunity to stand out as being part of an avant-garde in the matter of environmental-friendly consumer behaviour.

The solution was initially met with sceptic questions by the IKEA staff: "Why do you have to call it a collection?" (Sandø, 2023). This indicates that the staff did not fully realise the necessity of making a break with the customers' view of the company's products and thereby transform the current myth.

The Life Collection

Based on the positive results and the international attention of the Trash Collection campaign, the success was followed up by a new series of ads in 2022. It was directed both towards the national and the international market. "The Life Collection" depicted products that were in good shape but no longer needed and therefore had been discarded, due to changed life situations like childbirth, divorce, disease, and the like. The series had subtitles like "The Temporary Collection", "The Divorce Collection", and "The Death Collection" (IKEA, 2022). The objects were collected with the help of real estate agents, funeral homes and other enterprises that dealt with such situations. They were displayed in a way that dramatised

Figure 6.3 IKEA's advertising campaign "The Trash Collection" 2021. (*Franklin.*)

the situation, often in a gloomy light. This was different from the previous campaign as well as the IKEA tradition. The accompanying soundtrack was the pop group Simple Minds' sentimental hit "Don't you forget about me". The text told the history of each object in an emotional way and informed that the objects could be purchased in IKEA's second-hand shops. While the first campaign appealed to feelings of social responsibility and the wish to contribute to a green future, the second appealed to intimate personal feelings related to common family situations. The moving and slightly sentimental narratives had similarities with popular

Figure 6.4 IKEA's advertising campaign "The Life Collection" 2022. (*Toledo.*)

contemporary motion pictures in the "drama" genre. The campaign was just as shocking but less provocative than the former, leaving the recipient in a sentimental and irrational state of mind. It invited the customers to care for the members of their family and thereby for the environment, in particular SDG 3 *Good Health and Well-Being* (Figure 6.4).

The reception

Displaying a company's discarded products made available for repurchase and reuse, the Trash Collection campaign was one of the earliest of its kind. The public impact of the campaign was measured as strong, particularly among people between the age of 18 and 35 (Kantar, 2021). The provocative form also had few precursors. One of the most famous examples is Oliviero Toscanis's advertisements in the 1990s for the Italian clothing company Benetton, which displayed people with deadly diseases like AIDS surrounded by shocked family members and friends (Duffy, 2017). It was thereby throwing light on an urgent societal problem in a surprising and shocking way. Combined with Benetto's logo, it can be interpreted as either an example of the company's societal concern or a striking example of greenwashing. In the design community, the IKEA campaign went viral. This was due to its daring content and form, described as: "In its new campaign IKEA has chosen to display their products in a brutal and honest way" (Kreativt Forum, 2021). The international attention was considerable. In 2021, TRY was awarded the prestigious Cannes Gold Lion in the category of Print & Publishing for the campaign (https://www.kreativtforum.no/artikler/nyheter/gull-og-solv-til-try-og-ikea-i-cannes). Additionally, it was nominated in the subcategory of Cultural Insight and Market Disruption (Kreativt Forum, 2022). The campaign also got attention from the global IKEA community, among others in the USA (Sandø, 2023). National adaptations of it were implemented in Portugal, Denmark, and other countries. In this way, IKEA Norway had paved the way for others to follow.

"The Life Collection" received less attention in the design community, and its impact was not quite as strong. It was described as a maintenance of the effect of the former campaign, both as regards the number of resell and buy-back (Kantar, 2021). Still, in 2023, it received the Gold Lion of Print & Publishing in Cannes, as The Trash Collection did the previous year (Sandø, 2023).

The first campaign probably also helped IKEA to become second in the Norway branch of The International Sustainable Brand Index, a position that it maintained until 2022, when there was no campaign and they were surpassed by four companies, among those its most fierce competitors, the website for sales of used objects Finn.no and the low-price retail chain Clas Ohlson (https://www.sb-index.com/norway).

Reflections

The minimal number of products that were advertised and offered for sale had no impact on the multibillion turnover of IKEA and was not meant to be so. It was an investment in the company's future reputation by communicating values that corresponded with the SDGs and encouraged a change of lifestyle. But by inviting customers to the small second-hand stores in the warehouses, the campaigns could easily lead to the purchase of brand items from the regular product range and thereby increased consumption. The campaign can therefore rightfully be claimed to be a case of "greenwashing". The CEO of IKEA's international franchise company INGKO Group, Jesper Brodin, has argued that "greenwashing is less dangerous than silence" (Bloomberg TV, November 9, 2021). By this statement, he was pointing to the fact that such messages, however false, can make us aware of the importance of the topic and influence our attitudes and actions. On the other hand, there is the *Rebound* effect, meaning that people are buying more of a product if they have been convinced that it is sustainable (Zink & Geyer, 2017). It is unclear whether this fact has been considered by IKEA.

The elephant in the room is the economic system, the dependence of growth. A recent SWOT analysis displays that IKEA is strong in customer knowledge, supply chain integration, innovations to drive costs down, and brand reputation, but is facing intensifying competition. The opportunities are described as further expansion into developing countries, growing online sales, and expansion to the grocery markers.[3] This means that the company has to expand in some way, either by a broader product range or by expanding the market to the Global South, which will inevitably lead to exporting the problem of consumption and discard behaviour to one more part of the world.

Although attempting to pave the way for a more circular economy, IKEA is far from being able to implement it. The aim to "make sustainability affordable" for the customers (Contagious, 2021) might become a competitive edge in the future when an adaptation to a more sustainable development has been further developed but does not constitute a valid business model under the current economic conditions. Still, according to IKEA Norway's Director of Sustainability Siri Norhagen, the goal of becoming 100% climate positive and circular in 2030 is maintained (https://www.kom24.no/green-camp-ikea-siri-norhagen/ikea-onsker-velkommen-til-2030/481373). This means that the company has continued to be faithful to the SDGs, in spite of the challenges it comprises. At the same time, it mirrors the self-contradictions of the SDGs.

IKEA's insistence on its strategy might be interpreted as an adaptation to and preparation for operating under conditions where scarcity of resources and the necessity of a revised business model is a matter of survival. In this way it will also be equipped with means to compete with other companies, and to secure a good reputation. On the other hand, to "make sustainability affordable" also functions as a sales argument towards the customers that might lead to increased consumption.

In the attempt to secure the future existence of the company in a time of decreasing natural resources, increasing competition, and changing market demands, the advertisement campaigns "The Trash Collection" and "The Life Collection" serve as a fruitful mythological lens. It constitutes a conceptual space that enables IKEA to communicate narratives of a meaningful life for its customers within the framework of the SDGs and at the same time by involve them in the transformation process. It displays that the company and the consumers have shared interests in securing the future in an environmental-friendly way outside the conflicts in the real world. For the company, its staff, and the consumers, the campaigns seen as myths is an incitement to work together for a sustainable future. On the other hand, it might be regarded as a sophisticated way of greenwashing: a false conception fabricated by IKEA to increase sales figures and improve its reputation that needs to be revealed. This would, however, mean that the conceptual space of the myth would disappear, which would be a loss of a common imaginary sphere and the opportunity to change attitudes.

Notes

1 In 2022, it was measured to 83.2 out of 100 points, according to Brand Strength Index. (16.06.2022 https://brandfinance.com/press-releases/swedish-brands-return-to-brand-value-growth-despite-continued-market-turbulence).
2 Although the term originated in Greek antiquity, myths have existed in most human cultures since pre-ancient times. The term has many definitions and is used in various academic disciplines. It can loosely be described as an oral narrative concerning basic human matters, like religion, ethics, and folklore (Wikipedia).
3 Strategic Management Insight (2023) *SWOT analysis of IKEA 2023*. https://strategicmanagementinsight.com/swot-analyses/ikea-swot-analysis/ (Retrieved 10.04.23).

References

Barthes, R. (2009) [1957]. *Mythologies*. London: Vintage.
Baudrillard, J. (1996). *The System of Objects*. London: Verso.

Bloomberg TV. (2021). November 9, 2021.

Contagious. (2021). Insight & Strategy: Ikea Trash Collection (PDF).

Duffy, E.N. (2017). "Benetton's Most Controversial Campaigns". https://www.vogue.co.uk/gallery/benettons-best-advertising-campaigns (Retrieved 09.04.23).

Edvardsson, B. & Enquist, B. (2021). *Values-based Service for Sustainable Business: Lessons from IKEA*. London: Routledge.

Foster, H. (2002). *Design and Crime (and Other Diatribes)*. London: Verso.

https://about.ikea.com/en/newsroom/2020/02/27/breaking-the-trend-ikea-reports-a-decrease-in-climate-footprint (Retrieved 03.04.23).

https://ikeamuseum.com/en. 2023. (Retrieved 03.04.23).

https://ikeamuseum.com/en/digital/ikea-catalogues-through-the-ages/2010s-ikea-catalogues/2015-ikea-catalogue/ (Retrieved 03.04.23).

https://kampanje.com/reklame/2021/06/try-med-ny-ikea-kolleksjon/ (Retrieved 17.12.2022).

https://www.ikea.com/no/no/campaigns/the-life-collection-2022-pub84689c91 (Retrieved 21.12.22).

https://www.kom24.no/aparent-babyboom-cannes-lions-2023/try-vant-norges-forste-gull-i-cannes/623828?utm_campaign=TRY%20nyhetsbrev&utm_medium=email&_hsmi=264311635&_hsenc=p2ANqtz-8RFFXrxXXjKYURTbPpc58TIWxEhQ43097kBwNkbqGi_vXOJDIBZpKFdiMs00VqDKEL8HmRRetZP2jL03LdFx03RaMjXw&utm_content=264311635&utm_source=hs_email (Retrieved 23.07.23).

IKEA. (2018). *People & Planet Positive: IKEA Sustainability Strategy: IKEA Systems B.V.* https://www.ikea.com/ca/en/files/pdf/ec/0c/ec0cbb98/ikea_people_planet_positive_june2018_a.pdf (Retrieved 03.04.23)

IKEA. (2019). Sustainability Report. https://www.ikea.com/global/en/our-business/reports/sustainability-report-fy19-200227/

IKEA. (2022). Årsmelding og Årsregnskap 2021 (PDF). https://www.ikea.com/no/no/files/pdf/75/12/751246f5/2400-ikea-as-fy21.pdf.

Kantar. (2021). *Trash Collection ad tested July 2021* (PDF).

Kreativt Forum. (2021). https://www.kreativtforum.no/arbeider/the-trash-collection-2021 (Retrieved 21.12.22).

Kreativt Forum. (2022). https://www.kreativtforum.no/artikler/nyheter/cannes-gull-til-try-og-ikea (Retrieved 22.12.22).

Lury, C. (2011). *Consumer Culture*. 2nd ed. London: Polity.

Rodgers, C. (2020). Green Branding of IKEA: Without Greenwashing (PDF of lecture at Oslo Metropolitan University 14.02.20).

Rosenstand, N. (1981). *Mytebegrebet*. København: Gad.

Sandø, T. (2023). Interview with the Account Director of Try (26.01.23).

Southerton, D. (2020). *Time, Consumption and the Coordination of Everyday Life*. London: Palgrave Macmillan.

Torekull, B. (1999). *Leading by Design: The IKEA Story*. London: Harper Business.

UN. (no date). The 17 Goals. https://sdgs.un.org/goals

Zink, T. & Geyer, R. (2017). "Circular economy Rebound". *Journal of Industrial Ecology* 21:3, 593–601.

7 Cultivating responsibility through Instagram

Fashion, revolution, and narrative

Paige Street

Introduction: fashion and structural injustice

The study of responsibility for structural injustice has been an ongoing field of research in and beyond the fashion industry. Fashion is a useful industry to study responsibility because it occupies a liminal position between public and private life, where the personal and everyday practices of dress are implicated in a global network of capital. An analysis of the fashion supply chain provides a view on the raced, gendered, and classed division of labour with which questions of responsibility are concerned. The fashion supply chain operates on a 'vertically disintegrated' model, which separates production markets from consumption markets (Kumar, 2020, p. 4). This model is commonly viewed as a split between high production in the Global South and high consumption in the Global North (Brooks, 2015, p. 4). Value accumulation occurs at each 'stage' of the supply chain through labour-intensive work which pushes power to the Global North and extracts power from the Global South. Understanding fashion's operations in this way helps to frame an understanding of injustice as *structural*, whereby cases of exploitation and extraction in the Global South are not deviations from an otherwise fair system, but endemic to how fashion operates (Garwood, 2011, p. 55).

The foundation of this study is informed by the narratives of responsibility that emerged following the Rana Plaza factory collapse on April 24, 2013. The collapse occurred in Dhaka, Bangladesh, and was one of the deadliest manufacturing disasters in history (Kumar, 2020, p. 3), killing over 1,100 workers and injuring thousands more, most of whom were young women (Safi & Rushe, 2018). Found among the rubble of the eight-storey building were garments sold by fast-fashion brands, headquartered, and selling predominantly into the markets of the Global North. Rana Plaza ignited narratives of responsibility around the world which shifted blame between governments, corporations and consumers. In Bangladesh, legal attributions of responsibility formally charged 38 people with murder in connection to the collapse (Reuters, 2018) and at production sites around the world, women workers led efforts to transform the conditions of garment work (Quayyum, 2019). In the Global North, attention quickly turned to the responsibility of global corporations and fast-fashion consumers who were implicated in the disaster via their innocuous, everyday actions of getting dressed. For corporations,

DOI: 10.4324/9781003392705-11

Rana Plaza accelerated interest in corporate social responsibility as both a business model (Benedetto, 2017, p. 251) and as part of the marketing and communications between fashion brands and their consumers (Owen & Napoli, 2021). In parallel, consumers were agitated to 'shop responsibly' via the markets of the ethical fashion industry which situated itself as an antithesis to fast-fashion (Khan, 2016, p. 7). Consequently, part of the immediate aftermath of Rana Plaza was an anti-fast fashion scrutiny that echoed some of the activist narratives championed in the 1990s but featured more moral and neoliberal inflections. These narratives reconfigured 'older critical discourses whose targets have been corporate greed' to instead focus on individual consumers themselves (Khan, 2016, p. 7).

Fashion Revolution is one such organisation which was founded in response to Rana Plaza. The organisation uses the social media platform, Instagram, to call consumers to attention on the responsibility they have in addressing the conditions in which their clothes were made. Fashion Revolution's digital messaging is often led by its use of hashtags; the *#WhoMadeMyClothes* (WMMC) campaign and the *#LovedClothesLast* (LCL) campaign are two of its most popular and form the basis of my analysis in this chapter. In doing so, I intend to analyse how structural injustice and consumer responsibility are framed and consider how the digital context of Instagram impacts this narrative. What this chapter calls 'narratives of responsibility' are the stories of structural injustice which serve to cultivate a response among an audience. Following Schiff (2014), this response entails more than just an acknowledgement of one's involvement in structural injustice, but a more nuanced and affective 'disposition toward responsiveness' (Schiff, 2014, p. 1). Narratives that cultivate this disposition highlight the urgency of responsiveness and frame injustices in a way that 'demands a response' (Schiff, 2014, p. 20). What these narratives must inevitably contend with is the struggle to visualise injustice in a way that cultivates a response and which 'safeguards the legitimacy', voice and agency of Others (Chouliaraki, 2013, p. 54).

Instagram as a fashionable and political space

Whether by design or by coincidental dovetailing with the fashion industry's attention to the role of consumers in driving change, the Instagram platform is frequently adopted as a space for consumer-directed activism. Social media sites present a particular challenge for responsibility-taking, because of the way in which activism and political discourses are mediated alongside and within other more personal, commercial and algorithmic contexts. For example, while social media is one of the primary ways in which people read and access news and current affairs stories (Vorhaus, 2020), and the increased uptake of digital activism politicises the processes of being online, these platforms also have long-standing commercial interests and a fashionable cachet which favours paid advertisements. For this reason, it is important that digital media research also studies the context in which they exist; the embedded mechanisms and logics of social media platforms have implications for how users read, understand, and reproduce politics online and in everyday life (Highfield, 2016).

The Instagram platform has over 2 billion active users every month (Dean, 2024) and its commercial interests have lent themselves neatly to those of the fashion industry. Instagram is largely image-based and trend-focused and has adopted several e-commerce possibilities that make it easily 'shoppable' (Caliandro & Graham, 2020, p. 2). Fashion scholarship has been attentive to the fashion industry's use of Instagram as a marketing tool for branding (Cukul, 2015) and to sell fashionable lifestyles through the advent of the 'influencer' (Abidin, 2016). The kind of fashion communications and content which is commonly posted on Instagram has been found to make 'self-aestheticisation' (de Perthius & Findlay, 2019, p. 223) and self-branding possible through online identity creation and performance. The notion that *anyone* can communicate fashion online has created a market for user-generated content that is regularly concerned with ideas of authenticity and realness. However, this practice also requires that individuals draw on 'market logics to brand themselves' (Duffy, 2017, p. 6) and thus Instagram has been found to predominantly reproduce (de Perthius & Findlay, 2019) or even strengthen (Tolentino, 2019), the normative and exploitative structure of fashion.

The Instagram platform is also a space for activist communication. Political messages on social media are described as forms of 'everyday politics' (Highfield, 2016). While most digital media scholarship has favoured X (formerly Twitter) for the study of political activism, a growing body of literature recognises Instagram as an important platform for both personal-political expressions and collective political mobilisation (Highfield, 2016). The digital context and methods of this study follow Amgott (2018) to suggest a digitally-literate approach to critically reading online texts and interpreting online media. This involves accessing and analysing digitally native objects, such as Instagram posts, to understand the narratives and cultures of which they are a part of. Instagram activism uses images as symbols of solidarity, weaponises hashtag campaigns to shape social and industrial discourse, and forms digital 'movements' through its widespread reach (Hill, 2013, p. 58). Thus, the platform can be used to raise awareness of injustices and cultivate a sense of responsiveness among large audiences.

The fashion revolution case study

Fashion Revolution was founded in the United Kingdom by fashion industry insiders, Orsola de Castro and Carry Somers in 2013. The organisation emerged in response to the Rana Plaza factory collapse and Fashion Revolution has since renamed the anniversary of the disaster, Fashion Revolution Day. The organisation leverages social media, especially Instagram, to spread its message around the world. Fashion Revolution's Instagram page, @fash_rev, is an accessible platform that uses the language of social justice, mainstream feminism, environmentalism, and consumption politics to share information about global injustices in the fashion industry. Its messaging has a generally friendly tone and attempts to mobilise action against injustices by educating and inspiring its audiences to make 'positive changes' (FR, 2023a).

Fashion Revolution is made 'global' through its community of followers, who reshare and reproduce online. Fashion Revolution describes itself as the largest fashion activism movement in the world (FR, 2023a) and its popularity has mainstreamed certain forms of activism within the industry. Rather than challenging some of the commercial logics of Instagram communication which have been traditionally used to encourage consumption, Fashion Revolution can be seen to be appropriating prevalent Instagram fashion communication practices to advance its messaging. The organisation uses selfies, user-generated content, and tagged (@) branded content as part of its activism. By aligning itself with these practices on Instagram, Fashion Revolution's campaigns blend a critique with a reinforcement of fashionable Instagram cultures. The fact that this digital fashion culture is often portrayed as catering to young, white, female consumers has important implications for the narratives of responsibility that exist within it. Fashion Revolution has been found to draw on discourses of mainstream feminism and female solidarity within fashion, offering consumers a platform to engage in feminist politics online (Horton & Street, 2021). By extension, it's digital messaging consistently endorses a 'feminisation of responsibility' that frames a young female consumer as the assumed audience (Horton et al., 2022; Street, 2022). Young women's bodies are made highly visible in Fashion Revolution's Instagram posts, with the gendered aesthetics, language, and assumptions about consumers reinforcing this visibility and feminisation (Street, 2022).

I turn now to analyse the two campaigns and conclude by reflecting on the role of the campaigns in challenging or reinforcing the broader structures of the fashion system.

Who made my clothes?

Fashion Revolution's best-known campaign, Who Made My Clothes?, deployed via the hashtag *#WhoMadeMyClothes*?, encourages consumers to post photos of themselves and tag the brands of the clothes they are wearing, asking the question, 'who made my clothes?'. FR provide printable resources to hold in these images, and as of 2024, the campaign has received more than 1 million public posts on Instagram from both Fashion Revolution and other users participating in the campaign. The question works as a personal frame to stand in for a discussion on the conditions of garment work.

The Who Made My Clothes? campaign is complemented by several other hashtag campaigns that make up Fashion Revolution's digital outreach. These include #WhatsInMyClothes?, which focuses on fashion fibres and environmental impact, and #WhoMadeMyJewellery?, which addresses the origins of jewellery. Fashion Revolution has also introduced the I Made Your Clothes campaign in response, urging brands to share stories of their garment workers. This campaign, marked by the hashtag *#IMadeYourClothes*, has generated around 270,000 public posts on Instagram (as of 2024). It encourages brands to showcase their workers holding an I Made Your Clothes poster, promoting supply chain to promote transparency. The staging of the image—the worker holding up a branded Fashion

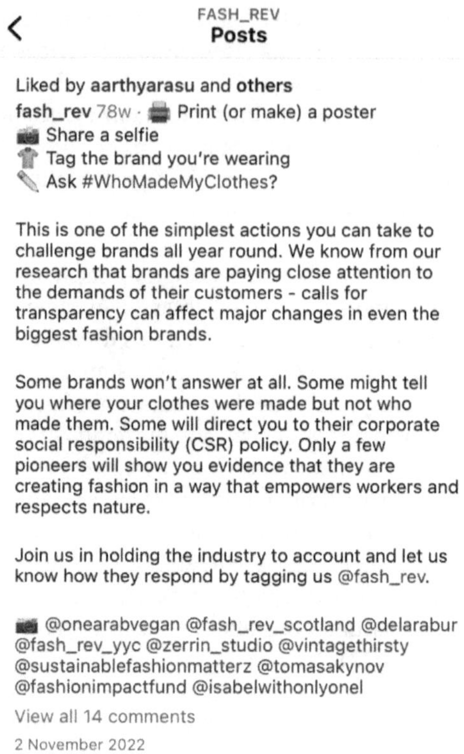
FASH_REV
Posts

Liked by **aarthyarasu** and **others**
fash_rev 78w · Print (or make) a poster
Share a selfie
Tag the brand you're wearing
Ask #WhoMadeMyClothes?

This is one of the simplest actions you can take to challenge brands all year round. We know from our research that brands are paying close attention to the demands of their customers - calls for transparency can affect major changes in even the biggest fashion brands.

Some brands won't answer at all. Some might tell you where your clothes were made but not who made them. Some will direct you to their corporate social responsibility (CSR) policy. Only a few pioneers will show you evidence that they are creating fashion in a way that empowers workers and respects nature.

Join us in holding the industry to account and let us know how they respond by tagging us @fash_rev.

@onearabvegan @fash_rev_scotland @delarabur @fash_rev_yyc @zerrin_studio @vintagethirsty @sustainablefashionmatterz @tomasakynov @fashionimpactfund @isabelwithonlyonel
View all 14 comments
2 November 2022

Figure 7.1 Screenshot of caption on @fash_rev Instagram post featuring #WhoMadeMyClothes?

Revolution poster in English—rebrands the garment worker away from narratives of exploitation (FR, 2017). Typically, brands that already prioritise ethics are the ones responding to the question of 'who made my clothes?', providing them the added benefit good press and social media engagement.

Figure 7.1 is an image of the caption on a Fashion Revolution Instagram post from November 2, 2022 (FR, 2022). The image on the post features a diverse range of people holding up 'who made my clothes?' posters. Fashion Revolution explains how to engage in the campaign and identify consumers as powerful because 'brands are paying close attention' to their demands. The caption continues with 'only a few pioneers will show you evidence that they are creating fashion in a way that empowers workers and respects nature' and finishes with a reminder to tag the @fash_rev Instagram account when brands reply. The caption is filled with agreeable 'emojis' and praise for the campaign, as well as a number of comments from the Instagram accounts of fashion brands promoting their own products and transparency practices.

While the Who Made My Clothes? Campaign can be seen to bring about awareness for supply chain transparency, it runs unsteadily on two assumptions: that consumers have a right/claim to the people who made their clothes, and that what brands say in response is accurate and truthful. Fashion Revolution suggest that by asking the question of 'who made my clothes?', consumers can 'get to know the people behind every piece of clothing' (Fashion Revolution, 2016). This draws on a long history of the use of the plight of the garment worker as a 'script of global capitalism' (Siddiqi, 2009, p. 156) to represent injustices 'quickly and credibly' (Brooks, 2007, p. xxvi). While older reproductions of the emblem of the garment worker might have depicted her as a suffering victim of capitalism, Fashion Revolution's campaign frames garment workers as content and even empowered by their subject position. The bodies, labour, and stories of garment workers are used by the campaign as photorealistic validation (Chouliaraki, 2013, p. 61) to prove that *someone* did make our clothes, *and* that they are happy and empowered doing so. This strategy cultivates responsiveness through a portrayal of workers as 'people like "us"' (Chouliaraki, 2013, p. 57).

The relationship between workers and consumers, and the frequent defaulting of these subjects as female, is used to evoke notions of a 'global sisterhood' in which engagement in the Who Made My Clothes? Campaign is the baseline for political solidarity. Fashion Revolution draw on quotes such as 'you cannot exploit women in one country to empower them in another' (FR, 2018a) to frame fashion as a 'feminist issue' (Press, 2017) because of the empirical presence of women in both production and consumption. These messages rightly prompt consumers to view the supply chain as a space of personal and political connections, highlighting 'unjust patterns of relationship[s]' (Khader, 2017, p. 608) among women. This is important, because the supply chain is the grounds on which responsibility is shared, and a 'cross-cultural, international politics of solidarity' (Mohanty, 2003, p. 140) among women would be revolutionary. However, this solidarity avoids attention at the broader institutional, corporate contexts shaping these relationships to instead draw a line between those exploited by fashion and those empowered by it.

Political narratives which focus on the empowerment of the consumer are troubling because the cultivation of responsiveness becomes an act of self-branding, where consumers are expected to publicly identify as politically attuned, to feel legitimised. This script is criticised in feminist literature for creating uncomfortable tensions at the point where contemporary logics of girl power in the Global North intersect with international development narratives that focus on 'empowering girls' (Banet-Weiser, 2015, p. 182). Fashion Revolution leverages this idea to create a *market* for empowerment which not only adds to claims of transnational solidarity but also separates garment workers in an evolutionary framing that reinforces the notion of production markets as less advanced. The practice of engaging in the Who Made My Clothes? campaign becomes a way of 'doing feminism' via a malleable assemblage of transnational discourses attempting to connect consumers and garment workers in solidarity but ultimately granting consumers more political power.

While the Who Made My Clothes? Campaign brings awareness to supply chain transparency, Fashion Revolution also addresses the environmental impact of clothing through its Loved Clothes Last (*#LovedClothesLast*) campaign. This campaign encourages consumers to consider the environmental implications of their clothing choices beyond just the production phase.

Loved clothes last

The Loved Clothes Last campaign is used to promote awareness of the environmental impacts of the use phase of a garment's life. The campaign provides tips on how to repair clothing and invites consumers to post photos of their favourite garments in a 'clothing love story'.

Figure 7.2 is an image of an Instagram post by Fashion Revolution on August 28, 2023 (FR, 2023b). It explains how to participate in the Loved Clothes Last Campaign and begins with a quote from Fashion Revolution co-founder, Orsola de Castro, 'the most sustainable garment is the one already in your wardrobe'. The caption encourages consumers to 'fall in love' with clothes again and that 'there's something transformation in forming a committed relationship with the clothes you already own'. The final sentence of the caption asks consumers to take a photo of themselves in their favourite item and 'share it' by using *#LovedClothesLast.*

The logics of the Loved Clothes Last build off findings from lifecycle analysis data which identify the use and laundering of a garment as one of the most resource and energy-intensive part of garment's life (Fletcher, 2014). The posts associated to this campaign are more informative, filled with statistics and empirical data on emissions reductions or rates of consumption. Statistics like 'doubling the useful life of clothing from one year to two years reduces the emissions over the year by 24%' (FR, 2018b) give its messaging empirical credibility. The arc of the campaign moves from material to symbolic as the domestic labour of clothing care practices turn to call on the affective labour of *caring* for clothes.

The clothing love stories shared by Fashion Revolution's followers reflect clothing's ability to hold memory, lives, aspirations, identity, and history. Material

Figure 7.2 Screenshot of @fash_rev Instagram featuring #LovedClothesLast.

culture studies concur on this practice of commodity attachment as part of the way clothes 'act' on us (Spivak, 2014). Holgar (2019) found sharing stories of garments is a way to cultivate a stronger attachment too them, fostering a more sustainable relationship to clothing. When the garment holds such power, it reflects a sort of affect back on the wearer – and the ability to feel something for what you own generates a sort of reciprocity, where 'we can love our clothes, and maybe they can love us back' (Spivak, 2014). This logic does little to respond to the poor quality of clothing circulating the fashion system today, or the fact that some clothing holds memories of uglier times and trends we now find difficult to love. In fact, contemporary popular calls to discard garments unless they 'spark joy' led to reports of clothing donation and disposal bins overflowing with the excess of commodities which had been affectively de-fetishised and outcast (Pitt, 2019). Affective gestures towards clothing here are not merely sentimental; they also reveal a complex interplay between personal narratives, societal values, and material objects, highlighting an intimate and dynamic relationship between individuals and their wardrobes.

In raising affect as a tool to respond to clothing, it is important to remember that clothes also 'have a particular capacity to create ambivalent feelings' because of the way they change through use and 'fail to remain pristine' (Sampson, 2023, p. 182). Fletcher (2014) argues that the use-phase of a garment matters, because we have a 'shared responsibility for material upkeep' (p. 92). In responding to garments in this way, taking responsibility becomes both a material and symbolic practice of clothing care. Following Gilligan (1982), these calls can be 'heard as feminine' (p. 89), because they rely on the relational and affective considerations typically part of women's psychological development and morality. The domestic context of these practices adds something more traditional, where taking responsibility is located the domestic spaces of the home and wardrobe. The historic and conceptual slippage of women's role in the home and her agency in domestic spaces remains. While once a point of critique, women's ability to feel and practice care on her clothes is repackaged here as her political empowerment. I turn now to analyse the implications of this and consider the campaigns as part of broader tensions of affect and agency in the fashion industry.

Affecting and cultivating a response

Clothing as a medium or witness to affective labour has persisted over time. The suggestion that a garment retains and reflects the lives and labour of those that hold it has been used by abolitionists and activists since the start of the industrial era (Sussman, 2000; Tu & Hatcher, 2023). Earlier narratives argued that 'free hands make light clothing', unburdened by forced labour (Tu & Hatcher, 2023, p. 84) and Fashion Revolution's campaigns hold a version of this to be true in the twenty-first century. Such narratives tend to 'reify out relationship to clothing' and instruct a close, tender, and sentimental attachment to the commodity itself. Situated as a marker of one's connection to differently displaced workers, the garments worn in 'who made my clothes' posts are further fetishised as signifiers of industry and Other. The claim that consumers can 'know' who made their clothes by seeing a photo of smiling workers intends to settle any consumerist anxieties on the conditions of their labour, attempting to reveal and de-mystify the production process through demands at an emotional response. Though, the methods of asking 'who made my clothes?' might serve to further separate consumers and workers from meaningful solidarity. Under the guise of concern for Others, it is the consumer who is empowered through their subject position to identify as properly caring. This narrative puts the consumer at the centre of a political discussion on garment work and gives corporations a platform to take credit and ownership of this labour. Left out of this discussion is the worker herself, who does not own her labour or her image, but finds herself standing in to represent her peers and colleagues as a symbol of transparency and a 'fashion revolution'. When brands take photos of their labour force for this purpose, their image online becomes a fetishised commodity itself – and the worker's existence is collapsed into the outcomes of their labour once more. The image of the worker does little to reveal the complicated and diverse manner of processes, people, and locations that go into making just one garment. The campaign stands as a 'feel good place to stall our minds' (Jansen, 2020) and helps to accept certain aspects of a world in which Others work for us.

The calls on the consumer's affective disposition extend from Others to things through the Loved Clothes Last campaign. While eschewing the fact that clothing's planned obsolescence and reduced quality and durability overtime is by systematic corporate design, that clothes are not 'lasting' is settled at the fault of the individual. Consumers are asked to take responsibility and love their clothes through tacit skills of clothing repair and a sentimental attachment to the commodity. Through this critique, I intend not to undermine the important role of simple clothing repairs in extending the life of garments. Repair presents both a real and poetic opportunity for intervention, reparation, and change. Nonetheless, it is precisely this care for clothing and one's empowerment and agency through it that is used by fashion brands and advertisers to sell more. The slippage between the consumer's ability to both resist and then draw upon their relationship to clothes makes for messy complications on the path for structural change. Fashion Revolution's campaigns situate the consumer as a central agent in a world of institutional and affective relationships. This narrative reproduces a 'patterned sensibility intimately connected to neoliberalism' (Gill, 2016, p. 610) which posits personal change as part and parcel of structural change. One of the central arcs here is that transformation of the empowered, consumer subject as a 'new feeling protagonist', whose feelings are helping to achieve global justice (Ferguson, 1992, p. 107). Thus, while the awareness-raising tactics of the campaigns remain successful, the fundamental hierarchies in the global fashion supply chain remain largely unchanged.

Stepping back to review the context in which these campaigns exist, the Instagram platform, which serves as a fashionable and political arena for activism and responsibility-taking, is also a platform driven by commercial interests and algorithms designed not to connect people, but to generate profit (Croeser, 2018, p. 28). This underscores the challenge of using social media as a tool for meaningful social change, as the platform's structure can easily co-opt activist messages for commercial gain. This is especially important in the fashion industry, where identifying as 'responsible' is a form of cultural cachet itself. Despite these challenges, Fashion Revolution's ability to leverage Instagram's reach highlights the potential for digital platforms to start conversations and cultivate action towards a more sustainable and ethical industry practices. Thus, while Fashion Revolution's campaigns succeed in raising awareness and engaging consumers in critical conversations, they also highlight the ongoing need for responses which properly challenge the structural injustices embedded in the system itself.

References

Abidin, C. (2016). Visibility labour: Engaging with influencer's fashion brands and #OOTD advertorial campaigns on Instagram. *Media International Australia*, *161*(1), 86–100. https://doi.org/10.1177/1329878X16665177.

Amgott, N. (2018). Critical Literacy in #DigitalActivism: collaborative choice and action. *International Journal of Information and Learning Technology, 35*(5), 329–341. https://doi.org/10.1108/IJILT-05-2018-0060

Banet-Weiser, S. (2015). 'Confidence you can carry!': Girls in crisis and the market for girls' empowerment organisations. *Continuum Journal of Media & Cultural Studies*, *29*(2), 182–193.

Benedetto, C. A. (2017). Corporate social responsibility as an emerging business model in fashion marketing. *Journal of Global Fashion Marketing*, *8*(4), 251–265. https://www.tandfonline.com/doi/full/10.1080/20932685.2017.1329023.

Brooks, E. (2007). *Unravelling the garment industry: Transnational organising and women's work*. University of Minnesota Press.

Brooks, A. (2015). *Clothing poverty: The hidden world of fast fashion and second-hand clothes*. Zeb Books.

Caliandro, A., & Graham, J. (2020). Studying Instagram beyond selfies. *Social Media & Society,* 1–7. https://journals.sagepub.com/doi/pdf/10.1177/2056305120924779.

Chouliaraki, L. (2013). *The ironic spectator*. Polity Books.

Croeser, S. (2018). Rethinking networked solidarity. In M. Mortensen, C. Neumayer, & T. Poell (Eds.), *Social media materialities and protest: Critical reflections* (pp. 28–41). Routledge.

Cukul, D. (2015, June). *Fashion marketing in social media: Using Instagram for fashion branding* [Conference paper]. Business and Management Conferences, International Institute of Social and Economic Sciences, Vienna, Austria. https://econpapers.repec.org/paper/sekibmpro/2304324.htm.

de Perthius, K., & Findlay, R. (2019). How fashion travels: The fashionable ideal in the age of Instagram. *Fashion Theory: The Body: Fashion and Physique*, *23*(2), 219–242. https://doi.org/10.1080/1362704X.2019.1567062.

Dean, B. (2024). *Instagram demographic statistics: How many people use Instagram in 2024?* Back Link. https://backlinko.com/instagram-users#how-many-people-use-instagram.

Duffy, B. E. (2017). *(Not) getting paid to do what you love: Gender, social media, and aspirational work.* Yale University Press.

Fashion Revolution. [@fash_rev]. (22 December 2016). *Get to know the people behind every piece of clothing.* [Instagram post]. Instagram. https://www.instagram.com/p/BOTGiAeBAQ.

Fashion Revolution. [@fash_rev]. (6 November 2017). *Thank you Abdul. #repost*. [Instagram post]. Instagram. https://www.instagram.com/p/BbIEJqOA9I5.

Fashion Revolution. [@fash_rev]. (31 October 2018a). *The power of influence: Since Meghan Markle appeared in @outlanddenim the brand has seen a 3000% increase in global traffic*. [Instagram post]. Instagram. https://www.instagram.com/p/BpmThpZhjdX.

Fashion Revolution. [@fash_rev]. (12 December 2018b). *N is for numbers*. [Instagram post]. Instagram. https://www.instagram.com/p/BrR7CHSHBc7.

Fashion Revolution. [@fash_rev]. (2 November 2022). *Print (or make) a poster. Share a selfie. Tag the brand you're wearing. Ask #WhoMadeMyClothes?* [Instagram post]. Instagram. https://www.instagram.com/p/Cka8RqpKlAG/?img_index=1.

Fashion Revolution. (2023a). About. https://www.fashionrevolution.org/about/.

Fashion Revolution. [@fash_rev]. (28 August 2023b). *The most sustainable garment is the one already in your wardrobe*. [Instagram post]. Instagram. https://www.instagram.com/p/CwfU0EjMARZ/?img_index=1.

Ferguson, M. (1992). *Subject to others: British women writers and colonial slavery, 1670–1834*. Routledge.

Fletcher, K. (2014). *Sustainable fashion and textiles: Design journeys* (2nd edition). Routledge.

Garwood, S. (2011). *Advocacy across borders: NGOs, anti-sweatshop activism and the global garment industry*. Lynne Rienner Publishers.

Gill, R. (2016). Post-postfeminism?: New feminist visibilities in postfeminist times. *Feminist Media Studies*, *16*(4), 610–630.

Gilligan, C. (1982). *In a different voice: Psychology theory and women's development*. Harvard University Press.

Highfield, T. (2016). *Social media and everyday politics*. Polity Press.

Hill, A. (2013). *Digital revolutions activism in the internet age, world changing*. New Internationalist Publications Ltd.

Holgar, M. (2019). *The wardrobe impact of worn stories: Exploring garment storytelling for sustainability* [PhD thesis]. Queensland University of Technology. https://eprints.qut.edu.au/133290/.

Horton, K., & Street, P. (2021). This hashtag is just my style: Popular feminism & digital fashion activism. *Continuum*, *35*(6), 883–896. https://doi.org/10.1080/10304312.2021.1993573.

Horton, K., Street, P., & O'Brien, E. (2022). When women owe women: Framing consumer responsibility in the context of fast fashion. *International Journal for Crime, Justice and Social Democracy*, *11*(2), 116–128. https://doi.org/10.5204/ijcjsd.2356.

Khader, S. (2017). Neoliberalism, global justice and transnational feminisms. In A. Garry, S. Khader, & A. Stone (Eds.), *The Routledge companion to feminist philosophy* (1st edition, pp. 607–619). Routledge.

Khan, R. (2016). Doing good and looking good: Women in 'fast fashion' activism. *Women & Environments International Magazine*, (96/97), 7–9. https://www.proquest.com/docview/1882372155?accountid=13380&pq-origsite=primo.

Kumar, A. (2020). *Monopsony capitalism*. Cambridge University Press.

Jansen, A. (2020). Connecting the dots—Or why I eschew the term 'garment workers'. *Research Collective for Decolonising Fashion*. https://rcdfashion.wordpress.com/2020/05/18/connecting-the-dots-or-why-i-eschew-the- term-garment-workers/.

Mohanty, C. T. (2003). *Feminism without borders: Decolonising theory, practicing solidarity*. Duke University Press. https://doi.org/10.2307/j.ctv11smp7t.

Owen, S., & Napoli, C. (2021). *Marketing forecast 2021*. Worth Global Style Network.

PITT. (2019, January 19). Marie Kondo creates boom for op-shoppers but bad news for oceans. *The Sydney Morning Herald*. https://www.smh.com.au/national/nsw/

marie-kondo-creates-boom-for-op-shoppers-but-bad-news-for-oceans-20190119-p50scu.html.

Press, C. (2017). Why ethical fashion is a feminist issue. *Fashionista*. https://fashionista.com/2017/04/ethical-clothing-fashion-feminist-issues.

Quayyum, N. (2019). Women workers in Bangladesh's ready-made garment industry: Building an infrastructure of dissent. *Journal of Labour and Society*, *22*(4), 835–852. https://doi.org/10.1111/wusa.12441.

Reuters. (2018, June 26). Luxury menswear growth to outpace womenswear. *The Business of Fashion*. https://www.businessoffashion.com/articles/luxury/luxury-menswear-growth-to-outpace-womenswear.

Safi, M., & Rushe, D. (2018, April 24). Rana Plaza, five years on: Safety of workers hangs in balance in Bangladesh. *The Guardian*. https://www.theguardian.com/global-development/2018/apr/24/bangladeshi-police-target-garment-workers-union-rana-plaza- five-years-on.

Sampson, E. (2023). Dirty pretty things: Stains, ambivalence and the traces of feeling. In R. Filippello, & I. Parkins (Eds.), *Fashion and feeling: The affective politics of dress* (pp. 179–194). Palgrave Macmillan.

Schiff, J. L. (2014). *Burdens of political responsibility: Narratives and the cultivation of responsiveness*. Cambridge University Press.

Siddiqi, D. (2009). Do Bangladeshi garment workers need saving: Sisterhood in the post-sweatshop era. *Feminist Review*, *91*(1), 154–174. https://link.springer.com/article/10.1057/fr.2008.55.

Spivak, E. (2014). *Worn stories*. Princeton Architectural Press.

Street, P. (2022). *Fashioning the revolution: Digital fashion activism and the narratives of responsibility on Instagram* [Master's thesis]. Queensland University of Technology. https://eprints.qut.edu.au/229144/.

Sussman, C. (2000). *Consumer protest, gender & British slavery, 1713-1833*. Stanford University Press.

Tolentino, J. (2019). The age of Instagram face. *The New Yorker*. https://www.newyorker.com/culture/decade-in-review/the-age-of-instagram-face.

Tu, T. L. N., & Hatcher, J. (2023). Can fashion feel? In R. Filippello, & I. Parkins (Eds.), *Fashion and feeling: The affective politics of dress* (pp. 83–96). Palgrave Macmillan.

Vorhaus, M. (2020). People increasingly turn to social media for news. *Forbes*. https://www.forbes.com/sites/mikevorhaus/2020/06/24/people-increasingly-turn-to-social-media-for-news/?sh=5c007ed23bcc.

8 Imagination and agency

On the role of fiction in ecological discourses

Dörte Linke

Introduction

"We're in the middle of the climate emergency and need a total transformation!". Such are the terms in which the so-called Letzte Generation calls for civil resistance on its website.[1] The grouping was very active in Germany when this chapter was written in 2023, targeting the major cities in particular and keeping them on high alert; one of the activists' tactics was to superglue themselves to roads and block car traffic for hours at a time. In February 2024, the group announced to stop this particular form of protest,[2] but their aim is still to secure measures including a speed limit on German motorways, an affordable ticket for local public transport and the convening of a citizens' assembly to work up plans for the phase-out of fossil fuels. The protests of "Letzte Generation" polarised, however: violent clashes flared up between "climate gluers" and motorists. Horrified reactions were provoked when potato puree was thrown at a Monet painting worth millions in the Barberini Museum in Potsdam in autumn 2022, and a paint attack on the "Basic Law 49" monument in front of the Bundestag, the national parliament of the Federal Republic of Germany, also drew fierce criticism. While the tactics and forms of protest first adopted by "Letzte Generation" are debatable, they also visibly manifest a sense of legitimate despair. Awareness of climate change and its catastrophic consequences is widespread, with regular media coverage, and there is broad political consensus on the principle of climate action. Yet even simple measures such as reducing the speed limit on motorways in Germany are not materialising in reality. Wherever one looks, the fatal consequences of climate change are plain to see and yet the majority felt mainly disturbed by those vehemently calling attention to the urgent need for action. Against this backdrop, the question is how the ubiquitous discourses on sustainability and the demands for resource-conserving action can be translated into reality? Why do people fail to change their behaviour even when all this is actually understood? Moreover, how can it be that the term "sustainability" is now degenerating into an advertising buzzword and hence adding further fuel to the biggest problem, unbridled consumption? How, one may ask, could messages and demands like those of "Letzte Generation" or "Extinction Rebellion" be mediated in such a way as to influence and change how humans act in the real world?

DOI: 10.4324/9781003392705-12

In this chapter, I will examine an area that seems, at first glance, very distant from the public debate and the practical action that is called for in society: the role of fiction in and for ecological discourses and the action taken by society to implement them. For some time now, humanities disciplines have been debating how they can contribute to countering the ecological crisis, as is evidenced by the establishment and differentiation of research areas such as Environmental Humanities[3] and the subdomain of Ecocriticism, in particular. The latter addresses questions within literary studies about how relations between humans and the environment are portrayed in fiction, how a dualistic separation between humans and ›nature‹[4] respectively our fellow life forms can be broken down, and how relationships between humans and ›nature‹ can be rethought.[5] But here one might pose the critical question as to whether, in reality, these scholarly endeavours can be of any real help in overcoming the current crisis? Or are they themselves part of the phenomenon, in which catchwords such as "sustainability" and "ecological" help to attract funding for the scholars' own research? Can storytelling help us create a more sustainable way of living? If so, how? And what kind of stories do we need? This is the line of inquiry I would like to pursue, by first discussing the significance of narratives for ecological action and concepts of ›nature‹ and then, making substantial reference to the theorist Donna Haraway, by exploring what might be thought of as ecological storytelling. Finally, I will take a closer look at three literary texts, *Hundenovelle* (2008) by the German author Marion Poschmann, and the novels *Den afskyelige* (2016) by Charlotte Weitze and *Om mørke* (2013) by Josefine Klougart, both from Denmark. Referring to these, I will show the many ways in which fiction can invite and contribute to reflection on Humanity's relationship with the environment.

The concept of ›nature‹ in fictional texts

Humans must create narratives in order to orientate themselves. That is why the contemporary German literary scholar Albrecht Koschorke refers to the human species as "homo narrans".[6] By means of narratives, people develop worldviews and try to grasp the world around them and communicate it to others. How we talk about our surroundings also has a great influence on how we act and how we create our own "life narrative". This applies equally to narratives about ›nature‹, which, like all other human narratives, remain bound to their originators. They say little about ›nature‹ itself, but much more about how humans see themselves within their relationship to the (material) environment, what needs they have, and how they situate themselves in the world. Thus, what ›nature‹ was understood to mean has varied greatly at different points in time and there has always been a close interplay between concepts of ›nature‹ and anthropological conceptions. It can therefore be said that ›nature‹ is not so much an entity with a real existence as an organising concept in the human cosmos of ideas.

One interesting observation is that the relation between humans and ›nature‹ repeatedly proves to be paradoxical. On the one hand, technological progress continually extends the possibilities for controlling material circumstances and utilising them for human convenience; at the same time, however, a yearning arises for closeness to ›nature‹. For instance, the first surge of industrialisation with its increasing mechanisation and urbanisation created the very conditions for the emergence of Romanticism, which established the thought that the human subject had a metaphysical closeness to ›nature‹, could empathise with it as an individual and give it a new voice and expression by means of poetic language. The construction of railways to access natural areas and the emergence of tourism were followed at the end of the nineteenth century by the first environmental conservation movements, which sought to safeguard ›nature‹ from human encroachment. When ecological modes of thinking intensified in the 1970s, the image of the blue, vulnerable planet took hold – although even this was predicated on the highly advanced technologies that made it possible to fly to the moon and capture images of this blue planet in the first place.[7] Today "Closeness to ›nature‹" is an appealing selling point – whether the subject be "forest bathing" and relaxation, foods, or organically produced goods. Yet there is simultaneous proliferation and use of medical and technological possibilities to neutralise and overcome the unruliness of ›nature‹ in any and all forms – be they the uncertainties associated with something like an illness, or the length of time that analogue communications or long-distance train journeys would take.

Seen in this light, the despair of the Letzte Generation is understandable. In the present day, ›nature‹ ultimately appears as an abstraction, an object of yearning and an ingredient of narratives expressing the human desire to live in a new harmony with one's environment, yet at the same time, there is a general reluctance to make any real changes to one's own behaviour and way of life. These "yearning narratives", which are primarily exploited by the advertising industry, gloss over a highly concrete problem, namely that to counter climate change, excessive consumption of resources and resultant phenomena such as species extinction, and consumption as such has to be massively reduced. But instead, the consumer's conscience is salved with an organic product. Narratives that create fantastical new ›nature‹ spaces rather than fundamentally calling old habits into question thus become a big problem as they might replace concrete ecological action.[8] It therefore seems important to critically question the very concept of ›nature‹, which is becoming increasingly problematic due to the anthropocentric worldview that it undoubtedly reflects. For example, the philosopher and publicist Timothy Morton argues for abolishing the concept of ›nature‹ since it will always be indelibly encoded with a dualistic worldview, an aestheticisation of natural phenomena and a distance which can result in an escape from the world and the urgent problems caused by our own destruction. What he advocates, instead, is ecology without ›nature‹ that lets humans jump back into "the mud" of the world, based on an acceptance even of death and the poisoned ground we live on. This seems reasonable, but I am a bit critical of Morton's concept as well, because ultimately it gives too little consideration to the human need to protect oneself from death and to create meaningful contexts.[9] At this juncture, I would like to propose a model that derives from the concept of "environment" (Umwelt) first formulated by the biologist and philosopher Jakob von Uexküll in the beginning of the twentieth century. His underlying assumption was that all life forms create meaningful environments for themselves, always subject to their own particular physical and mental conditions.[10] Therefore, there is not one environment, but rather a multitude of environments. In a similar vein, in our days, the artist and author James Bridle proposes expanding the concept of intelligence by regarding it as an interface that makes the world meaningful for living beings. Intelligence is then regarded as the ability to form meaningful environments for oneself based on one's own specificities, which means that it can also be ascribed to the non-human world.[11] From this perspective, the environments of all life forms contain and influence specific ecologies – that is to say, interrelationships and interdependencies with other life forms. Specific to humans is that they also create environments by means of language, and are thus capable of generating mental realities that transcend concrete materiality, outlast it and also reflect it.[12] In this model, ›nature‹ images and narratives become *one* component of human relationships with their environment, *one* aspect of human ecological relations, by describing foundational ideas that people conceive about their relations with the (material) world. These relations themselves are very much wider-ranging, however: besides physical processes of which humans are oblivious, they encompass technology, which can be seen with James Bridle as a foundational interface with the world, ranging in content from wool-processing for human clothing to artificial intelligence.[13] To sum up those short theoretical reflections, the first and most crucial thing to realise, then, is that narratives about ›nature‹ are primarily specific constructs which reflect human consciousness and ways of life and are bound to the era in which they arose. This applies just as much to the "ecological narrative", which represents *the* ›nature‹ narrative of the present day. Even in the face of the ecological crisis, people still do what they usually do – create a narrative that enables them to apprehend and understand the situation. The ecological narrative features humans as the destroyers of ›nature‹, despite its intrinsic goodness, when they really need to re-establish harmonious wholeness with it. While the first part of the narrative about the destruction of sensitive ecological balances and interrelationships is highly self-evident and plausible, the subsequent quest for a solution often bespeaks an attempt simply to reverse one's own developmental history, even though this does not help. There is no original ›nature‹ as an ontological entity that could be returned to, and even if there were, returning to it would not be a realistic objective because all the uncertainties and dangers that humans have overcome with the help of technology would then be reinstated. This is more than clear from the current inability to give up even a fraction of the standard of living that has been attained.

In my view, it makes more sense to concentrate largely on the concept of "ecologies", as interacting networks. This enables a holistic understanding of the current situation as an ecological crisis which amounts, essentially, to a destruction of meaningful and complex life-nexuses on many levels. Within this crisis, the ways of life of human and non-human life forms collide in many places. Accordingly, it is argued that the first step towards a "solution" would require each of us to pay conscious attention to our own ecological nexuses and to shape and change them as life-promoting. During the stress of the daily traffic jam, for example, one might reflect on the fact that it is currently part of the human ecology to travel from one place to another quickly, conveniently, and on schedule. Not that this is objectionable per se, but it is somewhat incompatible with other ecologies and environmental relationships that prioritise the conservation of resources and avoid CO_2 emissions. A solution might then be either to rethink prevailing cultural ideas and concepts or to develop appropriate technologies that make both compatible.[14] It is important to understand that rewinding history is not an option but "(hi)stories" must be consistently developed and improved upon. This is emphasised both by Donna Haraway, when she writes "We must think, think we must",[15] and by James Bridle, who advocates that "we might allow our own intelligence to flower into new forms and new emergent ways of being and relating. The admittance of general, universal, active intelligence is a necessary part of our vital re-entanglement with the more-than-human world".[16] It is thus a matter of having to create new, meaningful ecologies. A more concrete question to turn to now is what role fiction can play in this context?

Life stories – on the role of fiction in ecological discourse

For the purposes of ecological action, it is thus essential to pay conscious attention to one's own ›nature‹ narratives and to create new narratives about one's own ecological nexuses. Ecocriticism also refers to this when it calls for the discovery of alternative narratives within fiction about human-›nature‹ relations as a basis for establishing a new environmental consciousness. Nevertheless, especially in early Ecocriticism, but sometimes in more recent publications as well, there are signs of a tendency that calls for a rapprochement between humans and ›nature‹ and for humans to be reintegrated into natural nexuses on the basis of the relinquishment of anthropocentric views. The human being, the destroyer of beautiful ›nature‹, is called upon to reconcile with it and protect it again and it is an aim to make ›nature‹ visible again in its very being, and to elucidate its power, magnitude and significance in relation to human life, while theoretical approaches, such as Mortons concept, are seen more critical.[17] To my mind, this is due to an unreflected use and generalisation of a conception of ›nature‹ that has its specific place in the early environmental movement. A frequent sign of that one sole narrative of ›nature‹ is used here without further reflection is the uncritical conflation of the terms ›nature‹ and "environment".[18] This becomes understandable as motivation of the early ecocriticism was partly a didactic programme, in that the aim of addressing the environmental crisis and pointing out solutions was brought directly to the texts. In the meantime, research in the field of Ecocriticism has become substantially more nuanced and currently takes a much broader perspective on "›nature‹-human relationships" and in my opinion, this is important to realise the great possibilities fiction has. It does not go far enough when it is reduced to provide specific narratives which should foster certain modes of behaviour. Fictional texts are rather open-thinking spaces that shed multifaceted light on human beings' relationships with materiality and their fellow beings. Thus, completely new ways of thinking can be explored and Ecocriticism can only contribute to new developments when it does not entrench itself in old conceptions and dualistic views, but opens new spaces of thinking itself. Nevertheless, the problem remains how those spaces can result in common action. Charlotte Weitze, a Danish author I will deal with below, draws attention to the tension between free artistic creation and her desire as an author to develop concrete and collective options for action.[19] She talks about the problem of the "indirectness" of fiction, since it cannot calculate its own effects and degrades into propaganda if it has an obvious agenda.[20] Likewise, Josefine Klougart says with regard to the question of whether it is feasible and desirable for fiction to solve concrete societal problems: "Its purpose is to nuance the way we see the world and thereby help with finding better solutions to concrete societal problems. Art achieves the most as free basic research".[21] Hence, fictional texts can contribute primarily to drawing attention to and reflecting on people's narratives of ›nature‹ and their ecologies, meaning how they relate to the world, and thus potentially change them.

What is important in this regard is openness to the diversity of relations, phenomena, and processes that cannot and need not always be slotted into an ecological box. More crucial by far is what Kramsøj Flinker, lecturer in Danish literature, describes as the creative process that unfolds between the literary text and its readers:

> When we tell, and when we read, listen, see, or actively interpret narratives, this activity becomes a "tool" that organizes and supports our experiences and thinking in such a way that we can gain a foothold in reality. Expressed differently, the world-creative power of narrative is not a cognitive crutch for those who cannot manage to think in more rigorous ways; rather, it is a basic and general strategy for making sense of the world. [...] The idea is not that the reader can get a more accurate image of life in the Anthropocene by reading Weitze's The Abominable. Instead, in the reader's storyworld or reconstructions of the novel, they build a model of causal, temporal, spatial, ethical, and environmental structures that can scaffold the reader's dialogue with a complex world in change.[22] Above all else, fiction is a space for exploration in which new possibilities can be fathomed. This is all the more necessary at present time because it has to confront new phenomena, the like of which have never occurred before in the history of Earth and of humankind.[23] This is also the point of departure for the theorist Donna Haraway, who places great faith in stories and imputes them with considerable transformative power. At the same time, she criticises "Big History" which features humans, especially white men, as the crown of creation and as beings who dominate their entire environment:
>
> So much of earth history has been told in the thrall of the fantasy of the first beautiful words and weapons, of the first beautiful weapons *as* words and vice versa. Tool, weapon, word: that is the word made flesh in the image of the sky god. In a tragic story with only one real actor, one real world maker, the hero, this is the Man-making tale of the hunter on a quest to kill and bring back the terrible bounty. This is the cutting, sharp, combative tale

of action that defers the suffering of glutinous, earth-rotted passivity beyond bearing. All others in the prick tale are props, ground, plot space, or prey. They don't matter; their job is to be in the way, to be overcome, to be the road, the conduit, but not the traveler, not the begetter. The last thing the hero wants to know is that his beautiful words and weapons will be worthless without a bag, a container, a net.[24] Haraway's text makes it clear that humans have not always been good storytellers. This is partly because their narratives often have a "bad actor",[25] the human being, and everything around them becomes a by-product of their advancement. The contemporary situation makes it more than clear, however, that this story of development and progress is not approaching the happy ending it was intended to reach. With this in mind, Haraway also formulates her critique of the concept of the "Anthropocene", which rests on the assumption that human activity is changing the material world so profoundly and irreversibly that it can be defined as a new geological epoch.[26] Two possible reactions to this are an apocalyptic-heroic stance, facing up to its own demise on a devastated Earth, or alternatively, a self-perception which, with the help of even more intelligent technology, elevates itself to the position of its manager and saviour in a spirit of heightened responsibility.[27] In this, Haraway sees "an almost laughable rerun of the great phallic humanizing and modernizing Adventure",[28] which perpetuates anthropocentrism in a new guise. This hampers both the positive coexistence of all life forms and the invention or discovery of new stories that are spun jointly by both human and non-human life forms.[29] Equally problematic, in Haraway's estimation, is catastrophic thinking where one considers one's own future a lost cause.[30] Admittedly, even the narrative form of the dystopia is underpinned by a hidden struggle over the future, of which a gloomy picture is painted in order to shake up the present day. Nevertheless, there is a failure to map out constructive ways of acting or visions for a better future. Haraway counters this with a call for critical, imaginative, and speculative thinking and action, and invites the reader to enter new "collaborations and combinations"[31] and collectively create new stories – in a tentacular mode of thinking and being that enters all kinds of relationships with one's fellow life forms and a composting process that shreds outmoded narratives and produces new ones. So Haraway, too, is not concerned with a return to ›nature‹ of whatever kind, but with new ecologies that are processual, complicated, and multifaceted – with an attitude that does not rip through and destroy the fabric of the world but, rather, contributes to spinning more of it in ever new ways. Her texts are fascinating not least because they so clearly convey pleasure in both storytelling and action, and the aliveness each can hold.

At the same time, the question raised is what Haraway actually means when she speaks of narratives and stories, for she is obviously not concerned with printed books, nor with a metaphorical perspective on the world as decipherable text, which would tie in with another Big Story that viewed ›nature‹ as a book written by a divine author. Instead, Haraway develops her idea of a material-semiotic reality in which language and stories are bound up with materiality. Practical action in the world and storytelling about it now become impossible to separate; stories apprehend realities and, at the same time, create reality. Nor are they restricted to human storytelling, but are created and co-determined by all the actors involved. Haraway sees stories in this sense both as new practices supporting mutual empowerment and a heightened attention to the flourishing of life-promoting nexuses, and as the act of narrating itself: there is thus a close interplay between making good (life) stories and telling them or writing them down. Consequently, Haraway makes no distinction between fiction and research – she believes that much of the best research takes place in fiction, which can thus also contribute to new solutions. The prerequisite for finding and creating such stories is polite inquiry[32] which departs from well-trodden paths and asks oneself and others new questions: "The risk of listening to a story is that it can obligate us in ramifying webs that cannot be known in advance of venturing among their myriad threads".[33] Haraway strikingly conveys how places and contexts are, as it were, interwoven with new threads of meaning and acquire new meanings through these interweavings. This applies as much to the mutualistic relationship between ants and acacias in Africa[34] as to the complex interconnections around the ingestion of an oestrogen.[35] It is thus a matter of looking carefully and heeding details in order to discover and witness the stories of the world, to draw closer and make use of language and narratives for the purpose of better understanding what surrounds us, its beauty, and its potential.[36] A similar model is sketched out by James Bridle, who also points to the ever-greater complexity and intricacies that result from looking carefully at reality without attempting to apprehend it by schematic, systematising means.[37] Here, an anthropocentric view is called into question insofar as non-human beings are also taken seriously as intelligent interaction partners in their "creation of environments" and attention is drawn to the manifold connections to and dependencies on them. Yet at the same time, the human need for meaning and orientation is taken seriously, their specific way of creating environments and the fact that it is impossible to eliminate anthropocentrism as such, because ultimately humans can only perceive from their own perspective.[38] It thus seems crucial that the important resources of attention, care, imagination, and creativity are used to create the stories that are teeming with new connections and, in this way, come alive.[39] As in Kramsøj Flinker's description above, Haraway similarly assumes that these can have an effect on human thinking and create new worldviews and inner worlds, which, in turn, give rise to new ways of acting:

> Each time a story helps me remember what I thought I knew, or introduces me to new knowledge, a muscle critical for caring about flourishing gets some aerobic exercise. Such exercise enhances collective thinking and movement in complexity. Each time I trace a tangle and add a few threads that at first seemed whimsical but turned out to be essential to the fabric, I get a bit straighter that staying with the trouble of complex worlding is the name of the game of living and dying well together on terra, in Terrapolis.[40] Against this backdrop, three fictional texts will now be examined to illuminate how they can offer a response to the ecological crisis and motivate rethinking of it.

Destroyed relationship worlds – Marion Poschmann's *Hundenovelle*

The German author Marion Poschmann writes both prose and poetry in which ›nature‹ images as well as the destruction of the environment play a major role. In her writing, she repeatedly emphasises that the images of ›nature‹ as wholesome and communicative are constructs she sets out to encode in a material reality which in fact no longer sustains them. Yearning for harmonious closeness to ›nature‹ yet simultaneously maintaining a critical distance are indivisibly linked for this author.[41] The book *Hundenovelle* tells the story of a nameless female protagonist who increasingly slides into depression in the so called "Hundstage" of a hot August. This is expressed through her encounter with a "black dog", which is a metaphor for depression on the one hand and, at the same time, appears in the text as a real animal and insinuates itself into the protagonist's life. It is a device which shows how the society in which the protagonist lives shapes her relationship to "natural" phenomena, and particularly animals. In contrast to the protagonist's wild and unkempt animal, the dogs in the urban neighbourhood are well groomed and, like children, supplied with ample food and chances to play. When she buys the food, the protagonist stands in front of a shelf and sees "little bone-shaped biscuits, coloured red and green. Baked rolls cut into bite-sized morsels like sushi […], three-coloured strands twisted into each other, chalky pastilles, flat crackers"[42] and pragmatically decides on "two cans labelled 'Dog Food'. That was the cheapest sort".[43] However, this ostensible friendliness towards animals is quickly unmasked as a false pretence, by wrongly humanising them on the one hand, and by assimilating them into the submissive consumer society on the other. For example, the protagonist is decried by fellow shoppers when she has taken her dog to a shopping centre to choose himself a new collar; he blocks the escalator and she is unable to control him. Here he becomes a being who disrupts the smooth running of the shopping centre in which her fellow human beings wander about as a seemingly unconscious crowd.[44] The external perspective that the dog forces the protagonist to adopt shows a cultural appropriation of "natural" phenomena which masquerades as love of animals but is, in essence, intent on narcissistic self-validation and control. In the novel, it becomes problematic because people's love for the controlled animal outweighs their fellow-feeling for a dissenting human being, and thus leads to social rifts. The protagonist's distress goes unnoticed. As a human being without a function in a mechanistic consumer society, she is ostracised and grows increasingly close to her wild dog so that the animal takes on the appearance of a saviour and last-ditch companion but also a stigma that increasingly isolates her from society.

A similar relation of beautiful illusion is also present in the city's ›nature‹ reserve, where the protagonist goes walking with her dog. The said conservation area has been converted from the former "Rieselfelder" (irrigation fields) of a sewage plant. As the old designation has been retained, the protagonist now associates it with "a notion of freshness, local recreation, lawn sprinklers, even discreet background music […] and nothing like a sewage reprocessing plant that had funnelled a whole town's excreta onto fruit orchards and vegetable fields".[45] In this passage, two ›nature‹ images are blended into one another which belong together historically but not in the world of imagination. Both the irrigation fields as a consequential phenomenon of industrialisation and the notion, ironically heightened here, of ›nature‹ as a recreational green space emerged at the end of the nineteenth century. Here, the novel exposes the paradox cited at the outset: on the one hand, seemingly beautiful natural spaces are created, but ultimately these can only superficially cover up the fundamental destruction of ecological nexuses:

> But I knew better, knew about polluted liquids that had fertilized poor soils for decades [...] until it reached the point that the system broke down and there was no choice but to stop irrigating. Then the operatic overturning of the landscape, the scene-shifting, suspended platforms, new artificiality. Topsoil tipped from load beds [...]. Certain plant species prevailed against regraded masses of earth, conquered a terrain that wandered back and forth, laden with its past. Too many interventions, too much friction, too much of everything. Washed-out, fat-ridden, soap-sodden soil. The reforestation was a failure, almost all the newly planted trees withered immediately. Only the couch grass held its own. Couch grass steppe. Beggar-tick mire plants. Dry grassland fragments. [...] In the soil there were still heavy metals and dioxins. The ›nature‹ reserve belied all this, faked intactness, boasted bushes, trees and open spaces. All in all, a congenial location for dogs.[46] Here the images of beautiful ›nature‹ are transported into the cultural sphere and integrated with the economy – the ›nature‹ reserve and the adjacent industrial estate merge seamlessly into each other.[47] They correspond to the easily consumable images in the media which divert our gaze from the real destruction or, if consumption is prolonged, clear our conscience. What emerges clearly is both confirmation and critique of the ecological narrative: the catastrophe of environmental degradation and the economic exploitation of ›nature‹ are facts but cannot be managed with superficial measures. To sum up, the ›nature‹ reserve is shown as a devastated space which the heat of summer turns into a dry, shimmering desert where the protagonist develops hallucinations and suddenly sees the dog, an accusing and menacing presence in her path. No longer does this place hold mysteries like those the Romantics read into their landscapes, nor space for discoveries.[48] Poschmann's text shows that the destruction of landscapes goes hand in hand with the destruction of imagination and inner worlds of meaning.

Marion Poschmann's novel can thus be read as socially critical, revealing the entanglement of contemporary ›nature‹ images with economics and consumption as well as the rifts in (inter)personal relationships and ecologies caused by a narcissistic love for animals. These ecologies lack their former dynamism and aliveness because the ability to deal with the resistant, the uncontrollable and the unpredictable has been lost. What remains is a bleak uniformity and a one-dimensional culture which no longer allows room for individual inner worlds. But to change this, far from a return to imaginary, intact "natural" spaces, the prerequisite is critical reflection on and concrete engagement with the cultural environments that humans have created for themselves.

Climate crisis as sensual – Charlotte Weitze's novels *Den Afskyelige* and *Rosarium*

Of the authors presented here, it is Charlotte Weitze whose texts refer most directly to the environmental and climate crisis. This is motivated by her own intensive commitment to ecological issues – for example, she experimented with living sustainably with her own family in the public eye and was part of the attempt to found an ecological authors' network in Denmark inspired by the Norwegian model[49] – and stemming from that, her wish that her literary work should likewise help to bring greater attention to contemporary problems. At the same time, Weitze explicitly emphasises that fiction cannot present simple solutions, but rather contributes to making concrete nexuses experienceable and visible in other ways – notably through her use of fairy-tale and fantasy elements. From her point of view, this is necessary because it is precisely what enables her to capture the monstrousness of the climate crisis.[50] Her novel *Den afskyelige* (The Abominable Snowman)[51] centres on a couple, a woman named Heidi and a man named Kenneth who is gradually revealed to be a hybrid creature between a human and a snowman. The book describes how terribly he and his kin suffer from global heating: their constant sweating causes massive health problems, very few habitats remain that they still find bearable, and this situation drives them to intense aggression and despair. The novel draws partly on contemporary facts – it is set in a future in which a Gulf Stream shift, among other factors, has changed the Earth's climate to the extent that southern plants now grow in northern regions and polar ice-cap melt threatens to unleash massive flooding, which is becoming more and more of a reality at the time of writing.[52] At the same time, through the fantastical figure of the snowman and the change in perspective, the climate crisis is made much more palpable for readers than is otherwise the case in our latitudes. Moreover, the novel also depicts the difficulties and complex questions that arise during the attempt to make one's own life sustainable: for instance, the couple run their home computer using only muscle power generated via a bicycle, Heidi wrestles with the dilemma as to whether it is better to buy organic goods that have to be transported or local ones that are treated with artificial fertilisers and pesticides, and invitations to dine at relatives' and friends' homes become difficult. Their homemade porn film, part of a project named *Fuck for Forest* which donates the revenues received from viewers to reforesting the rainforest as a way of balancing the couple's CO_2 emissions and thus improve their overall carbon footprint, also strikes Heidi as a dubious project. Kenneth, in contrast, demands a kind of eco-dictatorship, a new strong leader to defend the climate. He becomes increasingly aggressive towards Heidi, and this not only casts him as a victim but also makes him seem an unlikeable and pedantic figure, certain aspects of which are very reminiscent of "Letzte Generation". The novel ends with a breached dam and a flood that largely destroys local civilisation, creating new conditions to which only the deformed child of Heidi's friend Mette is adapted since his fused legs endow him with a kind of fish tail. The author is also reflecting very thoroughly upon[53] the genesis of this very exciting novel in which the climate crisis and the complex challenges it poses to people are made experienceable on an emotional, sensual, and cognitive level:

> Even though there are fairy-tale elements in the novel, the scientific research still makes sense. My experience with the genre is that readers do not accept the magical unless the scientific facts are also correct. Without these, it is difficult to convince readers that the changes happening to the climate are real. But then again, without the fairy-tale elements, it is not possible to create a future world. The climate-changed world of the future requires the full power of our imagination.[54] The possibilities of fiction are thus used to convey the scientific facts once again in a different way.

Weitze's latest novel *Rosarium*[55] also deals with hybrid creatures and a blurring of boundaries between people and the world of plants. In the first part of the book, a brother and sister fleeing the war accompany their parents into the forest, where they are left to survive alone after the parents are murdered. The sister becomes pregnant – by the brother – and after ingesting the seeds of a special rose belonging to the tsar's son, exhibits more and more traits of this plant herself. The child she gives birth to is a hybrid between a human and a rose, Esther, who is so dependent on sunlight that its absence makes her aggressive. Esther, in turn, gives birth to twins fathered by Johannes, a transsexual botanist who wants to find and research a rose with human characteristics. At the end of the book, the special rose disperses throughout the world, spread by people taking flights, and its pollen causes respiratory problems that only one person survives – the sister's last descendant, Fine, who has a special connection with the plant world. Fine, for her part, brings forth from within herself a new civilisation of beings that are more plant-like. In this text once again, Weitze interweaves facts about the often unappreciated plant world with a fantastical story. The rose runs through the entire novel as a motif, representing a plant that symbolides not only the beauty of ›nature‹ but also, through its thorns, its resistance to humans. Charlotte Weitze herself says that she considered it important to write about ›nature‹ with all her senses, and thereby to demonstrate a new way of relating to ›nature‹:

> The hope with Rosarium is that readers will feel spurred on to connect with ›nature‹. A new respect will make us realize that we are dependent on it and part of it. Thereafter we will include that in the consideration of everything we do. There is also some hope in the fact that ›nature‹ always regenerates when we just let it be. Perhaps the novel's dystopian moral is just that we humans are merely a parenthesis in Earth's history.[56] While she sticks to the concept of ›nature‹ here on the argumentation level, on the narrative level, a dualistic separation is effectively subverted by portraying the mutual dependencies and interweavings. At the same time, the imagined view into the future calls present-day behaviour into question.

Weitze's novels are entertaining and stimulate the imagination and pleasure of fabulating. At the same time, they invite us to carry on exploring our own relations to "natural" phenomena and ecologies – in all their complexity and contradictions. Hence, the emphasis in Weitze's writing is more on imparting knowledge and making contemporary problems amenable to experience, its intention being to help relate the world views in people's heads to reality, on the one hand, whilst also leading them towards creative reflection about possible futures. In the process, Weitze also reflects on the contradictions of her own work, for example when a book about the climate crisis is presented on reading tours that necessitate flights,[57] highlighting once again the tension that exists between ecological thinking and action and is also inherent in literary writing about the climate crisis.[58] World-interweavings – Josefine Klougart's *Om mørke*

Josefine Klougart, another Danish author, creates a special narrative space in her novel *Om Mørke*. Other as in Charlotte Weitzes novel, a plot can barely be discerned. All that can be inferred is that it revolves around the separation of a couple, who briefly get back together, and a female first-person narrator who recounts the story. The text itself appears fragmentary and it is the readers who have to discover the connections and create meaning for themselves. So, in this text, even the form is "ecological", performing interconnections, and in the following, I will reflect on this in combination with observations on the content level. The first thing that is striking is the intensity of the images Klougart creates. The multitude of intersections, lines, and associations running back and forth between materiality, sensation, symbolism, and interpretation in this imagery allows a complexity of experience to be apprehended, although it cannot be firmly pinned down:

> Skin contracting round her body like boiled wool. / She is cold, and yet she sweats, perspiration seeps from her pores, a crystal rain of coldness, beading and trickling. / Both of them tremble with rage, shaking – why are we doing this, what are we doing here; / it was your idea, they say in turn, in different ways and with their healthy bodies.[59] The quotation is unremarkable at first glance, but at second glance, it opens up a whole world which merges the materiality of shrinking wool with the skin as tissue, and uses the image of sweat, which besides icy rain also evokes the association with a tinkling crystal chandelier, to visualise the strong but silent tension that reigns between the protagonists. The result is that physical, emotional, and cognitive aspects are all tied together in the reception process. Klougart thus makes particular use of ›nature‹ images and phenomena to create a common experiential level that can mediate the communication of mental content. This merits discussion because it may be that shared experiences of ›nature‹ are presupposed too uncritically here,[60] but at the same time, it takes language into a special relationship with being – in Klougart's conception, language permeates being, weaves and forges links, and thereby configures its own reality within the text with myriad connections.[61] It is this new reality, which tries to capture existence linguistically, that the reader must enter in order to really engage in a dialogue with it and make the text readable and

> meaningful – which, in turn, calls forth a new world of imagination that is linked to the reader's experience of being. Apparent here on the formal level is a great awareness of people's embeddedness in their material environment, which is always primary, and in sense-connections that far surpass humans as subjects. Moreover, a dynamic and processual network emerges, a framework, which makes no attempt to capture life's aliveness as a complex reality, but instead inscribes itself therein and perpetuates it in writing. As a result, a dualistic separation of humans and ›nature‹ is relinquished and called into question.

Formally, then, the text ties in very strongly with the material-semiotic realities put forward by Haraway in that it makes explicit new connections between language and being. It, therefore, seems surprising that on the level of content, the text also enshrines a strong distinction between humans and ›nature‹. In Klougart's novel, the most notable implication of the human body's unavoidable integration into material contexts is the need to come to terms with one's own transience and with death. This entails great sadness, which explains why reconnecting with ›nature‹ is expressly not an aim. Indeed, ›nature‹ also appears brutal because it takes no care of the particular individual but is a dynamic nexus in which individual phenomena are ultimately submerged. Here the nexus of the living world is shown to be at odds with human strivings: to cling to what one loves, to exist as an individual who wants not to die and to be remembered after death, and to create one's own world of ideas, which is linked to transient matter without belonging to it completely. This world of ideas is not therefore connected with the image of interconnections, like that of dark matter, but with that of reflections – a crystal whose multifaceted refractions of light counteract the dark interweavings and allude to human consciousness, which creates its own world of meaning. In this way, Klougart's text emphasises very clearly that although people are embedded in material life-nexuses, within them they shape their own environments which are necessarily anthropocentric:

> A person is the only thing that can move a person./ An absence of interest in ›nature‹ as it is found out there,/ or perhaps an interest in what is human in ›nature‹./ ›nature‹'s humanity, if that's something we can talk about./ Where everything is a directed approach./ What do we do with that which is *without* direction? Emotion undirected, and a feeling of being left out, always./ It's not combat; there isn't that much left to conquer, not in that sense. White flags. [...] Still the syntax of ›nature‹ exists, the sentence spoken: one voice among several./ Or writing emerged from under limewash, now simply *there,* a gaping wound affording sight of a time other than the one in which you want to be.[62] Klougart, too, presents these ›nature‹ images as beautiful illusions that obscure a much more complex reality in which the directionless processes of creation and destruction that characterise life itself are manifested. Within these processes, human beings cannot permanently establish their own sense-constructs; rather, these appear to be short-lived

> configurations that come and go within the universal dynamic of life itself. In this acknowledgement lies the strength of Klougart's text: it takes the human need for meaning and order seriously, but at the same time shows that this is at odds with life itself, and that life is impossible to pin down and control permanently. Klougart's text thus pushes beyond classical conceptions of ›nature‹ and exposes a considerably deeper, more complicated and also more dangerous connection to the material being.

Om mørke shows in a highly nuanced way how paradoxical ›nature‹ relationships are. On the one hand, it reveals how irrevocably humans are embedded in life-nexuses, since these determine and support not only their physical but also their mental being; on the other, it also takes seriously the fact that this causes great vulnerability, which people try to escape, not least by means of technological advances. The text helps us to develop an honest view of ourselves and brings into focus a topic that is rarely addressed in environmental discourses: part and parcel of living a good life, respecting non-human life forms and shaping one's own ecologies in relation to them is to come to terms with death and the limits of one's own life. Haraway, too, emphasises this when she writes that it is a matter of "developing a practice of learning to live and die well with each other in a thick present".[63] This appears to be a fundamental wisdom if the aim is ever to change human ecologies: only by coming to terms with one's own relationship to mortality, vulnerability, and resistance can a way of life be established that no longer primarily relies on security, control, and protecting human life, but that once again also reflects and integrates the relationship of human life to a complex being.

Concluding remarks

So to what extent can fictional texts and literary scholarship contribute to the search for solutions to the ecological crisis and a more sustainable way of life? The preceding discussion has shown that this happens mainly through the inherent potential of fictional texts to question, disrupt, and reconfigure traditional models of thinking. Fictional texts can critically reflect on images of ›nature‹ (Poschmann), can visualise and communicate contemporary issues multidimensionally (Weitze) and can deal with more profound anthropological and philosophical questions concerning the relationships of humans to the complex nexuses of life (Klougart). What also becomes clear is that fiction cannot transmit one-dimensional and concrete solutions, but offers remarkably versatile responses and varied approaches to the current ecological crisis. Foremost among these is to make readers conscious of the human narratives about our own being and our relationships to other life forms, our own ecologies, and to rethink and reimagine their respective configurations. Also included in this process are narratives of ›nature‹ and the term itself, which must be seen critically because it ultimately perpetuates a dualism that does not adequately represent the infinite complexity and entanglement of a being-nexus in which humans are integrally embedded.

The challenge is to rethink human being-ness as something vital, physical, mental, and mortal which is embedded in a larger nexus of life – without losing sight of the fact that humans, like all other life forms, rely on structuring and shaping specific environments in order to be able to exist meaningfully in the world. Narration is a foundational element of this as a tool for understanding oneself and the world. It will thus be a matter of learning to understand which structures and stories foster our own lives and the life of others. Which narratives help us to better understand ourselves and our relations to our surroundings and non-human life forms? Which narratives open our eyes to being-nexuses, and touch and change us? From this perspective, fiction becomes a reflecting and thinking space, in which memories, futures, conceptions and experiences, ideas and images, visions and materialities come into complex interplay. This makes fiction a genuine component of ecological discourses, as it invites people to rethink, reflect, and engage in dialogue about problems that are currently pressing.

Notes

1 “Wir sind mitten im Klimanotfall und brauchen einen umfassenden Wandel!” https://letztegeneration.de/ (accessed 24.4.2023). The “Letzte Generation” (Last Generation) is a group of environmental activists who want to use civil disobedience to force governments to take concrete measures to comply with internationally agreed climate targets. At present, “Letzte Generation” is mainly a German phenomenon. An example of a similar grouping on the international scene would be “Extinction Rebellion”, which also carries out high-profile protests but these appear less aggressive. There was a big discussion about “Letzte Generation” in German media and even an investigation whether the “Letzte Generation” is a criminal organization, because of their actions.

2 https://www.zeit.de/thema/letzte-generation (accessed, 6.2.2024).

3 Environmental humanities is understood to mean inter- and trans-disciplinary cooperation in the humanities dedicated to the issue of the ecological crisis and the quest for solutions to it.

4 I take a critical view of the term ›nature‹ as such and will comment on this in more detail later in this chapter. In this chapter, the term is therefore set in simple guillemets to show that the concept of “nature” is not a fixed one, but rather open to all sides and needs to be reconsidered and opened to inquiry.

5 This summary is necessarily schematic. Ecocriticism itself is a multifaceted and differentiated branch of research which comprises a wide variety of approaches. By way of an introduction, see Bühler, Benjamin: *Ecocriticism. Grundlagen – Theorien – Interpretationen.* Stuttgart: Metzler, 2016 and Dürbeck, Gabriele and Urte Stobbe (eds): *Ecocriticism. Eine Einführung*. Cologne: Böhlau, 2015.

6 Koschorke, Albrecht: *Wahrheit und Erfindung. Grundzüge einer Allgemeinen Erzähltheorie.* Frankfurt a.M.: S. Fischer Verlag, 2012, p. 9ff.

7 For a fuller treatment of this aspect, see Linke, Dörte: *Reflexionen und Verwebungen. Wechselwirkungen von ›Natur‹ und ›Mensch‹ in der deutschen und dänischen Gegenwartsliteratur.* Berlin: Nordeuropa-Institut der Humboldt-Universität zu Berlin 2021, p. 26ff.

8 On this aspect, see also Morton, Timothy: *Ecology without Nature. Rethinking Environmental Aesthetics.* Cambridge/London: Harvard University Press 2007, p. 113ff.

9 Morton, Timothy: *Ecology without Nature. Rethinking Environmental Aesthetics.* Cambridge/London: Harvard University Press 2007, p. 204f. For a full treatment, see also Linke, Dörte: *Reflexionen und Verwebungen. Wechselwirkungen von*

›Natur‹ und ›Mensch‹ in der deutschen und dänischen Gegenwartsliteratur. Berlin: Nordeuropa-Institut der Humboldt-Universität zu Berlin 2021, p. 42. On this point, I think that the concepts of Donna Haraway, which are in some aspects similar to Morton's thoughts, are more constructive. I will come back to this later on.

10 In this regard, see Bühler, Benjamin: *Ecocriticism. Grundlagen – Theorien – Interpretationen.* Stuttgart: Metzler, 2016, p. 38f.

11 Bridle, James: *Ways of Being. Beyond Human Intelligence.* London: Penguin Books 2022, p. 51f. Bridle discusses these different approaches and finally defines intelligence as something that exists everywhere and between everything and is inherent in every movement, every gesture, every interaction of the more-than-human world. Bridle, James: *Ways of Being. Beyond Human Intelligence.* London: Penguin Books 2022, p. 56.

12 See Hoffmeyer, Jesper: *Biosemiotics. An Examination into the Signs of Life and the Life of Signs.* Scranton: Scranton University Press, 2009, p. 15ff. See also Linke, Dörte: *Reflexionen und Verwebungen. Wechselwirkungen von ›Natur‹ und ›Mensch‹ in der deutschen und dänischen Gegenwartsliteratur.* Berlin: Nordeuropa-Institut der Humboldt-Universität zu Berlin 2021, p. 34ff. On the question as to the significance of language and of the human capacity for reflection, further work remains to be done. Current research reveals with increasing clarity the sophisticated intelligence of non-human life forms. Nevertheless, I still consider the linguistic worlds of humans to be very specific, allowing as they do for great variability in the conception and creation of worlds.

13 For a detailed discussion, see Bridle, James: *Ways of Being. Beyond Human Intelligence.* London: Penguin Books 2022, p. 174ff.

14 Bridle assumes that technology can be fashioned in such a way that it no longer aims to control and dominate the world but, instead, interacts meaningfully with a complex being. This makes it very clear that technology itself is not the problem, but rather, certain human modes of thinking that influence the way in which technology is used. Bridle, James: *Ways of Being. Beyond Human Intelligence.* London: Penguin Books 2022.

15 Haraway, Donna: Staying with *T*he trouble. Making Kin in the Chthulucene. Durham/London: Duke University Press, 2016, p. 5.

16 Bridle, James: *Ways of Being. Beyond Human Intelligence.* London: Penguin Books 2022, p. 57.

17 I am referring here to the recently published book by Hennig and Furuseth. What becomes evident is that for all the commendable appraisal of the history of Ecocriticism in Norway, basic assumptions and arguments of older authors within Ecocriticism are simply taken over when they really need to be critically questioned and differentiated in the light of current theoretical considerations, for example within queer theory, postcolonial studies, and indigenous studies. See Hennig, Reinhard and Sissel Furuseth: *Økokritisk håndbok. Natur og miljø i litteraturen.* Oslo: Universitetsforlaget 2023.

18 See the very title of the volume, and Hennig, Reinhard and Sissel Furuseth: *Økokritisk håndbok. Natur og miljø i litteraturen.* Oslo: Universitetsforlaget 2023, p. 14f. This is not true across the whole of the field of research, but it is a tendency that is noticed again and again. Ecocriticism is fruitful in those instances where it inquires in a nuanced and open way into the relationship between humans and a living reality.

19 Weitze sought dialogue with the public early on during the writing of the novel *The Abominable Snowman*" as a climate novel and, among other things, created a radio show and invited climate researchers, ice scientists, a psychologist and even missionaries to appear as guests. See Weitze, Charlotte: *Klimaet og kunstneren.* Sorø: U Press 2022. p. 65ff.

20 Weitze, Charlotte: *Klimaet og kunstneren.* Sorø: U Press 2022, p. 68.

21 Den skal nuancere vores opfattelse af verden og derigennem føre til en bedre løsning af de konkrete samfundsmæssige problemer. Kunsten når længst som fri grundforskning. Schütt-Jensen, Kasper: "Jeg har skrevet en eksistentiel thriller." In: *Jyllands-Posten* (1 December 2013), p. 23.

22 Kramshøj Flinker, Jens: "Econarratology, the novel, and Anthropocene imagination." In: *Academic Quarter* 25 (2022), p. 99f.
23 Weitze, Charlotte: *Klimaet og kunstneren*. Sorø: U Press 2022, p. 11.
24 Haraway, Donna: *Staying with the Trouble. Making Kin in the Chthulucene*. Durham and London: Duke University Press, 2016, p. 118.
25 Haraway, Donna: *Staying with the Trouble. Making Kin in the Chthulucene*. Durham and London: Duke University Press, 2016, p. 49.
26 See Haraway, Donna: *Staying with the Trouble. Making Kin in the Chthulucene*. Durham and London: Duke University Press, 2016, p. 66ff.
27 I am conscious that this is a selective and abbreviated account, as the discourse on the Anthropocene is extremely diverse, and that there are other narratives besides the catastrophe narrative mentioned here and the biotechnology narrative. For a detailed treatment, see Dürbeck, Gabriele: "Narrative des Anthropozän. Systematisierung eines interdisziplinären Diskurses." In: *Kulturwissenschaftliche Zeitschrift* 3 (2018), p. 1. https://content.sciendo.com/configurable/contentpage/journals$002fkwg$002f3$002f1$002farticle-p1.xml (1.9.2020). Further-reaching discussion of the Anthropocene is also found in Horn, Eva and Hannes Bergthaller: *Anthropozän zur Einführung*. Hamburg: Junius, 2020.
28 Haraway, Donna: *Staying with the Trouble. Making Kin in the Chthulucene*. Durham and London: Duke University Press, 2016, p. 47.
29 See the detailed summary of Haraway's critique concerning the Anthropocene in Haraway, Donna: *Staying with the Trouble. Making Kin in the Chthulucene*. Durham and London: Duke University Press, 2016, p. 49f.
30 Haraway, Donna: *Staying with the Trouble. Making Kin in the Chthulucene*. Durham and London: Duke University Press, 2016, p. 12f.
31 Haraway, Donna: *Staying with the Trouble. Making Kin in the Chthulucene*. Durham and London: Duke University Press, 2016, p. 4.
32 Haraway, Donna: *Staying with the Trouble. Making Kin in the Chthulucene*. Durham and London: Duke University Press, 2016, p. 127.
33 Haraway, Donna: *Staying with the Trouble. Making Kin in the Chthulucene*. Durham and London: Duke University Press, 2016, p. 132.
34 Haraway, Donna: *Staying with the Trouble. Making Kin in the Chthulucene*. Durham and London: Duke University Press, 2016, pp. 121–125.
35 Haraway, Donna: *Staying with the Trouble. Making Kin in the Chthulucene*. Durham and London: Duke University Press, 2016, pp. 104–116.
36 For a detailed discussion, see also Linke, Dörte: "String Games and Entanglements. On the Idea of »Interconnectedness« in the Works of Rosi Braidotti, Donna Haraway and Josefine Klougart". In: Special Issue of NORDEUROPAforum. Edited by Marie-Theres Federhofer and Dörte Linke. Berlin, 2021.
37 Bridle, James: *Ways of Being. Beyond Human Intelligence*. London: Penguin Books 2022, p. 58 and p. 85f, p. 102.
38 In this regard, see also Bridle, James: *Ways of Being. Beyond Human Intelligence*. London: Penguin Books2022, p. 68ff and p. 75f. Although the perspectives of other life forms can be imagined, ultimately all life forms have their own specific prerequisites for perceiving the world and cannot really feel what it is like to be another life form.
39 Bridle, James: *Ways of Being. Beyond Human Intelligence*. London: Penguin Books 2022, p. 118 and Haraway, who talks about the invention of new "attentive practices of thought, love, rage, and care." Haraway, Donna: *Staying with the Trouble. Making Kin in the Chthulucene*. Durham and London: Duke University Press, 2016, p. 56.
40 Haraway, Donna: *Staying with the Trouble. Making Kin in the Chthulucene*. Durham and London: Duke University Press, 2016, p. 29.
41 See in detail Linke, Dörte: *Reflexionen und Verwebungen. Wechselwirkungen von ›Natur‹ und ›Mensch‹ in der deutschen und dänischen Gegenwartsliteratur.* Berlin: Nordeuropa-Institut der Humboldt-Universität zu Berlin 2021, p. 152f.

42 "kleine Kekse in Knochenform, rot und grün eingefärbt. Gebäckrollen, wie Sushi in mundgroße Happen geschnitten [...], dreifarbig ineinander gedrehte Stränge, kalkige Pastillen, flache Kräcker." Poschmann, Marion: Hundenovelle. Frankfurt a.M.: Frankfurter Verlagsanstalt, 2008, p. 15.

43 "zwei Dosen mit der Aufschrift 'Hundenahrung'. Das war die billigste Sorte." Poschmann, Marion: *Hundenovelle*. Frankfurt a.M.: Frankfurter Verlagsanstalt, 2008, p. 22.

44 See in detail Linke, Dörte: *Reflexionen und Verwebungen. Wechselwirkungen von ›Natur‹ und ›Mensch‹ in der deutschen und dänischen Gegenwartsliteratur.* Berlin: Nordeuropa-Institut der Humboldt-Universität zu Berlin 2021, p. 176f.

45 "eine Vorstellung von Frische, Naherholung, Rasensprengern, sogar eine dezente Hintergrundmusik [...] und keineswegs eine Abwasserverwertung, die die Ausscheidungen einer ganzen Stadt auf Obstplantagen und Gemüseäcker geleitet hatte." Poschmann, Marion: *Hundenovelle*. Frankfurt a.M.: Frankfurter Verlagsanstalt, 2008, p. 29.

46 "Aber ich wußte es besser, wußte um verschmutzte Flüssigkeiten, die über Dekaden hin magere Böden düngten [...] bis der Punkt erreicht war, an dem das System kippte und man sich gezwungen sah, die Berieselung einzustellen. Dann die opernhaften Umstürze der Landschaft, das Auffahren von Kulissen, Schwebebühnen, neuer Künstlichkeit. Mutterboden stürzte von Ladeflächen [...]. Bestimmte Pflanzensorten setzen sich durch gegen umgeschichtete Erdmassen, gewannen ein Gelände, das hin und her wanderte, beladen mit Vergangenheit. Zu viele Eingriffe, zu viel Reibung, von allem zu viel. Rieselmüder, verfetteter, verseifter Boden. Die Wiederaufforstung scheiterte, fast alle neugepflanzten Bäume gingen sofort ein. Nur die Quecke hielt sich. Queckensteppe. Zweizahn-Schlammgewächse. Trockenrasen-Fragmente. [...] Im Boden befanden sich immer noch Schwermetalle und Dioxine. Das Naturschutzgebiet täuschte darüber hinweg, täuschte Intaktheit vor, wies Buschwerk auf, Baumbestand und unverbaute Areale. Alles in allem eine günstige Gegend für Hunde." Poschmann, Marion: *Hundenovelle*. Frankfurt a.M.: Frankfurter Verlagsanstalt, 2008, p. 29f.

47 In this regard, see Poschmann, Marion: *Hundenovelle*. Frankfurt a.M.: Frankfurter Verlagsanstalt, 2008, p. 31.

48 See Linke, Dörte: *Reflexionen und Verwebungen. Wechselwirkungen von ›Natur‹ und ›Mensch‹ in der deutschen und dänischen Gegenwartsliteratur.* Berlin: Nordeuropa-Institut der Humboldt-Universität zu Berlin 2021, p. 190.

49 See Weitze, Charlotte: *Klimaet og kunstneren*. Sorø: U Press 2022, p. 95ff.

50 Weitze, Charlotte: *Klimaet og kunstneren*. Sorø: U Press 2022, p. 49. In this regard, see also Weitze, Charlotte: *Klimaet og kunstneren*. Sorø: U Press2022, p. 47ff.

51 Weitze, Charlotte: *Den afskyelige*. Copenhagen, 2016.

52 Weitze, Charlotte: *Klimaet og kunstneren*. Sorø: U Press 2022, p. 25. This is also evidenced by the climate reports published at the time of writing this article in May 2023.

53 Weitze, Charlotte: *Klimaet og kunstneren*. Sorø: U Press 2022, p. 73ff.

54 Selvom der nu er eventyrlige elementer i romanen, giver den naturvidenskabelige research stadig mening. Min erfaring med genren er, at læserne ikke hopper på det eventyrlige, hvis der ikke også er styr på naturvidenskabelige facts. Uden dem er det svært at overbevise læserne om, at klimatforandringerne er virkelige. Men uden eventyrlige elementer er det til gengæld ikke muligt at fremskrive en fremtidsverden. Fremtidens klimaforandrede verden kalder på hele vores forestillingskraft. Weitze, Charlotte: *Klimaet og kunstneren*. Sorø: U Press 2022, p. 81.

55 Weitze, Charlotte: *Rosarium*. Copenhagen: Gutkind 2021.

56 Håbet med Rosarium er, at læserne vil føle sig ansporet til at forbinde sig med ›nature‹n. Et fornyet respekt vil få os til at indse, at vi er afhængige af den och en del af den. Derefter vil vi tage den med i betragtning i alt, hvad vi gør. Der ligger også et håb i, at ›nature‹n altid regenererer, når bare vi lader den være. Måske er romanens dystopiske pointe blot den, at vi mennesker kun er en parentes i jordens historie. Weitze, Charlotte: *Klimaet og kunstneren*. Sorø: U Press2022, p. 124.

57 Weitze makes this remark in a conversation with Maja Lunde, who is arguably the most famous woman writer of climate literature from Norway at the present time. See Weitze, Charlotte: *Klimaet og kunstneren*. Sorø: U Press 2022, p. 113f.
58 Weitze, Charlotte: *Klimaet og kunstneren*. Sorø: U Press 2022, p. 139.
59 Huden trækker sig sammen omkring kroppen som kogt uld. Hun fryser, men sveder, sveden hagler af hende, kulden hagler af hende i en krystalregn./ De ryster begge to af arrigskab, dirrer, hvad de skal til for, hvad laver vi her;/ det var din idé, siger de på skift på forskellige måder og med deres raske kroppe. Klougart, Josefine: Om mørke. Copenhagen: Gladiator 2013, p. 79f. Quotations from Klougart's novel in English are from the published translation, *Of Darkness* (2017), p. 69.
60 In this regard, see in detail Linke, Dörte: *Reflexionen und Verwebungen. Wechselwirkungen von ›Natur‹ und ›Mensch‹ in der deutschen und dänischen Gegenwartsliteratur.* Berlin: Nordeuropa-Institut der Humboldt-Universität zu Berlin 2021, p. 441f.
61 Klougart, Josefine: "Verden er en uredt seng. Essay om kærlighed og metaforens otruskab." In: Politiken (26.12.2012), accessible online at: https://politiken.dk/debat/kroniken/art5424317/Verden-er-en-uredt-seng (accessed 6.11.2018).
62 Et menneske er det eneste, der kan bevæge et menneske./ Et fravær af interesse for ›nature‹n, som den findes derude, eller måske som interesse for det menneskelige i ›nature‹n./ ›nature‹ns menneskelighed, hvis man kan tale om det./ Der hvor alting er en henvendelse med retning./ Hvad stiller man op med det *retningsløse*. Den retningsløse begejstring og en følelse af at stå udenfor altid./ Det er ingen kamp, der er ikke så meget tilbage at erobre, ikke i den forstand. Hvide flag. […] Stadig findes sætningen om ›nature‹n bare som én stemme ud af flere./ Eller som en skrift, der er kommet frem under kalken og nu bare står der som et åbent sår ind til en anden tid end den, man egentlig har lyst til at findes i. Klougart, Josefine: *Om mørke*. Copenhagen: Gladiator 2013, p. 13. Klougart, Josefine: *Of Darkness*. Dallas: Deep Vellum, 2017 p. 8.
63 Haraway, Donna: *Staying with the Trouble. Making Kin in the Chthulucene*. Durham and London: Duke University Press, 2016, p. 1.

References

Bridle, James: *Ways of Being: Beyond Human Intelligence*. London: Penguin Books 2022.

Bridle, James: *Die unfassbare Vielfalt des Seins. Jenseits menschlicher Intelligenz*. Munich: C.H. Beck 2023.

Bühler, Benjamin: *Ecocriticism. Grundlagen – Theorien – Interpretationen*. Stuttgart: Metzler, 2016.

Dürbeck, Gabriele and Urte Stobbe (eds): *Ecocriticism. Eine Einführung*. Cologne: Böhlau, 2015.

Dürbeck, Gabriele: Narrative des Anthropozän. Systematisierung eines interdisziplinären Diskurses. *Kulturwissenschaftliche Zeitschrift* 3 (2018), 1. https://doi.org/10.25969/mediarep/3602 (1.9.2020).

Haraway, Donna: *Staying with the Trouble. Making Kin in the Chthulucene*. Durham/London: Duke University Press, 2016.

Hennig, Reinhard and Sissel Furuseth: *Økokritisk håndbok. Natur og miljø i litteraturen*. Oslo: Universitetsforlaget, 2023.

Hoffmeyer, Jesper: *Biosemiotics. An Examination into the Signs of Life and the Life of Signs*. Scranton.: Scranton University Press, 2009.

Horn, Eva and Hannes Bergthaller: *Anthropozän zur Einführung*. Hamburg: Junius, 2020.

https://www.zeit.de/thema/letzte-generation (accessed, 6.2.2024).

Linke, Dörte: "String Games and Entanglements. On the Idea of »Interconnectedness« in the Works of Rosi Braidotti, Donna Haraway and Josefine Klougart." In: Special Issue of NORDEUROPAforum. Edited by Marie-Theres Federhofer and Dörte Linke. Berlin: Humboldt-Universität zu Berlin 2021a.

Linke, Dörte: *Reflexionen und Verwebungen. Wechselwirkungen von ›Natur‹ und ›Mensch‹ in der deutschen und dänischen Gegenwartsliteratur.* Berlin: Nordeuropa-Institut der Humboldt-Universität zu Berlin, 2021b.

Klougart, Josefine: "Verden er en uredt seng. Essay om kærlighed og metaforens otruskab." In: Politiken (26.12.2012), accessible online at: https://politiken.dk/debat/kroniken/art5424317/Verden-er-en-uredt-seng (accessed 6.11.2018).

Klougart, Josefine: *Om mørke.* Copenhagen: Gladiator 2013.

Klougart, Josefine: *Of Darkness*, translated by Martin Aitken. Dallas: Deep Vellum, 2017.

Koschorke, Albrecht: *Wahrheit und Erfindung. Grundzüge einer Allgemeinen Erzähltheorie.* Frankfurt a.M.: S. Fischer Verlag, 2012.

Kramshøj Flinker, Jens: "Econarratology, the novel, and Anthropocene imagination." In: *Academic Quarter* 25 (2022), 91–102.

Morton, Timothy: *Ökologie ohne Natur. Eine neue Sicht der Umwelt.* Berlin: Matthes & Seitz, 2007a.

Morton, Timothy: *Ecology without Nature. Rethinking Environmental Aesthetics.* Cambridge/London: Harvard University Press, 2007b.

Poschmann, Marion: *Hundenovelle.* Frankfurt a.M.: Frankfurter Verlagsanstalt, 2008.

Schütt-Jensen, Kasper: "'Jeg har skrevet en eksistentiel thriller'." In: *Jyllands-Posten* (1 December 2013).

Weber, Jutta: *Umkämpfte Bedeutungen. Naturkonzepte im Zeitalter der Technoscience.* Frankfurt a.M.: Campus Verlag, 2003.

Weitze, Charlotte: *Den afskyelige.* Copenhagen: Samleren, 2016.

Weitze, Charlotte: *Rosarium.* Copenhagen: Gutkind, 2021.

Weitze, Charlotte: *Klimaet og kunstneren.* Sorø: University Press, 2022.

Part 4

Literacy

9 Redefining digital literacy for sustainable mediation

Dagny Stuedahl

In a world where media, digitalisation, and information technology are closely linked to sustainability transformations, there is an ongoing discussion in various disciplines and research fields, from media studies to education and science and technology studies (STS), as will be shown below, of how to define the core literacies that are needed to support sustainable transformation in a digitalised future. The concept of literacy has a long history of trying to define the skills required for acquiring knowledge and information. Developing from a focus on skills necessary for doing reading and writing, the literacy concept has expanded into numerous definitions, some of them including interpretation, evaluation, and engagement, with visual, audible, and digital materials (e.g., see International Literacy Organisation).

Focusing on the mediation of the messages of sustainability, which is the focus of this book, we also need to discuss the literacy required for the practices of this mediation. A definition of sustainable mediation literacy would need to include skills and competencies in understanding the relation between mediation, behaviour, sustainable development, sustainable production, learning, as well as ways of thinking, and communicating knowledge of the complexity of sustainability. Knowledge and skills of sustainable mediation does as such diverge from the mediation of sustainability, with a broader literacy that include matters of construction, design, and performance coming into play when sustainability issues are communicated. Mediation of sustainability is characterised by the communication of sustainability issues necessary for sustainable transitions. Sustainable mediation points to the knowledge and practices needed for sustainability transitions by way of mediation. Sustainable mediation involves relating to the "wicked" problems that are difficult to solve, and are interconnected to a host of other problems highly resistant to resolution (Morris & Martin, 2009). Sustainable mediation asks for a competency needed to realise sustainability transitions by the way of mediators.

Technology is central to the 17 Sustainable Development Goals (SDGs) and 169 targets of the 2030 Agenda for Sustainable Development. The 2030 Agenda states: "The spread of information and communications technology and global interconnectedness has great potential to accelerate human progress, to bridge the digital divide and to develop knowledge societies". The SDGs are highly criticised for following the Global North tradition of development policy, and not to break up the power dynamics of global economy (see for example Ziai, 2017). This critique

DOI: 10.4324/9781003392705-14

could also potentially include the technology understanding, which is interwoven into the SDGs, but this is not the focus of this chapter. The aim here is to explore the literacy definitions that consequently are addressed by the 2030 Agenda, and that partly diverge and contradict an awareness of technology's potential environmental footprints.

In this chapter, I question how awareness of the environmental impact of computers, streaming and data storage, use of resources in production, usage of digital technologies, as well as the consequences of digital technologies obsolescence can be included in the literacy required for sustainable mediation. Sustainable mediation goes, as mentioned above, as a concept beyond the mediation of sustainability. The concept includes *all* aspects of the practices involved in mediating sustainable lives in digitalised contexts. This stimulates broadening our understanding of mediation as semiotic communication. And to include a critical understanding of how manufacturing, production, usage, and the lifetime of digital technologies and sociotechnical entities shaping mediation. In short, aiming to include the material aspects of technologies that both shape and are shaped by social, economic, and political conditions.

Understanding sustainable mediation as involving the material makes it necessary to ask what critical practices and literacies we include in our conceptualisation of mediation when we want it to contribute to sustainable living. How may a conceptualisation of literacy include an understanding of climate-friendly production and consumption of the digital technologies used for sustainable mediation? What skills, competencies, and capacities would support consumers in making choices of climate-friendly media production and usage, and equip literacy of sustainable mediation?

Paradoxes of sustainable technologies, the cloud and e-waste

Information and communication technology and digital media all come with challenges connected to usage, as well as storage and end-life phases of hardware devices. Internet technology paradoxically leads to challenges of server resources and increasing energy demand from data centres and data transmission networks for data storage which each account for 1%–1.5% of global electricity use, according to the International Energy Agenda (IEA, 2022). Recently the capabilities of artificial intelligence (AI) have rapidly progressed, with the consequence that the computational power required to develop machine learning models has doubled every five to six months since 2010 (IAE, 2023). In 2022, Google reported that machine learning accounted for about 15% of its total energy use over the prior three years (IEA, 2023).

E-waste is, according to the UN's Global E-waste Monitor 2020, the world's fastest-growing, domestic waste stream. E-waste is fuelled by higher consumption rates of electronic equipment, short life cycles, and few options for repair (Forti et al., 2020). In addition, computers for business and personal use put an enormous strain on power consumption, in addition to the chemicals and pollutants during manufacturing that the production of computers requires. The manufacturing, usage, and end-of-life phases of computers are three lifecycle phases which all have environmental impacts that need to be included in measurements of sustainable design, delivery, and use of digital technologies. Formal e-waste recycling is the safest way to manage e-waste. However, recent estimates suggest that only about 17.4% (9.3 Mt) of the global e-waste generated in 2019 has been collected and recycled in the formal sector, leaving the flow of the rest 44.3 Mt (82.6%) e-waste undocumented (Forti et al., 2020).

Also, data storage technologies such as the Cloud is material. Monserrate (2022) conducted a five-year ethnographic study of North American data centres, to show how we also need to reformulate and critically debate our understanding of the Cloud as information technology. Monserrate refers to numerous studies showing that data centres and data stored in the Cloud now have a greater carbon footprint than the airline industry (Cook et al., 2017), and annually data centres collectively devour more energy than some nation-states. Data centres account for 0.3% of carbon emissions. But if extended to include devices like laptops, smartphones, and tablets, the total carbon emission of data storage technologies was estimated to be 2.0% of global carbon emission in 2015 (Burrington, 2015).

It needs to be mentioned that data required to calculate carbon emissions is often proprietary, scholars and activists can only draw upon publicly available records, documents, and data provided voluntarily by companies like Amazon and Google (Monserrate, 2022). Also, the rapid changes and pervasive data gaps in traffic and network energy usage make accurate, up-to-date assessments difficult or impossible (Koomey & Masanet, 2021). But we might notice that Internet services have during COVID-19, for example, seen rise in usage from 40% to 100%, compared to pre-lockdown levels. Cities like Bangalore have seen a 100% increase in internet traffic. Video-conferencing services like Zoom have seen ten times increase in usage, and content delivery services have seen a 30% increase in content usage (Branscombe, 2020). Monserrates' study clearly illustrates the complexities inherent in digital sustainability, when carbon emission of digital technology usage must be solved according to SDG 4 (Quality education), SDG 5 (Gender equality), SDG 6 (Clean water and sanitation), and SDG 7 (Affordable and clean energy). Electronic waste, digital storage, and carbon emission represent a complex interconnectedness, not only of the material aspects but also of the contextual relations it is part of (Monserrate, 2022).

Purely technological solutions to problems might easily create or aggravate other problems, as Mulder, Ferrer-Balas, and Van Lente remind us of the paradoxes, perceptions, and possibilities involved in the concept of sustainable technologies. Some technologies may solve one articulated problem, but may aggravate new ones:

> The possibility of producing pollution-free energy based on recycling and renewable materials and energised by biofuels, wind turbines and, perhaps, even nuclear fusion will not bring sustainable development if it can only be achieved by introducing new forms of inequity, by suppressing resource-rich developing nations, by creating an arms race with poor migrants that are

> struggling for their future at the rich world's borders, by devastating our ecology and wildlife in order to get the renewables.
>
> (Mulder et al., 2012: 4)

Sustainable development has the characteristics of programmes of action that ask for transdisciplinary efforts, alignments and knowledge that equips for action. The question of how critical knowledge of material consequences of sustainable technology could be included in future digital literacies definitions is therefore important to raise. Also to ensure that future generations have the tools to assess how the "acceleration of human progress" becomes profoundly good for nature as well as the environment. A critical understanding of sustainable mediation includes, potentially questioning the idea of technology and progress as such, but more importantly, questioning the sustainability of digital materials and technologies. This chapter will not conduct a mapping of the diversity of disciplinary understanding of literacies. But it aims to present diverse translations of literacy that have the potential to be aligned in future conceptual development of digital literacy for sustainable mediation.

Sustainable mediation as a socio-technical entity

To realise this aim, the chapter will apply a socio-technical perspective. It starts with an argument for including a focus on the agency of the material aspects of digital technology in the literacy conception. As one anchor for this perspective, I draw on conceptual encounters between media studies and the field of social technology studies (STS) which have converged in a joint interest in mediation and materiality, though from very different research traditions (Boczkowski & Lievrouw, 2008). The other anchor for understanding material agency in sustainable mediation is the actor-network theory (ANT) because it suggests concepts and a theoretical perspective that allows us to analyse critically how material agency influences mediation.

ANT has both inspired and provoked with its semiotically grounded framework which gave agency to both human and non-human actors involved in science and technology development and innovation. Mediation, in an ANT perspective is understood as the encounter of different *programmes of actions*, negotiated between diverging actors (Akrich, 1992; Latour et al., 1991). Mediation and intermediates are central concepts for studying how diverging actors articulate and negotiate pieces of knowledge and how different assemblies covering diverging programmes of action are shaped to achieve the next phases of innovation and circulation of knowledge. ANT makes a distinction relevant to our focus on sustainable mediation, between *intermediaries*, which are passive entities that circulate without changing the translations, and *mediation* which actively changes and gives a new direction to the circulation. Another central concept in ANT is *translation*. Defining for example speech as circulating within things, with and through them (Callon, 2006), ANT developed a *sociology of translation* where translation processes were understood as the point where actors in a process define themselves and take roles. Translations in the form of definitions and dependencies are establishing complex issues. For example, the entities of speech are changing meaning when circulating, because different actors make different translations that influence each other and build assemblies that include each other's arguments resulting in new conceptual understandings. The focus on translation has been central in studies of information technology development (Walsham, 1997), design (Yaneva, 2015), and co-design (Storni et al., 2015), as well as in interdisciplinary negotiations in technology-design processes (Stuedahl & Smørdal, 2015). Mediation is in this perspective material-semiotic translations, and this understanding of media materiality represents the crossroad between ANT, STS, and media studies.

Understanding media materiality is central to shaping a new literacy framework required for sustainable mediation. To argue for this statement, we will now take a swift journey visiting different programmes of action related to literacy and sustainability conceptualisations within three relevant fields of research: media studies, computer science, and education. The different translations of literacy and sustainability do represent disciplinary programmes of action which can help us discover translations that have the potential to align and suggest a translation of interdisciplinary literacy to a conception of sustainable mediation.

The materiality of mediation

Media studies and STS originally represented two different theoretical approaches to studies of technology and mediation. There have been endeavours to bridge STS and media and communication studies because of the two fields' joint interests in mediation and a joint pragmatic turn over the last two decades (Badouard et al., 2016). Media studies were in the first period of internet appropriation dominated by an early understanding of media technology as constituting an extension of human senses and sensorial practices, as argued by McLuhan (1964), Ong (1982), and Stone (1991). These studies focused on the effects and impacts of media technology, and how technology can generate distinctive social effects as an object of inquiry worth social explanation (Boczkowski & Lievrouw, 2008).

Media studies focuses in this phase on digital technology as human extensions, giving attention to the complexity of media practices. This is thanks to a turn towards understanding mediation as constitutive to material articulations and an interest in the domesticating role of technologies mediating people's everyday lives (see for example Silverstone & Haddon, 1996; Silverstone & Hirsch, 1992). This interest STS studies and media studies did share. Mediation became to be conceptualised as comprising the artefacts, the social, the institutional as well as the organisational arrangements that constitute practices with media artefacts (Livingstone, 2009).

The STS field has from its grounding in constructivist sociology and history developed perspectives on technological research that focus on the social factors that shape technological development, presumably related to individual cases of technology development with modest conclusions. STS technology studies, therefore, were rather hesitant to say much about technology's large-scale social effects

(Boczkowski & Lievrouw, 2008) and focused on how technical artefacts were given status as mediators that change, alter, enhance, or lower the performativity of social actions (Hennion & Latour, 1993). In this, the STS field did define mediation as a result and not a cause (Badouard et al., 2016) of processes in the actor-network.

Digital materialities and agency

Digital technologies may challenge the understanding of media as material, as many digital services and digital media formats are immaterial, and the literacy concept related to digital media within media studies has been understood as related to the perception, appropriation, and usage of digital content. We should remember though, that the word digital comes from the Latin *digitus*, which means fingers and toes. The digital does therefore refer to something that can be manipulated by fingers, or digits. The digital is originally connected to counting and calculating with fingers but has since the entrance of the computer and the interest in binary codes been associated with digital and numeric data. Today's discussion of sustainable mediation and digital technologies gives meanwhile an opportunity to remember the material, the finger, and the action of *digit* as part of the semiotic base of the digital. To revitalise the concept of the digital as a material-semiotic concept is relevant to a programme of action that includes the materiality of digital media in its literacy conception.

Media materiality and the political economy of media devices

Inspiration for this material perspective is the discussion of media which has been central in German media studies; where for example Friedrich Kittler has been a leading figure in work at the cutting edge of media and literary studies, by emphasising media technologies as materials that structure human body and human agency (Gane & Hansen-Magnusson, 2006). Following Kittler, media technology structuring is "not merely dialectical but direct relationship between technology and physiology" (Kittler, 2002: 21). The German media scientist Wolfgang Ernst gives another example of this school of materially focused media studies, arguing for media archaeology studies to question for example the physical processes of copying and storing data (Ernst, 2021). Inspired by the work of Kittler and Ernst, media materiality has been connected to environmental and sustainability questions by media critique Jussi Parikka.

Parikka argues that media studies need to expand their boundaries, expanding from content analysis to "the study of material political economy of things and devices as well as from software to hardware perspectives" (Parikka, 2011). Parikka's programme of action is to argue for an ecological step for media theory. But also, to be specific on the need for media studies to include a view on the "materials that are necessary to build them (rare earth minerals), the global trade networks, the waste management, and so forth" (Parikka, 2011). Parikka is especially concerned about how to include media obsolescence and distribution in the concept of media practices, and to include a new understanding of temporality and capitalist politics of recycling e-waste:

> Hence, focusing on the materiality of components and waste of electronic media suggests extremely long and uneven networks of the spatial distribution – and also labour distribution – of media cultures, as well as a completely different temporality to that which is usually marketed as an aspect of digital technologies.
> (Parikka, 2011)

Also, the Australian media researcher, Sean Cubitt, has focused on the material-semiotic consequences of media productions, in his studies of the environmental impacts and the material resources used for manufacturing screens (see for example Cubitt, 2009). Cubitt argues for a confluence between Media Studies and Environmental studies involving both material and semiotic perspectives. While neither Parikka nor Cubitt discusses the concept of digital literacy for sustainable mediation, their arguments and perspectives provide translations of media relevant for extending existing literacy discussions to also include the material perspectives of production, obsolescence, and waste. This is relevant for future programmes of action for digital media literacy for sustainable mediation.

ICT, computer science, and sustainable mediation

Within computer science, researchers have for decades focused on how ICT designers are required to rethink central aspects of their discipline to include aspects of disposal, renewal, and reuse. A landmark research paper by Eli Blevis presented the term "sustainable interaction design" at the research conference CHI 2007. This represented the starting point of systematically thinking about environmental sustainability within the field of human-computer interaction (HCI). Blevis suggested a cultural paradigm shift away from technology novelty and induced consumption, towards an aesthetic of well-cared-for systems. Blevis' proposal argued for a programme of action, consisting of ten points questioning design issues of disposal, recycling, remanufacturing for reuse, achieving longevity for use, sharing, heirloom status, and active repair of misuse (Blevis, 2007). This programme of action focuses on the material effects of digital technologies and argues for reducing the rapid product obsolescence cycle.

In a review article in 2010, Di Salvo and colleagues find that the interest in the topic of sustainability has increased within HCI, but conclude that many of the papers analysed in the review focus on user behaviour as causing environmental problems, and therefore concentrate on user behavioural change as a main topic of sustainable HCI. The critical understanding of technology as part of the problem, therefore, seems to slip and the focus of the debate is on the consumer. Conceptual subthemes in the HCI research field, such as pervasive technologies, ultimately aim to let users know which aspects of their behaviours are environmentally problematic (Di Salvo et al., 2010). The programme of action within the HCI field stays with existing methods and orientations well known in the HCI field, which are applied to address problems of sustainability but without a change of the disciplinary programme of action.

A recent review focusing on how sustainability research had developed in the HCI field in the years 2010–2019 found that the sustainability challenges addressed under the umbrella term "sustainable HCI" still focus on user behavior. And that sustainability within the HCI community to a great extent is interpreted as a matter of negotiating (e.g. decreasing or shifting) individual resource consumption in the home through informed choices or persuasive systems and often based on eco-feedback and/or eco-visualisation (Hansson et al., 2021). The review illustrates how more than 80% of the publications matched to a single SDG, namely SDG 12 "Responsible Consumption and Production". Both Di Salvo et al. (2010) and Hansson et al. (2021) conclude with a call for a programme of action with a broader perspective within the research field, to explore interdisciplinary perspectives to reach a more holistic understanding of sustainable computer and interaction.

SDG's programme of ICT and digital infrastructure

The Agenda 2030 has a programme of action where technology is translated to accelerate human progress. This programme of action points to expectations of ICT to upscale critical services in health, education, financial services, smart agriculture, and low-carbon energy systems. Meanwhile, digitisation may come with a big dilemma, that is left out in much of the UN SDGs on technology in much the same way as in the main programmes of action presented above within media studies and HCI. These dilemmas are crucial for a critical awareness and sensitivity towards how digitisation is capitalist-driven and how this may undermine the sustainability of sustainable transition (Sareen & Haarstad, 2021).

ICT and digital infrastructure come with questions of carbon emission and energy use. For some, digitalisation is a major environmental threat – the United Nations estimates that information and communication technology operations may well already represent 20% of global energy demand (UN DESA, 2020). This creates vast opportunities but also new inequalities and new configurations of power relations in society, dividing those digitally connected from those who are not (Sareen et al., 2020). If we do not centre digitalisation more forcefully in our analyses, Feola (2020) cautions, we not only overlook a key driving force of sustainability transitions of the next decade but also may be complicit in producing forms of capitalist-driven change that undermine the sustainability of sustainability transitions.

The opportunities that digitalisation offers to sustainability require to keep high awareness that digitalisation can be a disruptive force that if unintended, uncontrolled, or underestimated, may negatively affect sustainability and its development (Andriushchenko et al., 2020; Carnerud et al., 2020; Flyverbom et al., 2019; Ghobakhloo, 2020; Guandalini, 2022). Digital sustainability may be considered a link between ICT and sustainable development but is a concept as complex as the two concepts from which it originated – digital and sustainability (Ribeiro et al., 2021).

Of the 17 SDGs, 169 objectives and more than 200 indicators, is ICT specifically mentioned in Goals 4, 5, 9, and 17 and their targets or indicators (van der Velden, 2018). Widening the scope into including terms such as "techno", "digital", "ICT", "communication", and "information" gives a mention in 19 targets directly related to 11 of 17 SDGs. Those goals are SDG 1 (No poverty), SDG 2 (Zero hunger), SDG 4 (Quality education), SDG 5 (Gender equality), SDG 6 (Clean water and sanitation), SDG 7 (Affordable and clean energy), SDG 8 (Decent work and economic growth), SDG 9 (Industry, innovation, and infrastructure), SDG 12 (Responsible production and consumption), SDG 14 (Life below water), and SDG 17 (Partnership for the goals). These 11 goals relates to 19 targets and are, therefore, oriented to technology to some degree (Ribeiro et al., 2021), but they do not link digital and sustainability. SDGs programme of action focusing on "basic needs do not include access to technology, at least not in a straightforward way. However, there is a need for basic technological infrastructure which contributes to people access, knowledge management, and city governance to reduce inequality" (Ribeiro et al., 2021: 242). The SDG programme of action misses a translation of *digits*, namely the material-semiotic character action with digital technologies.

For example, digitisation is central to Goal 9: Build resilient infrastructure, promote sustainable industrialisation, and foster innovation. Goal 9 encompasses the complexity and interrelated dependencies of sustainable development and resilience and is further defined in 9.4 as "resource-use efficiency and greater adoption of clean and environmentally sound technologies and industrial processes". In this example is information technology and digitalisation understood as the use of digital technology to transform social, economic, and cultural life (see, e.g., Bukht & Heeks, 2017) but neither equitable access to nor resource-use of digital technology is mentioned.

A joint report by Ericsson and the Earth Institute at Colombia University (ICT & SDG, 2015/2016) has analysed concerns related to SDG 4, 5, 9, and 17 and points to several challenges where ICT also may come with downsides and risks. The areas of concern in this report are identified with the following challenges: (1) Privacy and surveillance, (2) Cyber-security, (3) Loss of human skills, (4) Possible public concern about health effects, (5) Electronic waste and carbon emission, (6) Digital exclusion, (7) Child protection and responsible use of the Internet. For example, does the report's concern (5) Electronic waste and carbon emission seem the best fit to comment on SDG 9 Build resilient infrastructure, promote inclusive and sustainable industrialisation, and foster innovation and target 9.4*: By 2030, upgrade infrastructure and retrofit industries to make them sustainable, with increased resource-use efficiency and greater adoption of clean and environmentally sound technologies and industrial processes, with all countries taking action in accordance with their respective capabilities*. The report suggests a focus on efficient resource use and adoption of clean and environmentally sound technology and processes: "The industry therefore needs to manage its own energy performance through better network efficiency, new techniques and technologies, and greater use of renewables" (ICT&SDG, 2015/2016: 90)

The ICT & SDG (2015/2016) report conclusions do illustrate the need for an alignment of diverging interdisciplinary programmes of action concerned with challenges of materiality and digitisation. The report also illustrates the need for a sustainable literacy that equips industry and users with awareness of energy efficiency and reuse technologies.

Infrastructures and big tech assemblies

An international, interdisciplinary research collective called Tech Otherwise has gathered to create a manifesto for practitioners, scholars, and citizens on critical technology themes. The group inaugurated this manifesto within research conferences and gatherings and by collecting arguments in a report called Defund Big Tech report (Barendregt et al., 2021). The manifesto argues that digital sustainable design project involves programmes of actions that involve not only individual technological devices but also whole assemblies of different technologies that together create digital infrastructures which people are dependent on in their everyday lives. The recognition that many millions of people daily rely on big tech's services (e.g. search, email, social networking, news gathering, and sharing, mapping, and way-finding), making them in effect infrastructural utilities (Barendregt et al., 2021) gives concrete examples.

The report discusses the capitalist-driven revenues of big tech companies creating infrastructures into society, arguing that big tech has been developed based on science and research that rely at large on public funding, and argues; "it is the State, not private capital, that funds the long-term, high-risk research and development that underpins Big Tech" (Barendregt et al., 2021: 3). Meanwhile, the report argues, the state does not get the reward. Therefore, the report calls for "defunding big tech and recover the resources they have that made them so powerful, and to refund community by redirecting the resources towards areas that benefit society" (Rømcke, 2021: 32).

The Defund Big Tech report defines big tech as enterprises that play an outsized role in governance, and as forceful promoters of technological solutionism, prioritising technological answers to a broad range of social, economic, political, and environmental questions facing contemporary society, and marginalising less technology-intensive but possibly more appropriate responses (Barendregt et al., 2021: 6). Inspired by the Black Lives Matter anti-racist defund campaign, the Tech Otherwise group calls for: "recovering resources currently contributing to its hold on our information and communications infrastructure (defund), which can then be redirected to community-oriented services (refund)" (Barendregt et al. 2021: 7). Tech Otherwise proposes a programme of action containing 27 points for collective actions to exert the pressure and to reshape big tech's priorities and modes of operation. The 27 points of action are structured within fields such as governmental policing, tech professionals and researchers, civil society organisations, and social movements as well as individuals and consumers.

Relevant to a focus on literacy for sustainable mediation is the Tech Otherwise' point of action regarding public transparency and privacy policy, surveillance practices, data trafficking, political campaigning on social media and environmental impacts (energy consumption and sources), and the demand for big tech to support peoples' right to repair. Tech Otherwise demands big tech companies to extend their producer responsibilities and mitigate environmental harms and to support repair versus planned obsolescence.

The manifesto for a technology otherwise communicates a programme of action that implies an ethical redefinition of the accountabilities that are enmeshed in digitisation and technology-based capitalist economies. Besides the concrete points for actions, the 27 points create an ethical programme of action that takes departure in human participation and the right to condemn unethical actions. The Tech Otherwise programme of action proposes an alternative ethical position for sustainable digital technology, suggesting the interrelations between the social, the cultural, the economic, the natural, and the technical to define the just rights for resources. This ethical programme of action, including the just right to condemn actions on behalf of humans and nonhumans that do not have a status as a moral actor in society, may be relevant for shaping a literacy for sustainable mediation as well.

Programmes of action: from digital literacy to sustainable literacy and sustainable mediation

The questions of how awareness of the environmental impact of computers, streaming and data storage, resource use in media production and usage of digital technologies, as well as the consequences of digital technologies obsolescence, can be included in the literacy required for sustainable mediation. This brings us to existing literacy discussions within educational research. The term "digital literacy" is central in diverse fields and practices across education and media and has gained status among other well-established literacies such as reading, writing, and civil literacy to define the sets of skills schools should equip students with. Meanwhile, the concept of digital literacy is as fluent and expanding (Tinmaz et al., 2022) as the programmes of media literacy within media education and media studies. These conceptions of digital literacy change according to media industry development. A broadened conception of digital literacy, for sustainable mediation, will in addition to ethical and material concerns need to involve elements from sustainability literacy from environmental education to fully work as an interdisciplinary programme of action. The three different programmes of action related to the literacy concept from within education do suggest relevant elements for an interdisciplinary programme of literacy for sustainable development which will be discussed below.

Digital literacy

Digital literacy stems from ICT literacies and a focus on the digital skills necessary for handling computer-supported and internet-based services, the ability to locate, identify, retrieve, process, and use digital information. Digital literacy has developed to additionally include issues of communication and collaboration, content creation, safety, and problem-solving. Lately, also issues of digital identity and wellbeing have been included. Representative of this development is, for example, the UNESCO definitions which developed from mainly focusing on ICT and tech skills and information retrieval literacies in to UNESCO Global Framework to Measure Digital Literacy, that includes additional skills such as communication and collaboration, as well as problem-solving and career-related competence in its digital literacy definition. Another example is digital literacy definitions within the policy domain, where the Canadian Centre for Digital and Media Literacy 2022 gives a recent example, additionally including skills such as constructive social action, understanding use, access and distribution, creative thinking, cultural empowerment, simulation, and decision-making.

Within media studies, digital literacies are translated to the expansion of digital technologies, networked media, and social media which stimulated literacy discussion into how media increasingly mediate everything in society (Livingstone, 2009). The existing concept of media literacy has been reconceptualised to cover how people engage with the media and with society through the media (Livingstone, 2018), and represents a turn away from focusing on critical reception into awareness of the competencies needed for citizens to participate in society. Henry Jenkins gives one of the numerous examples trying to offer such a definition, in his studies of the emergence of participatory culture, and the "new media literacies" which embrace a set of cultural competencies and social skills that young people need in the new media landscape (Jenkins, 2009).

Recently, United Nations Educational, Scientific and Cultural Organization published the Media and Information Literacy (MIL) curriculum for educators and learners (UNESCO, 2021), proposing a framework for key twenty-first-century skills. Here we find the following definition combining media literacy, information literacy, and digital literacy emphasising critical understanding not only of the media but also of media institutions that distribute content as well as of the use of digital technologies: "Media and information literacy covers competencies that enable people to critically and effectively engage with communications content; the institutions that facilitate this content; and the use of digital technologies" (UNESCO, 2021: v).

This UNESCO definition of MIL is based on the promotion of information as a public good, which is argued to be indispensable if the SDGs are to be achieved by 2030. MIL contributes to the realisation of all the SDGs, as it aims to empower citizens with critical thinking to enable their informed and critical engagement with media institutions providing content and personal opportunities to produce and share content. MIL's focus on empowerment through media aims to: "support users' purposeful, and creative use of digital technology, and enhance knowledge of rights online, such as privacy rights, and ethical issues concerning access to and use of information" (UNESCO, 2021: 6). MIL aims to foster intercultural dialogue, gender equality, access to information, freedom of expression, peace, and "sustainable development in an increasingly digital society" (UNESCO, 2021). As seen, UNESCO focuses on social and cultural aspects of digital MIL, with little mention of the awareness and skills needed to handle the material dilemmas of media technologies.

Interestingly for a definition of digital literacy for sustainable mediation is that the latest definitions and framework of digital and media literacy from within the educational field include not only critical engagement related to content but also knowledge and critical thinking related to the providers of content, the institutions, and the providers of opportunities to produce and share content in the digital literacies' conception.

It could be argued that endeavours to broaden digital media literacy to include material aspects could build on this focus on providers and institutions as a programme of action that opens for a digital literacy conception that includes the individual knowledge to handle digital institutions influence on societal life. The argument could also be that this individual knowledge also includes critical understanding of how production of digital content depends on material and technical infrastructures and their obsolescence. This would include a critical awareness of how economic structures and big tech in the future have the potential to make production and sharing possible otherwise, and potentially may realise mediation in sustainable ways.

Sustainable literacy

The concept of sustainability literacies has a long history in the environmental education field, which influenced the Brundtland report (Brundtland, 1987) introducing the concept of sustainable development (Perkins et al., 2019). Education and literacy for sustainability and sustainable development has since developed until the Agenda 2030 established the 17 SDGs that include education goals that define quality and inclusion. Sustainability literacy as a field has evolved around the question of what and how to attain and access literacy for sustainability. Reviews of the literature have included frameworks of collective action, community participation, behavioural features, psychological aspects (Ansari & Stibbe, 2009), awareness of real-world issues related to sustainability, self-confidence, values, problem-solving skills, and creative thinking (Perkins et al., 2019). The concept of sustainable literacy is though challenged by the field's ambiguous terminology and fragmented literacy competencies, lacking theoretical justification and decontextualised problem-solving literacies (Perkins et al., 2019).

Relevant to broadening the boundaries for digital literacy for sustainable mediation, the field meanwhile informs us with a programme of action that focuses on handling complexity. This does existing frameworks for digital media literacy to a lesser degree. The broad definition of sustainable literacy as competencies includes equipping people to understand the need for transfer into a sustainable way of doing things, individually as well as collectively, with sufficient knowledge and skills to decide and act in a way that favours sustainable development. Sustainable literacy also includes recognising and rewarding other people's decisions and actions that favour sustainable development (Parkin et al., 2004).

In short, sustainable literacy is about the acquisition of knowledge and tangible cognitive skills to contribute to a more sustainable world and "entails more than simply knowing things about the environment, economics, or equity, but rather involves a willingness and ability to engage intellectually and personally to improve on the environment, economics, and equity" (Perkins et al., 2019). The focus on the agency of sustainable literacy argues for an action competence approach (Iversen & Jonsdóttir, 2019; Jensen & Schnack, 2006; Jegstad & Sinnes, 2015) as an endeavour in environmental education beyond issues of behaviour modification. The focus lies on the distinction between direct and indirect environmental actions. A perspective that also could include mediation.

Recent definitions of sustainability literacy seem to develop in equally expansive ways as digital literacy definitions reported above, and the potential of aligning perspectives and programmes of action seems fruitful. The field of sustainable literacy presents potential theoretical inputs and programmes of action relevant to digital literacy for sustainable mediation that include individual and collective actions taken and direct and indirect actions. These actions could potentially also in future include the sustainability of media materialities.

Discussion: towards an interdisciplinary understanding of literacy for sustainable mediation

This chapter raises a question about the need for developing interdisciplinary digital literacy for sustainable mediation that includes an understanding of climate-friendly consumption and production of digital technologies, and that defines the skills, competencies, and capacities relevant to equip our understanding of sustainable mediation and support making choices of climate-friendly media usage and production. The aim of this chapter aim was not to conduct a mapping of diverse areas but rather to look for elements that have the potential to be connected in a future further development of our understanding of literacy for sustainable mediation.

This swift visit to diverse programmes of action within disciplines and research areas have presented programmes of action that involve knowledge and practices as well as competencies relevant to sustainable mediation. Sustainable mediation has been presented as interconnected complexities where information and communication technologies are understood as means to meet the SDG and the target goals of Agenda 2030. The visits show how awareness of the environmental impact of digital technologies must be included in a literacy conception necessary for mediation to be sustainable and technologically climate-friendly in production and usage. The diverse conception of sustainability and technology within media studies, science and technology studies (STS), HCI, media education, environmental education, and digitisation studies has proposed the potential for further development of a cross-disciplinary endeavour to redefine digital literacy for sustainable mediation. The swift visits into disciplines and research areas have reported on programmes of action from diverging disciplinary fields that may be relevant to align in future literacy for sustainable mediation.

The endeavour contains a visit to the socio-technical discussions, with the materiality perspective in the understanding of media and mediation. This leads to allowing non-humans to be defined as mediators and even to allow the perspective of non-humans to have an agency for sustainable mediation. This ANT perspective allows the technology to be conceptualised as creating conditions and acting as a response to both human and non-human actors. Which paves the way for humans equally to act upon technologies with a will and with a programme of action, rather than being paralysed by technological determinism. Important literacy understanding relevant to sustainable mediation lies in the insight that the materiality of mediation is grounded in the will to act. This agency is implicated in the Latin origin of the digital, *digitus*, indicating the actions of the digits, the finger, or the toe, to be grounded in programmes of action. Material understanding of media, therefore, gives us an understanding of digitisation as being about acting and decisions of resource usage, including elements extracted from the earth as well as elements given back to the earth, such as e-waste and carbon emission.

From the field of HCI, we have learned a programme of action that includes an awareness of how technology usage is related to user behaviour, and how technology design may influence user change patterns. But also, that technology usage, as media usage in general, is still in the process of being conceptualised, and that more entities and interdisciplinary aspects need to be included to understand current technological complexities and interconnectedness between individual usage and platforms, systems, and infrastructures. The programme of action of sustainable HCIs reminds us that just access to technological devices is necessarily required if the basic technological infrastructures shall at all become relevant for sustainable mediation. It is this infrastructure, not the technological devices per se, that may contribute to access and govern an equality-based sustainable life. Technology infrastructures can for example secure an equal resource-use efficiency, or track the amount of electronic waste with infrastructural measurements, and in this way have a function for the good of global society. The human-computer programme of action seeks to define sustainable digitisation as a matter of design of infrastructures and technology assemblies that are both just and transparent. The initiative Tech Otherwise suggests a programme of action to focus on the capitalist mechanisms behind infrastructural technology, and how the income of technology development may be shared in more just ways by defunding and refunding programmes. The initiative manifest how technology professionals may work in other ways with community organisations and professional unities to envision, design, build, and manage alternatives to big tech.

The educational programme of action of digital literacy focuses on competency that gives abilities to engage critically with the content necessary to make decisions about actions that would support long-term sustainable development. Also, to understand how content is deeply enmeshed in the infrastructure of institutions and politics and economies making this content accessible. The programme of action of environmental education focuses, as reported above, on the importance of awareness of real-world issues within media production and usage. And how sustainability awareness relates on acquisition of knowledge, self-confidence, problem-solving skills, and creative thinking, in meeting dilemmas and wicked problems. The programme of action in environmental education focuses on the willingness to handle complexity and reward people's decisions to favour sustainable development.

The bundle of diverging programmes of action presented related to sustainability and technology during this visits are anchored in different disciplinary traditions and values, and are assembled here only to give examples of the spectrum of research areas that are relevant to define the kind of pieces of knowledge we need to handle future technological challenges. If technology is understood as the tool to reach the target and goals of SDGs, it requires that the understanding of digital literacy for sustainable mediation necessarily do harvest concepts and understanding from diverse fields. To create a literacy understanding that gives critical competencies in understanding the positive as well as the negative sides of technology requires understanding the interconnected and enmeshed forces of social, cultural, organisational, and economic power deciding infrastructures. To create a literacy for sustainable mediation requires an interdisciplinary conceptional assembling.

It seems like an overwhelming effort to create a digital literacy for sustainable mediation. A literacy concept that is easy to grasp and that is experienced as relevant for young people today. The density, complexity, and interwovenness of technologies from the global scale into individual private life can paralyse. Hence, I would like to end this article with the ending words of a student, who wrote her bachelor's thesis on *Big Tech and surveillance capitalism* – as her tactics to handle the issue was through being informed so that she had the tools to fight:

> Getting a better understanding for the power of big tech from its infrastructure of the platforms and multiplicity of the algorithms (and the workings of machine learning ones), to the surveillance capitalism that underpins the very business models of the big tech companies, it seems like the right and necessary thing to do to be a counter power to big tech, to fight for democracy and restore balance in every way we can.
>
> (Rømcke, 2021: 40)

References

Akrich, M. (1992). The de-scription of technical objects. In: W.E. Bijker, J. Law (Eds.) *Shaping Technology/Building Society, Studies in Sociotechnical Change*. Cambridge: MIT Press, 205–224.

Andriushchenko, K., Buriachenko, A., Rozhko, O., Lavruk, O., Skok, P., Hlushchenko, Y., Kondarevych, V. (2020). Peculiarities of sustainable development of enterprises in the context of digital transformation. *Entrepreneurship and Sustainability* Issues, 7(3), 2255–2270.

Ansari, W.E., Stibbe, A. (2009). Public health and the environment: what skills for sustainability literacy–and why? *Sustainability*, 1(3), 425–440. https://doi.org/10.3390/su1030425.

Badouard, R., Mabi, C., Sire, G. (2016). Beyond "Points of Control": logics of digital governmentality. *Internet Policy Review*, 5(3). https://doi.org/10.14763/2016.3.433

Barendregt, W., Becker, C., Cheon, E., Clement, A., Reynolds-Cuéllar, P., Schuler, D., Suchman, L. (2021). Defund Big Tech, refund community. Anti-trust is not enough, another tech is possible. https://doi.org/10.21428/93b2c832.e0100a3f.

Boczkowski, P.J., Lievrouw, L.A. (2008). Bridging STS and communication studies: Scholarship on media and information technologies. In: E. Hackett, O. Amsterdamska, M. L.

Lynch, J. Wajcman (Eds.) *New Handbook of Science, Technology and Society*. Cambridge, MA: MIT Press, 951–977.

Blevis, E. (2007). Sustainable interaction design: invention & disposal, renewal & reuse. *CHI 2007 Proceedings of the SIGCHI Conference on Human Factors in Computing Systems,* April, San Jose, USA, 503–512. https://doi/10.1145/1240624.1240705.

Branscombe M. (2020). The New Stack; 2020. The network impact of the global COVID-19 pandemic. https://thenewstack.io/the-network-impact-of-the-global-covid-19-pandemic/ April 14, 2020.

Brundtland, G. (1987). Report of the World Commission on Environment and Development: Our Common Future. United Nations General Assembly document A/42/427.

Bukht, R., Heeks, R. (2017). Defining, conceptualising and measuring the digital economy. *Development Informatics Working Paper no. 68*. https://doi.org/10.2139/ssrn.3431732.

Burrington, I. (2015). The environmental toll of a Netflix binge. *The Atlantic*, December 16. https://www.theatlantic.com/technology/archive/2015/12/there-are-no-clean-clouds/420744/.

Callon, M. (1984). Some elements of a sociology of translation: Domestication of the scallops and the fishermen of St Brieuc Bay. The Sociological Review, 32, 196–233. https://doi.org/10.1111/j.1467-954X.1984.tb00113.x

Carnerud, D., Mårtensson, A., Ahlin, K., Slumpi, T. P. (2020). On the inclusion of sustainability and digitalisation in quality management – an overview from past to present. *Total Quality Management & Business Excellence*, 1–23. https://doi.org/10.1080/14783363.2020.1848422.

Cook, G., Lee, J., Tsai, T., Kong, A., Deans, J., Johnson, B., Jardim, E. (2017). #ClickClean. Greenpeace. https://www.clickclean.org/international/en/about/.

Cubitt, S. (2009). *Digital Aesthetics*. London and New York: SAGE. ISBN 978-0761959007

DiSalvo, C., Brynjarsdóttir, H., Sengers, P. (2010). Mapping the Landscape of Sustainable HCI. In *Proceedings of the 2010 Conference on Human Factors in Computing Systems*. ACM Press. 1975–1984.

Ernst, W. (2021). *Technológos in Being: Radical Media Archaeology and the Computational Machine*. London: Bloomsbury.

Feola, G. (2020). Capitalism in sustainability transitions research: Time for a critical turn? *Environmental Innovation and Societal Transitions*, 35, 241–250.

Flyverbom, M., Deibert, R., Matten, D. (2019). The governance of digital technology, big data, and the internet: new roles and responsibilities for business. *Business & Society*, 58(1), 3–19. https://doi.org/10.1177/0007650317727540.

Forti, V., Baldé, C.P., Kuehr, R., Bel, G. (2020). The Global E-waste Monitor 2020: quantities, flows and the circular economy potential. United Nations University (UNU)/United Nations Institute for Training and Research (UNITAR) – co-hosted SCYCLE Programme, International Telecommunication Union (ITU) & International Solid Waste Association (ISWA), Bonn/Geneva/Rotterdam. https://collections.unu.edu/view/UNU:7737.

Gane, N., Hansen-Magnusson, H. (2006). Review materiality is the message? Optische Medien by Friedrich Kittler. *Theory, Culture & Society,* 23(7–8), 315–328. https://doi.org/10.1177/0263276406075080.

Ghobakhloo, M. (2020). Industry 4.0, digitization, and opportunities for sustainability. *Journal of Cleaner Production*, Article 119869. https://doi.org/10.1016/j.jclepro.2019.119869.

Guandalini, I. (2022). Sustainability through digital transformation: a systematic literature review for research guidance. *Journal of Business Research*, 148, 456–471. ISSN 0148-2963. https://doi.org/10.1016/j.jbusres.2022.05.003.

Hansson, L., Pargman, T.C., Pargman, D. (2021). A decade of sustainable HCI: connecting SHCI to the Sustainable Development Goals. *CHI Conference on Human Factors in Computing Systems (CHI '21)*, May, Yokohama, Japan. New York: ACM. https://doi.org/10.1145/3411764.3445069.

Hennion, A., Latour, B. (1993). Objet d'art, objet de science. Note sur les limites de l'anti-fétichisme. In: Sociologie de l'art 6: 7-24.

ICT & SDG (2015/2016). *How Information and Communications Technology can Accelerate Action on the Sustainable Development Goals*. Earth Institute Colombia University/Ericsson. https://people.climate.columbia.edu/projects/view/1513. Retrieved 19/03/2024.

IEA (2022). *Data Centres and Data Transmission Networks*. Paris: IEA. https://www.iea.org/energy-system/buildings/data-centres-and-data-transmission-networks, License: CC BY 4.0.

IEA (2023). *Why AI and Energy Are the New Power Couple*. Paris: IEA. https://www.iea.org/commentaries/why-ai-and-energy-are-the-new-power-couple, Licence: CC BY 4.0.

International Literacy Association, https://www.literacyworldwide.org/

Jenkins, H. (2009). *Confronting the Challenges of Participatory Culture: Media Education for the 21st Century*. Cambridge, MA: The MIT Press. ISBN 9780262513623.

Jensen, B. B., & Schnack, K. (2006). The action competence approach in environmental education: Reprinted from *Environmental Education Research (1997) 3*(2), pp. 163–178. *Environmental Education Research, 12*(3–4), 471–486. https://doi.org/10.1080/13504620600943053

Kittler, F. (2002). *Optische Medien. Berliner Vorlesung 1999*. Merve Verlag Berlin.

Koomey, J., Masanet, E. (2021). Does not compute: avoiding pitfalls assessing the internet's energy and carbon impacts. *Joule*, 5(7), 1625–1628. https://doi.org/10.1016/j.joule.2021.05.007.

Latour, B. (1991). 'Technology is society made durable'. A sociology of monsters. In: J. Law (Ed.) *Essays on Power, Technology and Domination*. London: Routledge, 103–131.

Livingstone, S. (2009). On the mediation of everything: ICA presidential address 2008. *Journal of Communication*, 59(1), 1–18. ISSN 0021-9916.

Livingstone, S. (2018). Media literacy: what are the challenges and how can we move towards a solution? October 25, 2018. https://blogs.lse.ac.uk/medialse/2018/10/25/media-literacy-what-are-the-challenges-and-how-can-we-move-towards-a-solution/. Retrieved 04/04/2023.

McLuhan, M. (1964). *Understanding media: The extensions of man*. New York: McGraw Hill.

Monserrate, S. (2022). The cloud is material: on the environmental impacts of computation and data storage. MIT Case Studies in Social and Ethical Responsibilities of Computing, no. Winter 2022 (January). https://doi.org/10.21428/2c646de5.031d4553.

Morris, D., Martin, S. (2009). Complexity systems, thinking and practice. In: A.E. Stibbe (Ed.) *The Handbook of Sustainability Literacy: Skills for a Changing World*. Totnes: Green Books, 156–164.

Mulder, K., Ferrer-Balas, D., Van Lente, H. (2012). *What Is Sustainable Technology? Perceptions, Paradoxes, and Possibilities*. Greenleef Publishing. https://doi.org/10.4324/9781351278485.

Ong, W. (1982). *Orality and Literacy: The Technologizing of the Word*. Routledge. https://doi.org/10.4324/9780203328064

Parikka, J. (2011). *Media Natures. The Materiality of Information Technology and Electronic Waste*. Living Books about Life, Open Humanities Press, JISC. https://www.livingbooksaboutlife.org/books/Medianatures.

Parkin, S., Johnson, A., Buckland, H., White, E. (2004). *Learning and Skills for Sustainable Development: Developing a Sustainability Literate Society*. London: Forum for the Future. https://classdat.appstate.edu/FAA/TEC/balllf/Files%20for%20Benton/Articles/learningandskills.pdf.

Perkins, K.M., Zepeda Quintana, D.S., Velazquez, L. (2019). Sustainable literacy. In: W. Leal Filho (Ed.) *Encyclopedia of Sustainability in Higher Education*. Cham: Springer. https://doi.org/10.1007/978-3-030-11352-0_231.

Ribeiro, D.M.N.M, Hourneaux Junior, F., Lara Cunha, C.L., Taeko Kaetsu, P., Fernanda Dionizio-Leite, P., Machado Junior, C. (2021). Digital sustainability: how information and communication technologies (ICTs) support Sustainable Development Goals (SDGs) assessment in municipalities. *Digital Policy, Regulation and Governance*, 23(3), 229–247. https://doi.org/10.1108/DPRG-11-2020-0159.

Rømcke, Y. (2021). Big tech, big infrastructure power dynamics in and through a technological media environment. Bachelor thesis, Department of Journalism and Media Studies, Oslo Metropolitan University.

Sareen, S., Haarstad, H. (2021). Digitalization as a driver of transformative environmental innovation. *Environmental Innovation and Societal Transitions*, 41, 93–95. https://doi.org/10.1016/j.eist.2021.09.016.

Sareen, S., Thomson, H., Herrero, S., Gouveia, J., Lippert, I., Lis, A. (2020). European energy poverty metrics: Scales, prospects and limits. *Global Transitions*, 2, 26–36. https://doi.org/10.1016/j.glt.2020.01.003.

Silverstone, R., Haddon, L. (1996). Design and the domestication of ICTs: Technical change and everyday life. In: R. Silverstone, R. Mansell (Eds.) *Communicating by Design: The Politics of Information and Communication Technologies*. Oxford: Oxford University Press, 44–74.

Silverstone, R., Hirsch, E. (Eds.) (1992). *Consuming Technologies: Media and Information in Domestic Spaces*. London: Routledge.

Stone, A.R. (1991). Will the real body please stand up? Boundary stories about virtual cultures. In: Michael Benedikt (ed.), *Cyberspace: First Steps*, MIT Press, pp. 81–118.

Storni, C., Binder, T., Linde, P., Stuedahl, D. (Eds.) (2015). Designing things together: intersections of co-design and actor–network theory. *CoDesign*, 11, 149–151. https://doi.org/10.1080/15710882.2015.1081442.

Stuedahl, D., & Smørdal, O. (2015). Matters of becoming, experimental zones for making museums public with social media. *CoDesign*, 11(3–4), 193–207. https://doi.org/10.1080/15710882.2015.1081245.

Tinmaz, H., Lee, Y.T., Fanea-Ivanovici, M. *et al.* (2022). A systematic review on digital literacy. *Smart Learning Environments* 9, 21. https://doi.org/10.1186/s40561-022-00204-y.

UN DESA. (2020). The Sustainable Development Goals Report 2020 - July 2020. New York: UN DESA. © UN DESA. https://unstats.un.org/sdgs/report/2020/

UNESCO (2021). Media and information literate citizens: think critically, click wisely! UNESCO [28104]. ISBN 978-92-3-100448-3.

van der Velden, M. (2018). Digitalisation and the UN Sustainable Development Goals: what role for design. *Interaction Design and Architecture(s) Journal - IxD&A*, 37, 160–174.

Walsham, G. (1997). Actor-network theory and IS research: current status and future prospects. *Information Systems and Qualitative Research*. https://doi.org/10.1007/978-0-387-35309-8_23.

Yaneva, A. (2015). Making the social hold: towards an actor-network theory of design. *Design and Culture*, 1(3), 273–288. https://doi.org/10.1080/17547075.2009.11643291.

Ziai, A. (2017). Die Sustainable Development Goals und die Hartnäckigkeit des Entwicklungsdiskurses. In: P. Lepenies, E. Sondermann (Eds.) *Globale politische Ziele: Bestandsaufnahme und Ausblick des Post-2015-Prozesses*. Baden-Baden: Nomos, 247–266.

10 Communicating sustainable uses of plastics in a museum setting

The case of the Museum of Design in Plastics

Louise Dennis

Introduction

'Museums'. 'Plastics'. 'Sustainability'. These are all words with wide-ranging connotations, some good, some bad, some in the middle. Museums can be seen as places of wonder and knowledge or as dusty and boring depending on your position. Plastics as utopian materials or as environmental disaster depending on your position. Sustainability as the answer to our environmental problems or a greenwashing tool depending on your position. This chapter will use the Museum of Design in Plastics (MoDiP) as a case study to explore the role of the museum in the mediation of plastics and their position in the sustainability agenda. For the sake of brevity, it will, like the museum itself, focus solely on plastics and the museum's communication of them without the debate of how they compare with other materials. It will demonstrate how MoDiP differs from other museums through its collecting practices, and builds visitor relationships with objects that they may not be familiar with as well as those that they would expect to see and how this enables a broader debate around plastics and sustainability.

Museums have traditionally used a variety of methods to communicate and engage with different audiences. Exhibitions with text panels and object labels provide a certain amount of information which satisfies a particular type of visitor, for example those who are happy to self-direct their visit. However, as 'every cultural organization today aims to reach larger and more diverse audiences' (Addis, 2023, p. 7), the repertoire of communication tools used by museums has been developing, which include, but are not limited to, audio guides, exhibition tours, workshops, and interactives. The tools used are decided upon depending on what drives the engagement for the museum, the visitor, and the context (Addis, 2023, p. 9). The museum is driven by the desire to share its collections to a range of audiences, the audience is driven by multifarious requirements including nostalgia, and emotional and educational engagement, and the context drivers are the 'physical, digital and social environments' (Addis, 2023, p. 12) where the engagement takes place. The material evidence, the objects that museums hold, is what makes a museum different from other educational establishments. For the most part, museums hold objects that have a tangible link to the history and story being told. Objects in museums, as in any other situation, have the potential to carry value and meaning which

DOI: 10.4324/9781003392705-15

is realised when they are associated with the other objects around them and with the people that engage with them. Museums have been seen as places for education and have relied on interpretation labels (Knell, 2007, p. 26) and object-information packages (Dudley, 2010, p. 8) to communicate information about the objects on display. The shift towards a 'two-way communication approach' (Giannotti, 2023, p. 17) where visitors add to the conversation as well as absorb information given to them is relatively new to museums. It is, however, a challenge for museums to offer 'customized and highly tailored ways, to establish free and dynamic dialogue to produce empathy and emotions' (Giannotti, 2023, p. 31). Visitors that want to engage with tailored mediation practices provided by any museum have been grouped into four types: The curious visitor, the passionate visitor, the involved visitor, and the expert visitor (Baldo and Minici, 2023, pp. 45–49). The curious visitor might be experiencing the mediation for the first time and are interested in what is involved. The passionate visitor might regularly engage with the mediation process to develop a deeper knowledge on the topic. The involved visitor is seeking an emotional experience. Whilst the expert visitor wants to interact with the qualified and expert museum professional to discover different perspectives on the subject matter.

Changes in museum practice have also come about in the form of non-neutrality, particularly when it comes to hard topics such as sustainability. Museums are seen as places of fact, and are in a 'powerful position to educate the public and enhance its ability to make decisions for their communities and themselves' (Rodegher and Vicario Freeman, 2019, p. 342). Sustainability science, through the work of museums, can help visitors to see where and how their actions can have an effect on the environment. It is recognised that in recent years 'museums have strengthened their social role, seeking solutions to social, environmental and economic problems and acting positively towards the urgent need for active responses to climate change' (Garlandini, 2023, p. 9).

Museum of design in plastics

MoDiP is the only UK Accredited Museum with a focus on plastics. To be an Accredited Museum in the UK, the organisation is required to provide evidence that it has policies, procedures, and plans in place to ensure the collection is being cared for and utilised appropriately for the good of the public. MoDiP has also been awarded Designated Collection Status by Arts Council England which recognises the collection as being of national and therefore international importance. It is based at Arts University Bournemouth (AUB) on the south coast of England, and welcomes visitors, researchers, and academics from within the AUB and beyond. It encourages engagement with its collections by museum professionals, the design and plastics industries, and the wider public of all ages (Figure 10.1).

The museum uses its evolving collection to develop understanding of the value of plastics within historical, contemporary, and sustainable contexts. Through its work, it aims to show how valuable plastics can be when used appropriately; acknowledge the negative impact the poor use and disposal of plastics materials

Figure 10.1 About plastics display, Museum of Design in Plastics. Photograph by Museum of Design in Plastics, Arts University Bournemouth.

has on the environment and health; and help manufacturers, designers, and consumers to make better informed choices today and into the future, by learning from the past. It provides the physical and mental space to look at objects made of plastics without the noise of other materials and asks visitors to think about the material value of the objects on display, to perhaps see that these objects are not necessarily 'cheap and disposable' but have an intrinsic and intellectual value; that they should be cared for whilst we use them and disposed of with careful thought when they are no longer needed.

All objects in the MoDiP collection relate in some way to its plastics focus. In addition, they conform to one of three other criteria; to be an interesting design, that is to say one that has been successful or, equally one that has failed as long as there is an understanding as to why it failed; they should provide insight into the society of which they are or were a part; and/or be documented in such a way that they add to the story and history of plastics. The collection comprises objects that describe a variety of uses and activities including the clothes we wear, the games we play, and the environments in which we live. Engagement of all kinds between the collection, the museum team, and visitors, takes place on the museum's website, www.modip.ac.uk, through physical exhibitions, and through group and individual activities to exchange knowledge and create debate.

Cultural relationships with plastics

Culturally, plastics materials and the objects that they are made into have had a varied and turbulent history with different perspectives generated by different people at different times. Today, the overarching connotations of plastics are that they are cheap, rubbish, throw away, and bad news. This position of negativity has been reached because we currently see the mismanagement of plastics waste as it blows about in the wind; we see it as rubbish in our streets, and as detritus in the oceans. To understand fully our current relationships with plastics, MoDiP uses its collections to engage visitors with the long history and culture of the material family which starts in the mid-nineteenth century with semi-synthetic materials, although the use of natural plastics, such as amber, horn, and tortoiseshell predate that significantly. Synthetic materials start to be developed at the beginning of the twentieth century and the use and misuse of plastics are publicly experimental. Initially, plastics were used as substitutes for other, usually natural, materials so it suffered from a lack of identity. The 1950s saw a rise in the number of objects made from plastics by a manufacturing community that was swamping the market with objects made from misapplied materials. This led to objects failing to fulfil the tasks they were designed to do. Plastics were therefore commonly seen as 'tacky, inferior and expendable' (Fiell and Fiell, 2009, p. 20).

In the 1960s, plastics offered Pop Culture perceived disposability, one of the movements' fundamental values. They then went through the 'ecological outcry of the 1970s' (Sparke, 1990a, p. 11) and were considered to be inferior to natural materials. The developments in plastics saw more increases in the late 1980s than in the previous two decades, and as such the image of the material family was constantly re-focusing. By this time, it has gained a more 'high-tech' image and the materials offered 'new textures, colours and moulding possibilities' (Katz, 1990, p. 145). Plastics were once again embraced for their almost infinite range of possibilities during the Post-Modernism era a 'culture which thrives upon pluralism' (Sparke, 1990b, p. 103).

Today, plastics and plastics objects continue to be used, developed, and purchased, whilst at the same time, there has been a number of campaigns that urge the boycotting of them, such as Plastic Free July ('Plastic Free July – Be Part of the Plastic Pollution Solution', n.d.), these are often focused on the encouragement of boycotting single-use plastics. Designers and manufacturers have also taken a stand against the use of such objects, including packaging and single-use carrier bags. As an example, MoDiP mounted an exhibition following the story of handbag designer Anya Hindmarch and her relationship with plastic through a triptych of bags (Museum of Design in Plastics, 2023a). The first of the three bags, 'I am not a plastic bag', launched in 2007, was a canvas tote bag designed to reduce the number of plastic carrier bags used by changing consumer behaviour, particularly that of middle-class women, to bring a carrier bag with them on shopping trips. The second, 'I am a plastic bag', from 2020, was designed to never be thrown away. It was made from a cotton canvas-feel material created using 32 half-litre plastic bottles and then coated with polyvinyl butyral (PVB) used to stop car windscreens from shattering. To promote the launch of the product range, instead of doing a London Fashion Week show, Hindmarch filled her three flagship shops in London with 90,000 bottles as a way of drawing attention to the waste generated by using single-use bottles. The third bag, 'Universal bag', 2021, was a large tote bag

Figure 10.2 A triptych of bags by designer Anya Hindmarch. 'I am not a plastic bag' 2007, 'I am a plastics bag' 2020, 'Universal bag' 2021. Photographs by Museum of Design in Plastics, Arts University Bournemouth.

made to contribute to the debate on the material value of plastics. It was made by the Solent Group (Solent International Ltd) for Sainsbury's, with another version available through Waitrose. The bag has a ten-year guarantee; however, when it gets to the end of its useful life, it can be easily returned to the manufacturer. By folding the bag into an internal pouch, it is turned into a parcel with a pre-paid Freepost returns label that can be placed in a post box. Once with the manufacturer, it can then be recycled locally. These three bags map some of the wider cultural changing attitudes towards plastics, that is to say, 'don't use plastics', 'use plastics thoughtfully', 'use plastics thoughtfully, then recycle them' (Figure 10.2).

Sustainability at MoDiP

Although plastic products are part of the environmental crisis by being poorly discarded and ending up in landfill or worse still in our landscapes and oceans where they break down to microplastics and cause significant damage, plastics materials can play a part in a sustainable future of designed products. They cannot be simply 'replaced without performance, cost, or safety trade-offs' (University of Birmingham, 2024, p. 10) including emissions and fuel consumption. They play important roles within the medical and utilities industries, some have durable and robust characteristics which are important when applied appropriately, they are part of various circular economies, they can be made from alternative feedstocks not just fossil fuels, and some can be recycled whilst others can biodegrade. These are all themes that are explored by MoDiP, and the museum employs the process of collecting, documenting, and exhibiting objects to find ways for the staff to think about plastics objects from an historical perspective but also from the immediate past and with contemporary products. These then help mediate connections and conversations about the topics raised between the visitor and the objects, between groups of visitors amongst themselves, and between visitors and the museum staff. The next few paragraphs will highlight some of the recent exhibitions mounted by MoDiP and will discuss some of the objects featured, all of which can be viewed in depth on the museum's website www.modip.ac.uk.

Friend and faux (Museum of Design in Plastics, 2021) explored the historical and contemporary use of plastics materials to replace animal products such as ivory, tortoiseshell, and fur. This usage may have been for economic or environmental purposes, either in pursuit of a more humane or cheaper option to natural materials. One particular theme looked at different forms of synthetic leather including a vinyl jacket from around the 1960s, as well as a contemporary sample card showing examples of Piñatex, a material made from pineapple leaves, and a modern pair of handmade boots made using a material derived from apple cores and skins which are by-products of the juicing industry. The exhibition also displayed two capes to demonstrate similar uses of real mole skin compared to a synthetic alternative. These capes have been used in close-looking and discussion sessions with visitors where comparisons are made and the merits of each are considered.

Endurance (Museum of Design in Plastics, 2022) displayed objects which showed how good design and the right choice of plastics materials can play a part in reducing risk to life and help people to survive in a variety of situations, including out at sea, in the air, and when travelling at high speed. In these themes, often the enduring nature of the materials is utilised to create objects which themselves are long lived and reliable. Such objects included an Indian-made water wheel designed to make the moving of water over long distances easier, a device that purifies water using the sun's rays, and a self-watering system designed to assist crop growing in dessert environments.

Reuse (Museum of Design in Plastics, 2023b) demonstrated ways in which the reuse of raw materials, as well as products, help to reduce our reliance on single-use plastics. Objects on display also showed how products can be designed to support recycling at the end of their useful life. These included a pair of shoes that were made to be disassembled once worn out and therefore the different materials used would be more easily recycled, a takeaway container that can be returned to the caterer for up to 1,000 reuses, a reusable ear cleaner to replace cotton buds, and a Coca-Cola bottle with an attached lid in line with the EU directive (European Parliament and the Council of the European Union, 2019) that requires all plastics single-use bottles up to three litres to have tethered lids to ensure they end up in the recycling system.

The current exhibition at time of writing, *Seen and unseen* (Museum of Design in Plastics, 2024) considers objects which are literally out of sight, alongside objects where the materials used may simply be unnoticed. On display is a roof tile designed to look like a terracotta tile, but which has an embedded unseen solar panel, a microplastic filter for inside a washing machine which itself is a hidden component but is also tackling an unseen menace, a biodegradable drinking glass which will become unseen in the right conditions, and more unusually a piece of furniture designed to do the same thing (Figure 10.3).

MoDiP as mediator

It is understandable that when we read that fragments of plastics waste can be found beyond areas of human population density including from 'soils to lake beds, from remote Antarctic island shores to tropical seabeds' (Barnes et al., 2009, p. 243) most people will see plastics as a bad thing. As such a contested group of materials,

Figure 10.3 Objects in the 2024 Seen and unseen exhibition. Photography by Museum of Design in Plastics, Arts University Bournemouth.

it can be difficult to see the good work that they do. Plastics are not just subject to changing environmental attitudes but also to changes in taste, acceptance, nostalgia and feel. With this in mind, how does MoDiP with its focus on plastics in design, help to mediate the sustainability agenda? By focusing on a single material family, the museum is able to reduce the complex material noise that will always put plastics at a lower rating than other materials. As an example, imagine three cups and saucers, one silver, one bone china, and one made of melamine. When looking at them closely and considering all aspects about them, such as, how old they are, who designed them, how were they made, how you feel about them, there will inevitably be value judgements made, not just financial value but cultural value, e.g. which is your favourite?, which is most precious? It is very difficult not to rank them with the melamine cup and saucer coming last each time and possibly, even subconsciously, with less consideration than the other two. Now imagine a constellation map coming out of each of the objects connecting them together with all of the thoughts you have about them, each thought has a line of connection taking you to other thoughts, these spread out beyond the objects themselves, there are so many lines and connection points that you can no longer see the objects. Now take out the silver and the china cup and saucer, leaving you with just the plastic example. The number of lines and connections are reduced. You are left with a quieter space. This is MoDiP. Now look at just the melamine cup and saucer, this time more closely, with more consideration, the constellation map of connections starts to grow again and likely become broader in scope.

This reduction of additional information in the single material family museum, such as MoDiP, allows the visitor to look at objects in the collection with fresh eyes and a clear focus. The conversations between the object, visitor, and curator are more focused than in a multiple material collection, with the clarity of a lens over the subject in hand. Visitors are then able to build freer relationships with the objects than if they were overwhelmed with information. The blinkers of 'plastics are bad' are lifted as the visitor steps through the door of the museum leaving behind the entrapments of material comparison and they may see a new, broader vista coming into view. The contested material is no longer just a low value, environmental disaster, the bigger picture is visible, and many other applications and relationships have the space to spring back to mind. The museum opens up a space for debate, not a prescriptive view but an opportunity to explore the subject without prejudice and it is at this point that the museum and the visitor are able to look at how the use, or anti-use, of plastics fits into the story of sustainability.

All activity at MoDiP is surrounded by objects. The exhibition space doubles up as an engagement room and research space. The objects are placed on display in glass cabinets, often on acrylic plinths and surrounded by mirrors which provide a 360° view of most pieces. The room is relatively dark which helps the museum to care for the objects but also draws the eye to them. The museum's exhibitions with their low-key text panels offer opportunities for visitors to engage with objects that they may not have encountered previously as well as giving them an opportunity to reengage with objects that they have. Alongside this traditional communication tool, the museum offers occasions to carefully handle objects in the collection through workshops and group visits; this is a tool which is used in a limited way in other museums. Researchers can interact with objects that they select and book to view through the website, they are able to have individual and tailored conversations with the museum staff who have in depth knowledge of the subject and the collection. The staff listen to the views and opinions of visitors, and hear what they have to say, they engage in conversation and will never steer people to the 'correct answer' or to a fundamental truth but will facilitate debate within a group and offer alternative views that perhaps are not the messages offered by other media.

One of the impacts of MoDiP as a mediator of sustainability is its potential to broaden the understanding of plastics by the public. In the current climate with the environmental damage caused by pollution being a key focus in the minds of many visitors, MoDiP can be a source of information of how plastics have been used in design in years gone by and in the present day. The ability for a museum to demonstrate the past assists visitors to 'understand the present and make informed choices about the future' (Morton, 1988, p. 141). Out of the visitors who have completed a simple evaluative 'comments postcard' during their visit to MoDiP, 92% suggested that visiting the museum had changed how they think about plastics. The most frequent changes in thought, described by the visitor, is that they leave the museum knowing that plastics are not all bad, that there is a positive side to the material family that they had not considered before, and that they are materials with a longer history than they had previously imagined.

These postcard responses from the museum's visitors (see Dennis, 2020) are rich with a commentary that evidences the impact MoDiP has on their understanding of, and relationships with, the plastics material family and its potential use in sustainable design. The comments can be anonymous and are placed in an opaque post box, meaning that visitors can be honest with their feedback to the museum. Respondents commented that it was interesting to see a side of plastics that was not normally shown. A number of visitors wrote that the museum expanded their knowledge of plastics; 'I never knew how much there was to know about plastics', and how a visit to the museum increased their awareness of how plastics linked to economic factors and the wider society. The opening up of the debate around plastics through MoDiP activities is demonstrated by statements such as 'plastics can be good and useful in the right places, and in other places a cause for destruction'; 'I thought plastic objects (plates, cutlery) look cheap and plain, but here I've seen some beautiful ones'; 'I used to think of plastic being just a water bottle or straw, but now I understand it has many possibilities in production'; 'You can do much more with plastics than I expected! It's easy to forget that plastics aren't just packaging'; 'They are a lot more interesting than you think'; and 'I never really realised how interesting plastics could actually be'. Respondents commented that the museum visit made them see a more 'positive' and 'revolutionary' side of plastics, that 'there's more than single use' to the material family, and that it was a good thing to think about the many reusable objects made out of plastics.

A visitor suggested that their time at the museum made them think about how, historically, plastics had been seen as valued materials and not always as those that are disposable. After visiting the museum, one respondent wrote about how the word plastics had negative connotations for them but that they now realise 'that plastics are much more than that'. Another stated that MoDiP makes central that the real issue with plastics objects is people's interaction with them. One postcard response confirmed that the museum

> has shown us a much more positive angle on plastics – it highlights their great uses for benefit in all our lives as well as ways to build up plastics and find new ways to produce them in more user friendly and especially environmentally friendly way[s].

A trip to the museum shows the visitor that a wide range of objects are made from plastics: 'I didn't know that plastic can be used in such different ways using interesting design'. A visit to the museum made one respondent 'think about the different forms and appearances of plastics, how they're made and the creation of the product'. Respondents commented that they 'hadn't realised how many different plastics we use'; 'I didn't realise plastics could come in so many types / functions'; and that 'I didn't realize how many types of plastics there are and how many products are made out of plastics'. Others suggested that their visit to the museum lead to them knowing 'more kinds of plastics', and that they learnt 'about different types of plastics, and all the different uses. I can now use this new knowledge in my own work'; and that 'plastic can be made from many materials'; as well as 'the variety of plastics is amazing and I've never thought about it'.

For some visitors, the museum offers 'a more extensive view on how much plastic is used in daily life', and 'illustrates how indispensable plastic has become in everyday life and how essential it is to develop affordable recycling/disposal facilities'. MoDiP has enable visitors to 'focus on details and how plastic can be manipulated to create different designs', enabling them to 'think about how it can be used in design, all the different ways, shapes, techniques to produce all these products'. There are uses of plastics, which are not obvious, such as their use in textiles. Visits to the museum are described as expanding the knowledge of the use of plastics materials, for example, 'I was surprised plastic is used for not only solid products but also flexible product such as cloth'; 'Today I realized that clothes can also be made of plastic materials and the ideas were so cool, I didn't even think about it, can't imagine how they make it'; and 'I was previously unaware of the term composite plastics'. In response to seeing the displays and interacting with objects in the museum, one commenter stated that 'a lot more objects relate to plastics than I thought, and I didn't consider plastic being around so long ago, I tend to think of only modern plastics'. Others corroborated this sentiment by writing that 'I learned that plastics are much older than I thought'; 'plastic has been used throughout history, not necessarily a 21st century thing'; 'plastics have been around longer than I expected'; 'some objects are a lot older than I thought'; and '[I was] amazed at the history behind plastics'.

There are a number of visitors who will not move from their preference for natural materials, for example, one commenter wrote: 'I really am a traditional materials type of person. I do appreciate the need for plastic but prefer the "real" thing where possible'. This use of the word 'real' demonstrates that it is still difficult for some individuals to see plastics as anything other than substitute materials even in the early twenty-first century. Others simply do not like plastics because of the negative connotations that surround them, for example, 'I see plastic as a bad thing for our planet and even though some of them are recycled once they are thrown away, they are a negative impact';

> I'm not keen on plastics as a material since it is so widely used without thought into how it will affect the environment. I understand that it is a very useful material and is interesting in terms of history. But I wouldn't design using new plastics;

and finally 'It's still plastic'. Statements like this have been generated despite conversations and activities in the museum and show that the visitor has had the opportunity to have an open and unrestricted debate about the material family but that they are still free to form or keep their own opinions and beliefs.

General comments about MoDiP is that respondents find their visit to the museum to be very interesting and informative, comments include 'I learnt so much more about plastic and I already thought I knew quite a lot!';

> As a museum professional, the idea of a museum of plastic is truly fascinating, unexpected, and bold – in an era that is definitely anti-plastic, preserving it in a way that resonates with contemporary culture is not just interesting but absolutely vital;

'I love the idea of MoDiP, I really hope they will have more and more interesting products to show us'; and 'Overall, I really like the museum, the staff are nice as well, as they explain about objects and answer our questions'. The collection gets particular praise with such remarks as 'An amazing collection of products made from a range of plastics and techniques'; 'Complex and visually satisfying materials which are made out of plastic which I didn't think would be'; 'Interesting objects! Plastics are very normal things in daily life. It was a first time to look deeply'; 'Who knew plastic could be so beautiful?'; 'Wonderful! Hoping to return when I have more time – and grateful for the online access to the collections!'; and

'Didn't realise the wide range objects you had from different eras. Also how easy it is to search online and to collect objects'.

It is interesting to see the comments from visitors who see the value of the museum and reflect on this through their responses. Visitors see the museum as a place to visit more than once: 'There are always new practical and decorative examples of plastics whenever I come to MoDiP'; 'Every time I come in here I see something new and different'. Others see it as a source of inspiration: 'It's inspired me with how I can use plastics. The use of trapping objects inside of shapes has inspired me'; 'It has made me aware of the many ways plastics can inspire not only my own projects but lots of other courses projects too'; and 'It's made me aware of all the processes and craft behind it. I love all the attentions to detail it inspires me to be that attentive in my work'.

Conclusion

The mediation of plastics and sustainability is part of a package of communication tools, including those traditionally used by museums, that are available to MoDiP. The museum engages with many different types of visitors, including those that want a tailored engagement who are curious, passionate, involved, and expert as previously described. All of these types of visitor desire a form of attention, which can only be provided if the resources to do so are in place, small teams can struggle in larger organisations to reach the public due to numbers of people and having large engagement teams employed to engage at a specific level with visitors can mean that the public are not often able to interact with the curators, the so-called experts. There are some visitors who wish to debate the subject, share their understanding and opinions, or argue a case, so they want to be engaging with a perceived expert. MoDiP is made up of a small team who can provide a personalised experience if they are available. It has found, however, that team members who have been employed to directly engage with visitors in this way have good interpersonal skills but are not necessarily the ones with the expert knowledge in the subject or in the collection and need support with some engagement from other staff. This has meant that, for a rich mediation session, more staff resource than first anticipated is needed.

The topic of plastics and the environment is an emotive one which can cause heightened tension if the museum team are not able to temper the discussion. Museums should be places for debate but not for argument. During a mediated group visit, MoDiP had a very passionate visitor who wanted to hold council with their fellow visitors to show their opposition against what they felt was the position of the museum. They talked about plastics and their environmental impact, they pointed out objects that they felt were 'bad', and declared that they would not see merit in anything in the collection. Rather than becoming defensive about the objects in the museum's care the team chose to use the energy of the individual to demonstrate some of the pieces that were going to be shown to the group. The team showed the visitor objects designed to capture microfibres in washing machines, reusable alternatives, and objects made from bioplastics, they then voluntarily shared the objects with the group. They were able to maintain the position of authority that they had established, and rather than being antagonistic with the collection they found positivity. The tension was defused, the visitor was not told they were wrong, and they found their own way of engaging happily with the subject having felt heard.

There are visitors whose preferred way of interacting with collections is quietly and at their own pace, they might not want to be part of the debate or conversation or become the focus of attention. They might need time to explore what is on offer, build their own thoughts, and draw their own conclusions before joining in in their own way. They may wish to ask a question, then continue reading, and perhaps ask another question about something else in their own time. There is a danger of museum staff overwhelming visitors with their enthusiasm for their subjects and their keenness to impart their knowledge when engaging with people. The risk is that the staff member becomes the centre of attention and draws the visitor away from the objects without the visitor's consent and therefore becoming a distraction. Getting the balance right and reading the individual is extremely important to ensure that the visitor has the experience that they want and need.

As a design museum, MoDiP, can, and should, use its powerful position to help mediate the decision-making processes of designers, makers, and consumers in how they sustainably and responsibly use plastics in their work and in their everyday lives by both traditional and contemporary tools and layering their interpretation through written texts and other forms of engagement. As demonstrated by the postcard responses, MoDiP's activities are helping visitors develop deeper value-based relationships with plastics materials and objects. In the near future, the museum will build on its mediation skills and activities with various audiences through the development of a new research centre at AUB. The Plastics Innovation and Curation research centre has been funded under Research England's Expanding Excellence in England (E3) grant scheme (Arts University Bournemouth, 2024). It will see the museum working alongside creative technologies colleagues and will consider how plastics degrade over time in different environments. One focus of the centre will be to work with designers and manufacturers to support the development of new plastics-based products. The research outcomes of the group will help to inform MoDiP's public engagement, ensuring a continuing profile of knowledge, mediation, and activity relating to plastics and sustainability.

References

Addis, M., 2023. Audience Engagement, Its Drivers, and Its Implications for Museum Cultural Mediation, in: Addis, M., De Stefano, I., Guerrisi, V. (Eds.), *Cultural Mediation for Museums: Driving Audience Engagement, Routledge Focus on the Global Creative Economy*. Routledge, Abingdon & New York, pp. 6–16.

Arts University Bournemouth, 2024. AUB Awarded £1.6 Million Grant for Research into Plastics Innovation. URL https://aub.ac.uk/latest/aub-receives-1-6-million-grant-for-research-into-plastics-innovation (accessed 4.26.24).

Baldo, R., Minici, A., 2023. Understanding Visitor Value in Museum Cultural Mediation, in: Addis, M., De Stefano, I., Guerrisi, V. (Eds.), *Cultural Mediation for Museums: Driving*

Audience Engagement, Routledge Focus on the Global Creative Economy. Routledge, Abingdon & New York, pp. 34–54.

Barnes, D.K.A., Galgani, F., Thompson, R.C., Barlaz, M., 2009. Accumulation and Fragmentation of Plastic Debris in Global Environments. *Philosophical Transactions of the Royal Society of London B: Biological Sciences* 364, 1985–1998.

Dennis, L., 2020. A Matter of Material: Exploring the Value of the Museum of Design in Plastics (PhD Thesis). University of Brighton.

Dudley, S.H., 2010. Museum Materialities: Objects, Sense and Feeling, in: Dudley, S.H. (Ed.), *Museum Materialities: Objects, Engagements, Interpretations*. Routledge, London & New York, pp. 1–17.

European Parliament and the council of the European Union, 2019. *Directive (EU) 2019/904 of the European Parliament and of the Council of 5 June 2019 on the Reduction of the Impact of Certain Plastic Products on the Environment*. European Parliament and the council of the European Union.

Fiell, C., Fiell, P., 2009. *Plastic Dreams: Synthetic Visions in Design*. Fiell Publishing, London.

Garlandini, A., 2023. Foreword: Museums, Ecomuseums and the Global Challenge of Sustainability and Climate Change, in: Borrelli, N., Davis, P., Dal Santo, R. (Eds.), *Ecomuseums and Climate Change*. Ledizioni, Milan, pp. 7–26.

Giannotti, Z., 2023. Museum Cultural Mediation: From Competences to Best Practice, in: Addis, M., De Stefano, I., Guerrisi, V. (Eds.), *Cultural Mediation for Museums: Driving Audience Engagement, Routledge Focus on the Global Creative Economy*. Routledge, Abingdon & New York, pp. 17–33.

Katz, S., 1990. Plastics in the '80s, in: Sparke, P. (Ed.), *The Plastics Age: From Modernity to Post-Modernity*. Victoria & Albert Museum, London, pp. 145–151.

Knell, S.J., 2007. Museums, Reality and the Material World, in: Knell, S.J. (Ed.), *Museums in a Material World*. Routledge, London & New York, pp. 1–28.

Morton, A., 1988. Tomorrow's Yesterdays: Science Museums and the Future, in: Lumley, R. (Ed.), *The Museum Time Machine: Putting Cultures on Display*. Routledge, London & New York, pp. 128–143.

Museum of Design in Plastics, 2021. Friend and Faux. URL https://www.modip.ac.uk/exhibitions/friend-and-faux (accessed 2.29.24).

Museum of Design in Plastics, 2022. Endurance. URL https://www.modip.ac.uk/exhibitions/endurance (accessed 2.29.24).

Museum of Design in Plastics, 2023a. Anya Hindmarch - A Triptych. URL https://www.modip.ac.uk/blog/2023/01/anya-hindmarch-triptych (accessed 3.2.24).

Museum of Design in Plastics, 2023b. Reuse. URL https://www.modip.ac.uk/exhibitions/reuse (accessed 2.29.24).

Museum of Design in Plastics, 2024. Seen and Unseen. URL https://www.modip.ac.uk/exhibitions/seen-and-unseen (accessed 2.29.24).

Plastic Free July – Be Part of the Plastic Pollution Solution, n.d. Plastic Free July. URL https://www.plasticfreejuly.org/ (accessed 3.2.24).

Rodegher, S.L., Vicario Freeman, S., 2019. Advocacy and Activism: A Framework for Sustainability Science in Museums, in: Janes, R.R., Sandell, R. (Eds.), *Museum Activism, Museum Meanings*. Routledge, Abingdon & New York, pp. 337–347.

Sparke, P. (Ed.), 1990a. *The Plastics Age: From Modernity to Post Modernity*. Victoria & Albert Museum, London.

Sparke, P., 1990b. Plastics and Pop Culture, in: Sparke, P. (Ed.), *The Plastics Age: From Modernity to Post-Modernity*. Victoria & Albert Museum, London, pp. 93–103.

University of Birmingham, 2024. *The Sustainable Plastics Policy Commission: Key Findings for Government*. Birmingham.

11 Indigenous approaches to mediation of the climate and nature emergency

A conversation with Vanessa Andreotti

Lisbeth Løvbak Berg

Mediation of sustainability, as well as the proposed political solutions, are dominated by Western ideas, where "indigenous knowledge is not wanted at the level of *how,* only at the level of *what*" (Yunkaporta, 2020, p. 42). Indeed, the concept of sustainability itself is a Western conception, grown out of concern over the environmental effects of increasing consumption and consumerism produced by Western economic and political systems. Despite sustainable development being on the agendas of global institutions since the release of the Brundtland Report in 1987, environmental impacts and global warming continue to increase globally.

Western media largely attribute attention to climate change and related international treaties, technologies and solutions, over other sustainability issues (Barkemeyer et al., 2018). When we hear of Indigenous peoples' concerns, it's most often related to their struggles to protect their lands, and as such portrayed as a struggle for survival, literally and/or culturally; e.g., the Sami in Norway, Sweden, and Finland protesting river dams, mining, windmills, etc.; the Kaypayo in the Amazon fighting against illegal mining; the Wet'suwet'en First Nation in Canada fighting oil pipelines. What is less communicated is the continuous work that many Indigenous groups do to raise awareness and fight for action on the climate and natural emergency (CNE). Their engagement with nature and land is founded on ecocentric worldviews, as opposed to Western cultures' egocentric/anthropocentric world views.

On a scholarly level, however, Indigenous struggles as well as their stories are attracting more attention (e.g., de la Cadena & Starn, 2007; King et al., 2009; Porsanger, 2004), along with Indigenous scholars and writers gaining attention (e.g., Kimmerer, 2013; Yunkaporta, 2020, 2023) and the need for diverse perspectives is also getting some attention from the European Environmental Agency (Strand et al., 2023). Different narratives of humanity and nature also come from within Western knowledge traditions (e.g., Harari, 2014; Haraway, 2016; Jackson, 2009; Quinn, 1992; Raworth, 2017; Trebeck & Williams, 2019), while the ideas we have of the world, which narratives dominate, and how they shape the trajectory of the future are increasingly examined (e.g., Beckert & Suckert, 2021; Jasanoff & Kim, 2015).

Hence, slowly new stories are being told, or old stories are coming to light but still, we struggle to find ways of doing which will move us out of the crisis and not

DOI: 10.4324/9781003392705-16

just perpetuate the same, growth-based systems that we currently have. As Ghosh (2018, p. 9), puts it: "For let us make no mistake, the climate crisis is also a crisis of culture, and thus of the imagination". As such, making space for other cultures and other worldviews, for other stories, and other ways of thinking about the world, is ever more important to be able to move from a system that exploits and extracts towards one that can be sustained within the limits of the planet's carrying capacity. One of the scholars working pedagogically to bridge the gaps between Indigenous and Western knowledge in order to find collective ways of moving in the direction of a sustainable future is Vanessa Andreotti.

In this chapter, Indigenous refers to the groups of Indigenous peoples in Canada, the USA, and South America with whom Andreotti works. Though many Indigenous groups share cultural traits such as ecocentric worldviews, collectivist social systems and a distinct connection to land and their local habitat, and as such oppose Western egocentrism/anthropocentrism, individualism, and globalism, their educational approaches will vary.

The work of Vanessa Andreotti

Vanessa Andreotti,[1] dean of education at the University of Victoria, Canada, is a scholar, educator, and the author of *Hospicing Modernity: Facing Humanity's Wrongs and the Implications for Social Activism* (2021). Her work involves a variety of educational settings, from universities to organisations. As the interim director for the Peter Wall Institute for Advanced Studies (PWIAS) at the University of British Columbia (UBC), she led the 2022/2023 Climate and Nature Emergency Catalyst Program, connecting "scholars, students, artists, disciplines, sectors, and communities to activate new ways of knowing and acting together in these challenging socio-ecological times" (Andreotti et al., 2023, p. 4). This project also included a third aspect of the emergency: the health crisis. At UBC, she has also been involved in work such as the UBC 2020 Indigenous Strategic Plan (ISP), outlining eight goals and 43 actions the university will take to implement Indigenous People's human rights (UBC, n.d.).

Andreotti's work has grown out of opposition to formal education systems, and work with educational and development programs led her to see to what extent modernity is influencing educational processes across the world: these enduring manifestations of colonisation, a global hegemony of power relations that benefit particular groups can be referred to as *coloniality*, while *colonialism* refers to the formal occupation of land and the accompanying subjugation of their original peoples (Quijano, 2000). The juxtaposition of modern(ity)-colonial(ity) often seen in her work further highlights the interconnection between the two.

Decolonisation became a driver for her and the Gesturing Towards Decolonial Futures (GTDF) Arts/Research Collective, which she co-founded. The collective is:

> a transnational, intergenerational, and inter-disciplinary collective of activists, students, educators, volunteers and Indigenous knowledge keepers who

work closely together to develop public pedagogies and artistic interventions at the interface of two sets of questions:

1 questions related to confronting historical, systemic and ongoing social and ecological violence, and
2 questions related to the unsustainability of modern-colonial systems and ways of being.

(Anticipation Conference, 2022, p. 150)

Neither she nor the GTDF Arts/Research Collective, however, offer precise definitions of decolonisation:

> In our research, teaching, community engagements, and other forms of cultural production and pedagogy, we do not offer normative definitions of decolonization, nor put forth prescriptive plans for action. Rather, we seek to facilitate the development of "radars" for potential circularities and short-circuits, and to identify opportunities and openings for responsible, context-specific collective experiments that enact different kinds of relationships, and different possibilities for (co)existence, without guarantees.
>
> (Stein et al., 2020, p. 45)

Rather they offer a pedagogical approach to work with decolonisation:

> In this pedagogical approach, we emphasize complexity, complicity, and uncertainty, and draw on multiple interpretations and dimensions of decolonial theory and practice – in particular, its ecological, cognitive, affective, relational, and economic dimensions. We undertake this work with a sense of humility, recognizing that our lives and livelihoods are underwritten by systemic, historical, and ongoing colonial violence. Thus, we can only "gesture" towards the direction of decolonization, and we will undoubtedly make mistakes in the process, for which we are also accountable. Yet these mistakes also offer important learning opportunities.
>
> (Stein et al., 2020, p. 45)

Among Indigenous peoples, Andreotti works particularly closely with the Huni Kui Indigenous people of the Amazon and their hereditary leader and elected President of the Huni Kui Federation of the State of Acre, Chief Ninawa Huni Kui.[2] Together with the GTDF, they have formulated a particularly hard-hitting critique of Western-oriented modern education from an Indigenous perspective, highlighting the incapability of colonial societies to create grown-ups as one cause for the current inaction on the climate and nature emergency (CNE), along with denial. (Note that the CNE is denoted as one crisis, with two interlinked elements.) The crisis is also of a relational nature, of the relationship between man and nature. The critique further exposes the "cracks in the house of modernity"

(Stein et al., 2017) and the fallacies in the narrative of modernity as the epitome of human development.

> Modernity is a single story of progress, development, human evolution and civilization that is omnipresent.
>
> (Machado de Oliveira, 2021, p. xxi)[3]

As with colonialism, Andreotti does not provide a precise definition of modernity but rather encourages us to recognise the voice of modernity in ourselves, which Western culture is built on, through the use of pedagogical exercises. She draws our attention to how modernity creates hierarchies of people, living beings, knowledges, experiences, needs, etc., all the while emphasising that perceptions of and relationships to modernity vary greatly, from strong attachment to complete rejection. Herself, she is among those who "believe that a genuinely new system is only possible if we are able to learn the lessons that modernity has to offer in its decline" (Machado de Oliveira, 2021, p. 17).

It follows that Andreotti's work goes further than current discourses that blame capitalism for the ills of today and discusses modernity itself as the root cause of the unsustainability and violence we see today: "Modernity's violence and unsustainability are usually interpreted within modernity as *complicated problems* that can be solved rather than *complex predicaments* that need to be confronted" (Machado de Oliveira, 2021, p. 30).

Andreotti's scholarship emphasises that there are no quick fixes: the violence and unsustainability are intrinsic to modernity – what modernity is based on. In this also lies that modernity's views of technology, progress, education, and pedagogies prevent us from seeing other ways of living and being, with other humans as well as nature. Andreotti's book *Hospicing Modernity* (2021), however, offers some hope or relief to those of us disillusioned with the current system. Here she posits that it's a dying system but through hospicing it, we "act with compassion to allow a system to die with grace, and to support people in the process of letting go – even when they are holding on for dear life to what is already gone" (Machado de Oliveira, 2021, xxii). The book also encourages learning from modernity to be able to do better to enable this, it offers a psychological journey of observing and untangling the complexities and contradictions within oneself relating to modernity and how we live our lives.

Drawing on the pedagogy and the Indigenous wisdom of the people with whom she has worked over the years, Andreotti further challenges us to grow up and face modernity's inherent violence and unsustainability but points out that, because we are so conditioned to seeing through its lens, it is hard to imagine other ways of being and doing – even to imagine humanity as being anything other than destructive. Here, her work, similarly to that of the French philosopher Ricoeur (1976), and many other thinkers, highlights the situated nature of imagination, and its cultural limitations. The words we use to describe the world betray our worldview, or in Haraway's words, "it matters what stories tell stories" (2016). With this in mind, this conversation explores Andreotti's pedagogical approaches to sustainability mediation and unlearning modernity's doctrines, and the following reflection discusses and contextualises this approach.

Conversation

On one of the sunniest Oslo afternoons in August 2023, I sat down in front of my computer to connect with Vanessa Andreotti from her home in Canada. True to her pedagogical approach, Andreotti started the conversation by asking me the important question of what would resonate with my audience.

> The themes of this anthology are mediation and communication of sustainability, greenwashing etc. In a Norwegian context, we also have our own history of coloniality, as I know you are aware of, regarding the Sami people, most recently the building of wind farms on Sami land.
>
> (Huni Kui & Andreotti, 2022)

When we talk about sustainability, we have to be thinking about sustainability of what and for whom. Who decides? In whose name? For whose benefit? And how come? We are in this situation. How did we arrive at the present and at whose expense? At whose expense do we have the system that we have today and what are the implications of sustaining this system, the current system, which is inherently harmful and unsustainable? I think we have come to a point where we already acknowledge that the current social, cultural, and economic system that we have in the mainstream is overshooting the limits of the planet, the planet has boundaries, and we can't have continuous growth and consumption to the levels that we have today in a finite planet. So, then the question is, how do we define sustainability – sustainability of what? And do we even know what a sustainable system would look like?

How would you answer those questions?
Whenever we get to this question generally, we have put on the table the fact that many Indigenous cultures, if not most Indigenous cultures have had sustainable systems that could live in partnership with or even sometimes as entangled in their environment in ways that secured the possibility of life, both human and non-human, for incoming generations. Their decisions were based on that responsibility to secure and sustain life. So, if we are thinking about sustainability in the broader sense, it's systems that can sustain life not only for human beings but also for non-human beings, and this sustainability is a regenerative one, it does not exploit, extract, and just consume, but it is one that is in tune and in line with a regenerative nature of Earth as a living system. It doesn't see earth as a property or resource to be consumed, but as something that we are a part of. And on those aspects, Indigenous peoples have developed their sciences and technologies to an advanced stage.

I work with Chief Ninawa Huni Kui who talks about Western culture developing to a very advanced stage with sciences and technologies for building things but that are often used for exploitation, expropriation, destitution, dispossession, genocide and ecocide, while Indigenous peoples have developed technologies and sciences of respect, reverence, reciprocity, regeneration, and responsibility to an advanced stage. And these sciences of respect and responsibility are missing in Western societies, and I think that's a very compelling argument for us to sober up, and to grow up, and show up differently.

There are increasing efforts to decolonise education/curriculum by including more diverse authors and perspectives. What are your thoughts on these efforts? How would an Indigenous curriculum look?

Part of the Indigenous critique is also that Western culture is in a self-infantilising state – and it is a young culture from their perspective too – and in Indigenous education, you cannot teach people directly, you have to create the context where they find it out for themselves, they figure it out, so going to Indigenous cultures and asking them to teach us is not going to look like a curriculum, it's going to look like "go and figure it out for yourself, the crisis will teach us, and the planet will teach us by showing us the implications of our choices". Basically, it's this idea that we as products of Western culture, we need a culture that produces grown-ups. We need to grow up and this process of maturing and of adulting and then of becoming elders to our relations of human and non-human beings is something that within modernity – which is our current story of progress, development and civilisation – is really not there. It's all about being functional within capitalist economies and creating value within this economy so that you can justify why you are alive. Hence, eldering and maturity, aging well, living well and dying well are teachings that have been exiled from our current system. Then how do we bring these values back without appropriating Indigenous cultures, creating them from Western culture itself?

This is a recurrent theme in your work, including in Hospicing Modernity, where you speak about growing up and learning to compost our "shit". So, what do you mean by growing up?

For me, growing up means facing the mistakes that have been made and are repeatedly made so that we can make different mistakes in the future, but also activating the sense of visceral responsibility. Visceral responsibility is not the kind of responsibility that is an intellectual choice, it's not about morality or feeling superior to each other, it's about doing what's needed even if that goes against your self-interest, and it's a different neurobiological state, not a state where you're seeking dopamine, or where you're seeking status: it's a state where you do what needs to be done, be it cleaning toilets or composting shit, even if you're not going to see the result of that work, even if it's not going to benefit you, it's going to benefit other people.

And it's interesting because Chief Ninawa Huni Kui, the chief from the Amazon, who we work very closely with, talks about colonialism as a separation of humans from nature, that then creates all the other problems of hierarchies, of value, of everything needing to be commodified, and so on so forth. He says that this separation, which he calls colonialism, is neurobiological, a neuro-physical impairment that is imposed upon us so the chemistry that we have to have to keep functioning in the current society is an impairment. So, we are missing out on so much, so many other states where we can be well without having to resort to consumption or competition and status-seeking. How do we then activate this other neurochemical/neuro-biological state that is possible, to engender a different system? Because part of the problem, I think, is that we have this neuro-chemical setup, and then we try to imagine something different, but because this setup is embodied – it's neuro-physical – we can only imagine the same thing in different clothes. And if we had a different state of being, our imagination might manifest differently, because our imagination is already also colonised.

So, if we're thinking about climate change, and how to approach the problem, in fact the big challenge that we have is that people are not conditioned to be able to sit with reality, especially the unpleasant parts of it. For example, complexity is unpleasant for many people; they prefer to have things reduced to something simple.

Complexity and education

Your, and the GTDF collective's, pedagogical approach is based on unlearning the teachings of modernity:

> One, we need to unlearn what we have been cognitively, affectively and relationally conditioned to think, feel, relate, hope and imagine in modern/colonial systems, which includes our formal education systems. Two, we need to learn to expand our capacity to hold space for multiple, moving layers of complexity, complicity and uncertainty.
>
> (Andreotti et al., 2023, p. 102)

However, these unlearning processes can be extremely painful and if forced, elicit denial and feelings of protectiveness towards what is familiar, i.e., modernity. How do you approach this pedagogically?

So, part of my work with these Indigenous groups and also with the collective here in what is known as Canada today is that we need to figure out a way of putting this information on the table while we raise the emotional threshold. So, the first invitation is for people to expand their capacity to sit with difficult, complex, and painful things without feeling overwhelmed, immobilised, or demanding quick fixes or demanding to be rescued from the discomfort. If we can't do that there's no point in continuing because the information that will come next is the information that most people have been conditioned to deny. And when we are dealing with denial, it's very different from dealing with ignorance. Ignorance is just lack of information: fine, you present the information and you're done, and people say: "Oh, ok, now I get it". But when you deal with denial or disavowal, it's a very different process because you present the information and people freak out. And then generally, when they freak out – they shoot the messenger. Then they have a defensive reaction against you because they cannot process the anxiety and the frustration that emerges with that.

> You write that "[b]efore we know it (literally), modernity's desires for universal formulas, consensual definitions, creative solutions, and hopeful futures hijack our attempts to grapple with the complexities of its own death" (Machado de Oliveira, 2021, p. 30). Why is complexity so challenging for us?

The first challenge we face is that we are not conditioned by education, psychology or the media to sit with the aspects of reality that are unpleasant, so there are lots of escape mechanisms that we find, and it has to do with our emotional threshold, what we can take. So, if people can't take the complexity we have in terms of the destruction of biodiversity because of the clothes we wear, the food we have, the food systems and the transportation and the economics and all of that, people feel overwhelmed. We have not been equipped to process the frustrations, the anxiety and the negative emotions. We are unequipped to deal with it and what we want is just an escape into an idealised reality or a simplistic solution that will just make us feel and look good but that won't really get to the root of the problem. And then we have a market system that exploits it. So, in many ways, we have become these consumers, primarily consumers in a market and if we demand simplistic solutions, the market says: "that's exactly what we're gonna give you!"

In our education systems and even Western psychology, functionality in the current system is about being happy and hopeful, but this "happy and hopeful"-thing is a liability to us actually facing what we need to face together, and figuring out another way of being well and coordinated together without having to the unpleasant aspects of reality, without having to deny our complicity in harm, without having to deny that for us to exist as we are right now in the Global North, we do that at the expense of other people, at the expense of the planet, at the expense of other species. All this violence we need to deny the things we want to enjoy. But there is another way – it's not either you enjoy or don't enjoy, either you are great, or you are worthless. This is precisely what we have been conditioned to think. But there are other ways where you can stay with the trouble, where you can compost the "shit" and still find joy. It's not that you're going to be completely depressed. In the current system, in the current neuro-biological setup, either you are avoiding and denying the same things and you're happy or you're acknowledging these things and you are depressed.

How can we move away from this and learn to "hold space for complexity"?
There are other ways in which we can hold everything together and still find well-being without having to deny and turn our back to reality – to the reality of

our own harmful impact. It's a different kind of education, it has to trick the ego, bypass the defences of the ego, and invite people into a very different process of maturing emotionally. So, we talk about *a compass* that we need in Western society. The compass[4] we are testing out in my research group [GTDF] is a compass of four things:

Number one is *emotional sobriety* or *serenity*, which means interrupting these immature compulsive impulses to sometimes deny reality or addictions that we have to consume.

Number two is *relational maturity,* which is about learning to build relationships that are not transactional, "you give me this, I give you that", but about trust, consent, reciprocity, respect, and accountability, which are very difficult to build. And we still need to figure out how to do that within Western societies.

Number three is *intellectual discernment,* which is about learning to approach reality and ourselves in it and language itself and knowledge in a layered way. Within modernity, we are taught to flatten everything to a linear thing that has a beginning, middle and end, that is very flattened and imposes coherence. But what we're inviting people to do is to be able to hold the moving layers of complexity and identify contradictions and paradoxes and ambiguity and not feel overwhelmed by it.

The last thing in the compass is *intergenerational responsibility,* so that part is about understanding yourself as part of a continuum, it can't be just about you, it has to be about something bigger than yourself, and not only human, tight, so we are responsible for the other generations of other species and we have been extremely irresponsible in interrupting many genealogical lines in order for us to have the comforts that we have today.

False solutions to the CNE

You have worked with many Indigenous groups over the years, but maybe closest with Chief Ninawa Huni Kui. How does his pedagogy inspire what you do?

One of the things that we did with Chief Ninawa and the federation of the Huni Kui people of the Amazon was to try to create pedagogical tools, we call them "technologies of inquiry", meaning a tool that people can engage with so that they can have a co-inquiry. One of them has just been published as a draft, and is called ClimateFRAUD, which is an acronym [of false solutions] (see Box 11.1). It's very critical of false solutions to the CNE, and it tries to summarise what the false solutions are. We, think that the tool will change because of the problem of the emotional threshold: if people can't process it, they will feel overwhelmed and they shut down. So this tool, right now, is only for the veterans [those who are looking for ways to engage with their complicity in the CNE and coloniality] – I wouldn't use it with the novices [those new to questioning their complicity in the CNE and coloniality] in the field because it can throw you into the deep end too soon. We are trying to see how the tool can be adapted and more defined to be used across novices and veterans.

Box 11.1 ClimateFRAUD (draft) Framework (GTDF, 2023). Reproduced with the permission of Andreotti.

Disclaimer: The ClimateFRAUD framework may upset those not ready to question their complicity in the CNE.

ClimateFRAUD is a draft framework that can be used to identify false solutions proposed in the context of the climate and nature emergency (CNE). It was originally created by the Federation of the Huni Kui Indigenous Peoples of Acre, in the Amazon, and collaboratively redesigned in the context of the Moving With Storms CNE Program of the Peter Wall Institute for Advanced Studies, at the University of British Columbia.

The draft framework spotlights not just the actions of governments, corporations, and NGOs, but also those of the broader public. Many of these actions seemingly offer solutions, but in reality, they perpetuate a reckless, violent, and unsustainable economic system. This system, founded on exponential growth, extraction, and overconsumption, has been responsible for dispossession, destitution, genocides, and ecocides, and is now placing humanity on the path of premature extinction.

It is not rocket science: if our economic system exceeds the planet's boundaries, the system must be overhauled. Simply put, the market and the paradigms that have created and that exacerbate the problem ultimately cannot save us from climate disaster or ecological devastation.

The ClimateFRAUD draft framework challenges the prevalent narratives of techno-solutionism and greenwashing, urging us to question the allure of quick fixes that fail to address the systemic root causes of overshooting the planet's ecological limits.

C – Carbon colonialism (CO2lonialism)
L – Land-grabbing
I – Indigenous co-optation
M – Mandatory growth and consumerism
A – Absurd Promises of Carbon Sequestration
T – Toxic hope in the continuity of violent and unsustainable systems
E – Externalization of costs
F – Financialization of nature
R – Regulatory loopholes
A – Arrogant techno-solutionism and techno-salvationism
U – Ubiquitous greenwashing
D – Distorted narratives and deceptive claims

C – *Carbon colonialism*: the appropriation of land and resources in the Global South to fulfil the carbon dioxide reduction demands of the Global North. Under the guise of carbon offsetting, the Global North perpetuates business-as-usual practices of exploitation, extraction, and expropriation, effectively treating the Global South as a carbon dump.

This unequal arrangement allows wealthy nations to avoid and evade their responsibilities for reducing emissions while further burdening vulnerable communities in the Global South with the consequences of climate change and environmental degradation.

L – *Land-grabbing*: the unjust acquisition or occupation of land and natural resources for purported climate initiatives, such as green energy projects. This often happens without meaningful engagement with affected communities, particularly Indigenous and local peoples, without their free, prior, and informed consent, and without adequate protections and government oversight. Land grabbing results in displacement and often forced labor, as well as threats to cultural sites and traditions, including traditional ways of land management that also protect long-term food sovereignty. This dynamic creates "green sacrifice zones" that perpetuate environmental racism and contribute to energy inequity.

I – *Indigenous cooptation*: the strategic mobilization of Indigenous individuals and groups by governments and corporations to endorse deceptive climate solutions, aiming to appease criticism from Indigenous communities advocating for genuine ecological protection. This pattern involves manipulating community engagement or leaders to prioritize and emphasise the short-term financial benefits of false solutions while obscuring and downplaying the externalized and future risks and costs of these initiatives.

M – *Mandatory growth and consumerism*: the perpetuation of endless economic growth and consumerism as non-negotiable components of what are deemed acceptable climate "solutions". This pattern reflects a deeply ingrained belief that growth and consumption are indispensable for underwriting societal progress and well-being, despite the evident consequences of overshooting the planet's ecological limits.*A* – *Absurd promises of carbon sequestration*: The propagation of unrealistic and exaggerated claims surrounding large-scale carbon sequestration technologies. By promoting carbon sequestration as a panacea for the problem of carbon emissions, this pattern diverts attention from the critical need to address emissions at their source, thereby hindering meaningful climate action and perpetuating the status quo of unsustainable economic growth and consumption.

T – *Toxic hope in (and desire for) the continuity of violent and unsustainable systems*: the detrimental belief in the possibility of sustaining the current trajectory of existing systems and institutions through minor fixes and superficial measures, perpetuating the illusion of a sustainable future. Toxic hope focuses on superficial measures while ignoring or deferring necessary transformative changes in societal values and behaviours, preventing meaningful movement towards addressing the climate and biodiversity crises at their roots and leaving people unequipped to face the difficult and painful dimensions of reality.

E – *Externalization of costs*: the unethical practice of shifting environmental and social burdens onto systemically marginalized communities so that systemically advantaged communities can continue their existing consumption levels without consequence. This can be seen in the mining of minerals for green technologies, carbon trading, green energy projects like hydropower dams and wind farms that disrupt fragile ecosystems and food sources, and e-waste disposal in the Global South. It can also be seen in extending timeframes and deferring action addressing the crisis that disproportionately threatens systematically marginalized communities.

F – Financialization of nature: the commodification, monetization, and commercialization of nature, treating it solely as a financial asset for profit. This pattern prioritizes economic gains over genuine environmental protection and perpetuates the harmful separation of humans from nature. Many Indigenous communities attribute the climate and biodiversity crises to this imposed sense of separation and the reduction of nature to mere property to be owned and exploited by humans.

R – Regulatory loopholes: the crafty exploitation of gaps in government regulations and policies that enable companies to sidestep their responsibilities and evade the necessary actions to meaningfully address their contributions to the climate crisis. For instance, some corporations may take advantage of weak emissions reporting requirements, allowing them to understate their environmental impact and continue business as usual without making substantial changes.

A – Arrogant techno solutionism and techno salvationism: the unwarranted confidence in technological solutions as the sole answer to the complex challenges posed by the climate and biodiversity crises, disregarding the necessity for comprehensive systemic changes. Emphasizing technology in depoliticized ways without addressing historical and systemic inequalities and broader social, economic, and cultural issues perpetuates the notion that quick-fix solutions can single-handedly address the complexities of these crises, while reinforcing the objectification and instrumentalization of nature.

U – Ubiquitous greenwashing: represents the pervasive practice of using deceptive environmental claims to present governments, corporations, and organizations as environmentally friendly, while substantial changes to their practices remain lacking. Greenwashing is a marketing tactic to improve a public image while preventing the cultural shifts that are necessary to interrupt the continuity of violent and unsustainable systems.

D – Distorted narratives and deceptive claims: denotes the intentional manipulation of information and communication to present a distorted view of climate-related issues, policies, or technologies. Astroturf organizations, as a significant manifestation of this pattern, are deliberately formed or financially supported to simulate grassroots movements and public support for specific climate policies or technologies, including obfuscating systemic harm with tokenistic claims of intersectional empowerment (e.g., claiming to empower women entrepreneurs). Employing various tactics, such as paid social media campaigns, fake online personas, and orchestrated letter-writing campaigns, these astroturf groups aim to create the illusion of widespread backing while concealing their true origins and motivations.

The ClimateFRAUD framework is about identifying false solutions to the CNE. What other sources would you recommend on this topic?

I've been working with this group of Indigenous peoples in the US called the Indigenous Environmental Network,[5] and there's also the Huni Kui people in the Amazon, who are very strong advocates against false solutions. There is also a very good book that was published by a US group called *Hoodwinked in the Hothouse* (Amorelli et al., 2021), which really explains how we're being deceived with solutions that say that the market itself – the system that created the problem – will be able to provide the solutions in the form of carbon trading, for example.

They have a very strong critique of carbon trading, carbon credits, and the financialisation of nature. And it is very difficult to put this critique on the table because everything that you see when you put climate change on the table are the solutions, and every single solution is about the continuity or sustainability of the current system so that what we imagine is that we address climate change while we go on with business as usual. We do not see that it is business as usual that is creating the problem, and that is actually placing humanity on the path of premature extinction.

Disillusionment and inquiry

Many people are disillusioned and feel like whatever they do they are contributing to harm. How can we think pedagogically about this?

So, what happens with people who realise that everything is harmful, or most things are harmful? I think seeing that realisation as a good thing is important: in Modernity, we are used to this mindset of mastery, we have to be masters of things, and again, it's a dopamine stage, and it's about your position in the hierarchy of the "know-what-verse" [a society that bases worth on knowledge and mastery]. And what this requires is not even a mindset, it's a body-set, of anchoring and collective anchoring. And yes, a lot is harmful, but there's a lot of potentials there in the cracks [of Modernity] for moving things to generative places. And that involves the composting of shit, which, in the mastery mindset, is not something we do. But in the inquiry mindset, it's about finding joy in doing that, finding joy in the epiphanies as we dig deeper and relate wider. And as we learn to process these things, or remember how to, because I think before we were buffered from responsibility in the current system we used to have ways to process things collectively. So, figuring out how to create a community not around identity or belonging, it's not about that, it's about inquiry: it's about figuring out together how to live in these times that are so challenging and how to have different states of well-being that are not about "I'm worthy" or "I'm worthless". This is a dichotomy that has been imposed on us. There is intrinsic value in everybody's lives.

And then we see that partly, the disillusionment, the disenchantment that happens when we learn that a lot of the things that are harmful have to do with our ego feeling hurt because our self-image as good people is falling apart. But that ego is part of the problem too, and we are more than that ego and we can connect and relate beyond that. We exist beyond that. And tapping into this existence beyond what has been constructed for us as who we are is where I think hope can lie. I don't have hope in the future, I have hope in the present, for us tapping into that thing, repairing relationships, and weaving different relationships NOW. And entering this collaborative inquiry with more humility NOW.

How have we come to be in this situation and how can we get out of it?

We have come to be in this situation partly out of a choice for comfort, but also was imposed upon us collectively. It is a kind of collective illusion that we can have this way of living permanently. The inquiry into how to get out of that requires us to be ok with making mistakes, with trying new things, experimenting, and being accountable to these experiments. And being much more humble, much more honest. To do this, we need humour. And we need hyper self-reflexivity. This is like walking a tightrope between two kinds of abyss, the abyss of desperate hope and of desperate hopelessness. And you don't want to fall into either. On this tightrope, you can't stand still, you have to continue. You want to walk this tightrope with relational rigour, with intellectual rigour, with honesty, humility, humour, with hyper self-reflexivity towards this compass of emotional sobriety, relational maturity, intellectual discernment, and intergenerational responsibility. This is super exciting! It's hard and painful but it's also super exciting. It's a different way of learning, a different way of being.[6]

You have developed many pedagogical tools. Which would you recommend for the veterans who want to further their inquiry and unlearning process and capacity to hospice modernity?

We have made a course called *Facing Human Wrongs* (2022). It's now offered through the University of Victoria, and here we go deeper into the psychological processes. The course gives kind of an initiation into a vocabulary and 30% of the course is based on the book [*Hospicing Modernity*], so you will see me talking about grounding concepts in the book but there are many more exercises and it's better when it's done with a network, a supportive network. You can also join a group from all over the world, but generally, those people say, "I need somebody close by", and I say "Yeah, you do"! At least one person. Learning to deal with complexity is like moving from a state where if in modernity you have to drive a truck, which is relatively safe and straightforward, in this other context, it's more like navigating a raft in rapids. Here you have some control, but not a lot. There's a lot of uncertainty but you can do it – once equipped you're not going to drown in the pain or be overwhelmed by it. You're equipped to navigate turbulent times with some confidence and understanding that you need other people to be with you.

Reflection

In her work, Andreotti puts forward a systemic critique of modernity-coloniality through the lens of education. She posits that modernity's worldview is instilled throughout modern societies, systems and pedagogies. This includes a propensity to break the world into small comprehensible pieces and simplify messages and learning processes in order to acquire specific skills, what she calls *mastery education*. The pedagogies of the Indigenous peoples that she works with underline the complexity of nature, treating nature itself as a teacher, in what she calls *depth education*, or *inquiry education*, in the conversation above. She further posits that the latter approach better prepares us to engage with the complexities of the CNE and take action – indeed, the way we are educated largely explains why we are ill-equipped to act.

Through this critique, she highlights an important fallacy in the sustainability agenda – sustainability is a much more complex issue than the impression that much of the sustainability debate and solutions may give. The Indigenous approach instead proposes that the issues that we are facing may be so complex that solutions may be futile as an approach, and can also come in the way of deeper change. However, sustainability is often communicated through numbers, facts, and solutions rather than as a way of being, a normal part of life, through stories, values, etc., leading to simplistic and reductionist public discussions of the CNE and the proposed solutions. In this conversation, Andreotti takes this reasoning a step further when pointing out that our focus on solutions in itself is problematic as they are framed by the same way of thinking that created the problems in the first place and ultimately are about sustaining a system that is unsustainable. Consequently, doing differently is dependent on our ability to unlearn the ways of modernity-coloniality and deal with these complexities, in essence, accept that sustainability is a "wicked problem", or a predicament of the current systems, that requires persistence and perseverance to work our way out of. Another, underlying premise for this work is uncertainty:

> In fact, I would be suspicious of, and encourage others to be suspicious of, people who declare that they have the answers. The mess we find ourselves in is unprecedented and we all have a lot of work to do.
>
> (Machado de Oliveira, p. xxi)

In her book *Hospicing Modernity* (2021), Andreotti introduces the reader to her pedagogy or educational philosophy, not through explicitly described goals (though decolonising the mind clearly is an implicit goal), content and methods but by taking the reader on a pedagogical journey gesturing at ways out of the state of being ill-equipped. This journey is full of stories and encounters with different perspectives on modernity-coloniality. The "technologies of inquiry" here come in both to convey messages and as ways of to examine your own positioning and feelings towards the subjects. Calling them "technologies of inquiry" rather than pedagogical tools sets them apart from the Western pedagogical approaches that she criticises and signals the process of enquiry and openness towards different ways of thinking that they are meant to facilitate. It also signals that they are not solely meant for formal educational settings, but rather for all the potential contexts where learning can happen. In the context of this book, we may call them "mediation devices".

When Andreotti uses the word technology, it also seems to be a deliberate subversion of the dominant idea of what technology is, meaning something highly technological, electronic, etc., or its definition "the practical, especially industrial, use of scientific discoveries" (Cambridge Dictionary, n.d. b). It further subverts the definition of science as "the careful study of the structure and behaviour of the physical world, especially by watching, measuring, and doing experiments, and the development of theories to describe the results of these activities" (Cambridge Dictionary, n.d. a). Indigenous knowledge, though not scientifically documented, has been proven over generations, and as such challenges the Western hierarchy of knowledge where rationality and modern sciences sit on top. In her work, technology is the application of Indigenous science in the creation of mediation devices, among other things.

While Andreotti does not deny modern scientific knowledge's merits, it is clear that it also has its limits: within the context of the CNE, it is unlikely that it will provide us with definite answers and a clear path forward. Relying on it may therefore delay action. Its numbers and figures can also be all too overwhelming, leading the receiver to shut down and become protective, rather than take action. It also lacks the ability to convince climate deniers at a larger scale: their denial is rather a reaction to the perception of Western culture being under threat (Jacques, 2012; Klein, 2015). In this context, the shortcomings that Andreotti and the Indigenous knowledge she draws upon point to are of relevance: the propensity to put head before heart, body, and land. Their approach instead says to educate the heart and the head will follow. Here we may begin to touch upon what she means when she, in the conversation above, says that sciences of respect and responsibility towards the planet as living entity are missing in Western societies. We may also reflect on how modern sciences often seek knowledge and quantifications of natural occurrences in ways that benefit human exploitation and enable extractive technologies.

This focus on positionality; of the receiver, the messenger, of what sustainability is, is a striking aspect of Andreotti's work. Along with this comes attention to the emotional threshold of the receiver: sustainability issues must be communicated in ways that do not provoke denial and hopelessness. Sustainability and in particular climate change are also subject to polarisation, right vs. left-wing politics, climate deniers vs. climate alarmists, climate action vs. nature protection, and so on. In addition, the Indigenous teachings connect modernity-coloniality to the CNE, which puts further responsibility on the receiver of the message. Therefore, it is important to mediate in ways that avoid deflecting by saying "I cannot be responsible for what generations before me, did". Instead, accepting that the order of the world is still very much influenced by coloniality and that one's position in the world and privilege are due to this, and furthermore, that one is perpetuating the injustice and inequalities that they created and so they become your responsibility, is an important part of moving forward.

Her attention to the unfinished state of the ClimateFRAUD framework presented in the conversation above (Box 11.1), must be seen in light of this focus on positionality. The framework gives pointers to the kind of solutions which will perpetuate the same system, rather than solve the problems in the long run: if the issues that arise are systemic, then solving them one by one is akin to treating symptoms rather than the underlying disease. It does so by presenting some statements and guidelines, while not being prescriptive, instead inviting us into a more open-ended enquiry. Is promoting solutions that sustain the same system yet another form of greenwashing? Moreover, the framework may elicit strong feelings, conflicts of interest, or complete rejection from the "novices", those not ready to receive this information.

The attention to its unfinished state must also be seen in the light of her positionality: Andreotti, mainly working with Indigenous peoples in Canada and South America, also writes from an American/Canadian context with a very different history of coloniality and Indigenous peoples, even with sustainability, than social-democratic Norway, where most political parties support action on climate change in some way or form. Therefore, the Indigenous messages may be received differently, where I sit as a listener and reader. (Or where you sit as a reader.) An important factor may also be the knowledge of these historical facts and the way in which they have been acknowledged and/or perpetuated to this day.[7] Still, there is an aspect of "them" vs. "us" rhetoric, or majority vs. minority rights, even though many ethnic Norwegians and Norwegian environmental organisations have joined the Sami in their protests. As such, we (Norwegians, like myself) may be under the illusion of being more respectful towards the Sami people and their culture than we are. In the same way, we seem to be under the illusion that we are good at preserving nature despite being a high-consuming country, top three in Europe (Eurostat, 2023), and 5,000 square metres of Norwegian wilderness making way for human constructions every hour (Nessemo, 2024). We also have a very high rate of climate denial on a European level, with one in four Norwegians not believing in manmade climate change (Delebekk & Flem, 2023), which would suggest that other ways of mediating the CNE are necessary.

Pedagogy also has a positionality and must be seen situated within its context(s) and as such Western education is not a uniform landscape, nor are the pedagogies practised, with distinct traditions related to time and space: Greek (Sokrates), German (Herbart), French (Rosseau), to name a few (see e.g., Compayré, 1886). Andreotti's argument is, however, that Western mass education is under the cultural hegemony of modernity/coloniality. For Andreotti, it is, however, also important that we recognise that education happens not only in formal educational institutions but also throughout society, how systems are set up, what behaviour is "rewarded", messages we receive through the media, advertisement and marketing, etc., through what Daniel Quinn (1992) in his philosophical novel calls the "whispers of Mother culture". That our ways of thinking and doing are like "the air that we breathe" is exactly the premise for Andreotti's work: we are so used to them that we cannot fathom other ways. For sustainability, this has serious implications, as many of these ways of thinking and doing are unsustainable. This normalisation also makes it hard to confront our ideas without creating resistance and protectiveness.

It is here that the above-mentioned concept of unlearning comes into play. In Western education too, it is recognised that a part of learning is unlearning ideas and conceptions to be able to take on new learning or more complex understandings of what was previously learned in more simple terms. The unlearning that Andreotti speaks of is of a much deeper sort – of unlearning the ways we see the world and questioning what we take for granted as the natural way of things. As an example, growth is the reasoning behind much decision-making: when a municipality clear-cuts forests for industrial usage, it is to allow them to grow. But why do they need to grow? This premise is taken for granted. The approach of enquiry allows us to see what we are taking for granted and whether we would like to change this. Why do we need growth? And if we do, what kind of growth?

In Western education, it is also acknowledged that any learning is difficult through concepts such as scaffolding (see e.g., Shvarts & Bakker, 2019): temporary adaptive support in a learning process making learning easier by avoiding the discomfort of being in a liminal state for too long. The Indigenous approach seems a stark opposite where the learning is also about handling these liminal states of not knowing for sure what to do next, not coming up with the answer straight away. Managing these situations, she argues, requires us to reach a more profound state of maturity. Andreotti's notion of maturity has similarities with Western theories of human development (e.g., Piaget, 1976) – being able to perceive more complexities as we approach adulthood. However, it also adds the ability of accepting responsibility for one's actions, managing and dealing with the complexities we perceive along with the uncertainty they bring to light, and self-reflexivity to this adulthood stage that is not present in most Western theories. In our conversation, Andreotti uses several metaphors for these kinds of situations – walking a tightrope, a raft in rapids. These are difficult endeavours but that one can learn to handle. Here the importance of seeing sustainability (and life) not as an end goal or a finite place you can reach but as a journey, a path to walk on that will require constant work, constant movement, is emphasised.

When Andreotti points out the need to start acting now, it is not only out of the urgency of the crisis but because it is by acting in the now that we are starting to shape the future. It was also within the context of futures that I first encountered Andreotti's work as she, together with Chief Ninawa Huni Kui delivered the keynote speech "Gesturing Towards Decolonial Futures (GTDF): A Decolonial Approach to Systems/Complexity Education" at the Anticipation Conference 2022.[8] Overall, these teachings have great importance for futures literacy: "the competency that allows people to better understand the role of the future in what they see and do" (UNESCO, n.d.), not the least because actions can be seen as manifestations of hopes and fears for the future (Bazzani, 2023), but because self-reflexivity about the origin of the narratives that shape one's actions can open the door for other ways of doing and other possible futures.

These are futures we need to create together and despite putting forward what some would find rather harsh critique of modernity, Andreotti's approach is more one of coming together than one of othering. The idea of *Hospicing Modernity* is not a complete rejection of modernity. Rather it's about learning from modernity, preserving what is well done, detaching from what is not and moving towards something better, implicitly asking what we actually want to sustain. The approach then also acknowledges that it is impossible to go back in time – we cannot all go back to living as hunter-gatherers but must find ways to go forward.

In highlighting the Indigenous perspectives, there is also an important counter-narrative of the implicit narrative of the Anthropocene, that *Man has caused the Anthropocene. Man is bad for nature. Man cannot act in any other way.* Andreotti instead proposes *an* approach that integrates Indigenous critiques and Indigenous deep learning pedagogies – one way of moving forward, not perfected, not universal, but a step in the direction, a gesture towards decolonial futures, and towards "living and dying well" in the wake of the CNE. Here, Andreotti's and the GDTF's approach brings a message of hope: *Man is not modernity*. Hence, we are capable of different, better – of growing as human beings.

Acknowledgements

I would like to thank Vanessa Andreotti for allowing me to present her work through this conversation and for allowing us to reproduce the ClimateFRAUD (draft) Framework in this anthology.

Notes

1 Vanessa Machado de Oliveira Andreotti is also a Canada Research Chair in Race, Inequalities and Global Change and David Lam Chair in Multicultural Education. Originally from Brazil, and of Indigenous/German immigrant heritage, she has previously held academic positions internationally, e.g., in New Zealand and Finland, and she has worked with Indigenous peoples in Peru, Brazil, the USA, and Canada. She works particularly closely with and is authorised to speak on behalf of the Huni Kui Indigenous people of the Amazon and their Chief Ninawa Huni Kui.
2 Chief Ninawa represents 118 communities and a population of more than 16,000 people. The Huni Kui indigenous people are part of the Amazon rainforest and risk their lives to protect it. Chief Ninawa has been a strong voice against false solutions to the climate crisis (i.e., solutions that perpetuate business as usual) and a global advocate for placing the rights of nature and Indigenous rights and lives at the centre of the agendas of climate change and biodiversity loss.
3 The book *Hospicing Modernity* is published under Andreotti's maiden name Machado de Oliveira, referencing Andreotti's family history (Machado de Oliveira, p. 94).
4 The compass can be found on the GTDF website, www.decolonialfutures.net, as the «SMDR compass».
5 Established in 1990 in the USA, IEN was formed by grassroots Indigenous peoples and individuals to address environmental and economic justice issues.
6 For more on walking on tightropes, see Machado de Oliveira (2021, pp. 240–242).
7 Though there are similarities in the strategies of forced cultural assimilation undertaken, Norway's history of the Sami differs from South American, US and Canadian history of their numerous indigenous peoples. Norwegians and the Sami arrived in this part of

the world at similar times and for a long time lived side by side. From 1850 to 1980, a policy of assimilation, similar to many other contexts, was attempted through schooling, prevention of speaking their own language and enacting their own culture, etc., was enacted, while today the official stance is that Norway was founded on the territory of two peoples, the Sami and the Norwegian, that have equal rights to develop their cultures and societies. Year 1989 saw the creation of the Sami parliament and an apology from the Norwegian King Olav during its opening, followed by an apology by King Harald in 1997, and Prime Minister Kjell Magne Bondevik in 1999 for the violence that the Sami endured during the assimilation period. The Supreme Court of Norway (2021) ruled that wind firms were built on Sami lands in breach of Sami Indigenous Rights.

8 The Anticipation Conference is concerned with anticipation as a means of engaging with the climate emergency, transitional justice, AI and ethics, energy security, social inequalities, public health and wellbeing, socio-technical systems, cultural values, activism, the right to protest, and more. https://anticipationconference.org/.

References

Amorelli, L., Gibson, D., & Gilbertson, T. (Eds.) (2021). *Hoodwinked in the Hothouse: Resist False Solutions to Climate Change* (3rd ed.). climatefalsesolutions.org. Available at: https://climatefalsesolutions.org/wp-content/uploads/HOODWINKED_ThirdEdition_On-Screen_version.pdf.

Andreotti, V., Stein, S., Wittman, H., Arefin, R., Valley, W., Slaymaker, O., Cardoso, C., & Evans, R. (2023). *Moving with Storms: PWIAS Climate and Nature Emergency Catalyst Program (Not Your Typical) Report 2022/2023*. P. W. I. f. A. Studies. Available at: https://blogs.ubc.ca/movingwithstorms/.

Anticipation Conference 2022. (2022, November). *International Conference on Anticipation, Conference Proceedings*. Tempe: Arizona State University.

Barkemeyer, R., Givry, P., & Figge, F. (2018). Trends and patterns in sustainability-related media coverage: A classification of issue-level attention. *Environment and Planning C: Politics and Space*, 36(5), 937–962. https://doi.org/10.1177/2399654417732337.

Bazzani, G. (2023). Futures in action: Expectations, imaginaries and narratives of the future. *Sociology*, 57(2), 382–397.

Beckert, J., & Suckert, L. (2021). The future as a social fact. The analysis of perceptions of the future in sociology. *Poetics*, 84, 101499.

Brundtland, G.H. (1987). *Report of the World Commission on Environment and Development: Our Common Future*. Geneva, UN-Dokument A/42/427. Available at: https://sustainabledevelopment.un.org/content/documents/5987our-common-future.pdf.

de la Cadena, M., & Starn, O. (Eds.) (2007). *Indigenous Experience Today*. Oxford: Berg.

Cambridge Dictionary. (n.d. a). *Science*. Cambridge Dictionary. Retrieved 22 Jul. 2024, from https://dictionary.cambridge.org/dictionary/english/science.

Cambridge Dictionary. (n.d. b). *Technology*. Cambridge Dictionary. Retrieved 22 Jul. 2024, from https://dictionary.cambridge.org/dictionary/english/technology.

Compayré, G. (1886). *The History of Pedagogy* (W.H. Payne, Trans.; 1st ed.). Routledge. https://doi.org/10.4324/9781315650449.

Delebekk, N.F., & Flem, S.F. (2023). Hver fjerde nordmann er klimaskeptiker. *Faktisk*. Available at: https://www.faktisk.no/artikler/jx882/hver-fjerde-nordmann-er-klimaskeptiker.

Eurostat. (2023). Actual Individual Consumption Per Capita in 2022. Available at: https://ec.europa.eu/eurostat/web/products-eurostat-news/w/ddn-20230620-2.

Facing Human Wrongs. (2022). Facing Human Wrongs Online Course. Available at: https://facinghumanwrongs.net/.

GTDF. (2023). Unmasking Climate Deception: The ClimateFRAUD Framework. Available at: https://decolonialfutures.net/climatefraud/.

Ghosh, A. (2018). *Uncanny and Improbable Events. Vel. 6. Green Ideas.* Dublin: Penguin Books.

Harari, Y.N. (2014). *Sapiens: A Brief History of Humankind.* Toronto, ON: Random House.

Haraway, D.J. (2016). *Staying with the Trouble - Making Kin in the Chthulucene.* Durham, NC: Duke University Press.

Huni Kui, N., & Andreotti, V. (2022). *Views from COP27: How the Climate Conference Could Confront Colonialism by Centring Indigenous Rights.* The Conversation. Available at: https://theconversation.com/views-from-cop27-how-the-climate-conference-could-confront-colonialism-by-centring-Indigenous-rights-194223.

Jackson, T. (2009). *Prosperity without Growth: Economics for a Finite Planet.* London: Earthscan.

Jasanoff, S., & Kim, S.-H. (Eds.) (2015). *Dreamscapes of Modernity: Sociotechnical Imaginaries and the Fabrication of Power.* Chicago, IL: University of Chicago Press.

Jacques, P.J. (2012). A general theory of climate denial. *Global Environmental Politics*, 12(2), 9–17. https://doi.org/10.1162/GLEP_a_00105.

Kimmerer, R.W. (2013). *Braiding Sweetgrass: Indigenous Wisdom, Scientific Knowledge, and the Teachings of Plants.* Minneapolis: Milkweed Editions.

King, M., Smith, A., & Gracey, M. (2009). Indigenous health part 2: The underlying causes of the health gap. *The Lancet*, 374(9683), 76–85. https://doi.org/10.1016/S0140-6736(09)60827-8.

Klein, N. (2015). *This Changes Everything: Capitalism Vs. The Climate.* New York: Simon and Schuster.

Machado de Oliveira, V. (2021). *Hospicing Modernity: Facing Humanity's Wrongs and the Implications for Social Activism.* Berkeley, CA: North Atlantic Books.

Nessemo, J.W. (2024). Ligger løsningen på naturkrisen her? *NRK.* Available at: https://www.nrk.no/dokumentar/xl/slik-kan-vi-stanse-nedbyggingen-av-norsk-natur-1.16687202.

Piaget, J. (1976). Piaget's Theory. In: Inhelder, B., Chipman, H.H., & Zwingmann, C. (Eds.), *Piaget and His School.* Springer Study Edition. Berlin and Heidelberg: Springer. https://doi.org/10.1007/978-3-642-46323-5_2.

Porsanger, J. (2004). An essay about Indigenous methodology. *Nordlit*, (15) (July), 105–120. https://doi.org/10.7557/13.1910.

Quinn, D. (1992). *Ishmael.* New York: Bantam.

Quijano, A. (2000). Colonial power and Eurocentrism in Latin America. *International Sociology*, 15(5), 215–232.

Raworth, K. (2017). *Doughnut Economics: Seven Ways to Think Like a 21st-Century Economist.* Windsor, VT: Chelsea Green Publishing.

Ricoeur, P. (1976). Ideology and Utopia as cultural imagination. *Philosophic Exchange*, 7(1), 5.

Shvarts, A., & Bakker, A. (2019). The early history of the scaffolding metaphor: Bernstein, Luria, Vygotsky, and before. *Mind, Culture, and Activity*, 26(1), 4–23. https://doi.org/10.1080/10749039.2019.1574306.

Stein, S., Hunt, D., Suša, R., & Andreotti, V. (2017). The educational challenge of unraveling the fantasies of ontological security. *Diaspora, Indigenous, and Minority Education*, 11(2), 69–79.

Stein, S., Andreotti, V., Suša, R., Amsler, S., Hunt, D., Ahenakew, C., Jimmy, E., Cajkova, T., Valley, W., Cardoso, C., Siwek, D., Pitaguary, B., D'Emilia, D., Pataxó, U., Calhoun, B., & Okano, H. (2020). Gesturing towards decolonial futures: Reflections on our learnings thus far. *Nordic Journal of Comparative and International Education (NJCIE)*, 4(1), 43–65. https://doi.org/10.7577/njcie.3518.

Strand, R., Kovacic, Z., Funtowicz, S., Benini, L., & Jesus, A. (2023). *Exiting the Anthropocene? Exploring Fundamental Change in Our Relationship with Nature* (Narratives for Change). EEA. Available at: https://www.eea.europa.eu/publications/exiting-the-anthropocene.

Supreme Court of Norway. (2021). Licences for Wind Power Development on Fosen Ruled Invalid as the Construction Violates Sami reindeer Herders' Right to Enjoy Their Own Culture. Available at: https://www.domstol.no/en/supremecourt/rulings/2021/supreme-court-civil-cases/hr-2021-1975-s/.

Trebeck, K., & Williams, J. (2019). *The Economics of Arrival: Ideas for a Grown Up Economy.* Bristol: Policy Press.

UBC. (n.d.). *UBC Indigenous Strategic Plan*. Available at: https://isp.ubc.ca/.

UNESCO. (n.d.). *Futures Literacy.* Available at: https://www.unesco.org/en/futures-literacy.

Yunkaporta, T. (2020). *Sand Talk: How Indigenous Thinking Can Save the World*. New York: HarperOne.

Yunkaporta, T. (2023) *Right Story, Wrong Story: Adventures in Indigenous Thinking*. Melbourne: Text Publishing.

Index

Note: **Bold** page numbers refer to tables; *italic* page numbers refer to figures and page numbers followed by "n" denote endnotes.

MIX
Papier | Fördert gute Waldnutzung
FSC® C083411

Kolibri 360 GmbH
Ferdinand-Jühlke-Straße 7
99095 Erfurt, Deutschland
produktsicherheit@kolibri360.de